WEATHERING RELATIONSHIPS

MAKEUP OR BREAKUP · CLARITY · HEALING · RELATIONSHIPS

Making Up   Moving On

DR. MICHAEL ACTON
Psy. D., M.Ed. (Psych.) Hons., M.A. C.Psych.

MPA
mind.com

Published by Life Logic Publishing LLC 2024

Text © Life Logic Publishing LLC 2024
Cover Design © Kate Turner 2024

A CIP catalogue for this book is available from the British Library.

Paperback ISBN 978-1-8383527-3-8

Also by Dr. Michael Acton

Power of You: Raw Facts From Real Parents*
Power of You: Learning How To Leave*
Narcissism & Codependency: Walking You Away From Toxic Relationships
Narcissism & Codependency: Both Sides of the Coin
*also available on audiobook

Typeset in Adobe Garamond Pro 9.7/14 by Life Logic Publishing LLC

CELEBRATING DIVERSITY

Kissing Sculpture, Brighton seafront, UK:
Dominic Alves. Licensed under Creative Commons 2.0.
https://creativecommons.org/licenses/by/2.0/

Praise for
WEATHERING RELATIONSHIPS

"Sometimes life can get messy. At 54, I often wonder how I can be a highly educated and successful entrepreneur, yet not manage that same assertiveness and order in my relationships. I've read all of Michael's books and *Weathering Relationships* has helped me understand why I should apply the skills and boundaries which have helped me grow and succeed in my professional career to my personal life. Moreover, the book provides valuable tips in identifying that 'AHA' moment, where trauma began, much earlier in life. Michael not only guides you in navigating relationships, but in setting healthy boundaries, too, something I've failed to do my entire life. The suggestions and recommendations offered have empowered and emboldened me to get 'unstuck,' acknowledge my truth, take ownership, and improve my communication skills so I may be at peace and move forward. Consider this piece as a valuable resource and tool to achieving the best 'you,' as it is currently doing so for me."

-Ana

"When life makes you have to put up with mean and ugly people, just think of them as sandpaper. They may scratch you, rub you the wrong way. But eventually, you end up smooth and polished, and the sandpaper? It's just gonna be worn out and ugly."

- Beyonce -

"What compassion, Sir! Thank you Dr. Acton (aka ACTION)"

- Anika -

ACKNOWLEDGEMENTS

I would like to thank Sigmund Freud, Carl Gustav Jung, John Bowlby, Elisabeth Kubler-Ross, and Victor Frankl for their scholastic input, and for giving me a tight framework within which I have been able to safely explore other innovative ways of working with people in crisis and trauma throughout my career.

I want to thank professor Arthur Hayes, grief expert and dear friend, for his wisdom, insight, and encouragement in my work.

I'd also like to thank everyone who has come into my life over the past sixty years. I don't regret one moment of my life, and I thank all of you for enriching it and getting me to this place of peace and happiness. Thank you to my wingman, Neil Hocking. Without your patience, understanding, support, and belief in me, I wouldn't be where I am today.

Most importantly, to all the souls - my patients - that have worked with me over the past three decades. I want to say that it has been a privilege to work with you. You have enriched my experience and expanded my wisdom through your own amazing coping mechanisms, ideas, insights, and reflections. I have brought together the three dimensions of my personal life, my scholastic life, and my working life with patient input to bring this most amazing book to you. This book is written for you: the people that are wise, the people that reach out for help, and the people that understand that there must be a different way of doing it.

And lastly, I'd like to thank Andy (Droidy, Roo) for coming into my life and showing me so much love, understanding, respect, and comfort.

PREFACE

I started working with the concept of writing a book about moving on and making up in relationships. I was determined to create something of value that people couldn't find simply by typing a query into Google or ChatGPT.

This book was an exponentially bigger challenge than my previous titles simply because to make sense and to cover this well, I needed to bring together so many moving parts. It is vital to harness these moving parts in order to achieve several important and inter-related goals.

First and foremost, Weathering Relationships introduces a new post-relationship breakup model that goes beyond the limited grief-based models that psychologists are trained in. My model, which I developed during recent research, combines elements of task-based, stage based, and dual-process models of grief in a context of relationship breakup.

This book also includes practical steps for managing a successful relationship reunion, making use of my Relate relationship training and the experience I have gathered from patients and my own relationship experiences - good and bad.

Weathering Relationships also incorporates the 'Acton Model for Gatekeepers of Domestic Violence (SOS DV8),' a 'first aid' style guidebook giving first responders eight simple rules for handling situations involving domestic violence.

But writing this book has been much more than a cognitive exercise in bolting these things together. I also went to great pains to pin down the ineffable wisdom of the soul, interweaving meditations and case studies to help readers relate to the emotional turmoil of the breakup and makeup journey, and to remember that they, you, are not alone.

The result is a living, breathing book which is different to anything else that is out there, and accessible by all people. Whether you are a scholar, a person struggling in life, working in a bakery, being in an academic department, it doesn't matter. This has been written for you, to be understood and to be helpful.

"Beautiful. Thank you so much for guiding all of us."

- Oliver -

CONTENTS

"Your compassion, empathy and care is so evident. Thank you for sharing with us."

- Omar -

PART I

A CATEGORY FIVE STORM

"Reading books to me is the ultimate privilege. They are my wisdom. They are my friends."

- Dr. Michael Acton -

"So much to unwrap with this topic. Thank you so much for your work and experience."

- Pierre -

ABOUT THE AUTHOR, MICHAEL

Michael's journey towards writing this, his latest book *Weathering Relationships*, actually started off in a car, many years ago. After narrowly surviving a dysfunctional and challenging childhood, he was struck down with meningitis and lost the ability to read and write. He then found himself living in a friend's car, at the age of 17. His life changed from that moment onwards, and Michael takes up his story.

"A Trinidadian lady took a chance on me and rented me a basement room in her house where I learnt how to read and write again - and, more importantly, how to build my life. She's now 83 and still a very dear friend. I was confused sexually, and I had a child at 21. I was going to be a Roman Catholic priest as a teenager, but I left the faith, although I was mindful not to leave the lessons of The Bible behind.

"Over the course of my life - I'm now in my early Sixties - I attained four degrees, travelled the world, dived into so many different cultures, and became a successful, highly paid psychologist. I've worked in hospitals and in private practice, and now I'm a consultant. Clinically, I'm trained in chronic pain management, disability, and addictions, and I've worked and been trained in clinical psychology, counseling psychology, and systemic family psychology. I did all this studying and improvement because I wanted to be the best I could be for people coming to me for help. I have certainly been in a position where I needed help at different times in my life myself, and it was the strength of that help I received that kept me going and helped make me the best version of myself today.

"I'm very humble, and I'm truly grateful every day for the opportunities I've got. I've always said that my cup is half full, even during my darkest days, when I was in extremely abusive relationships. Yes, it happened to me, too. I'm now with a beautiful man in a beautiful relationship and I'm grateful every day for that. Before I started writing, I considered returning to faculty, to teach at a university, but I realised that I have learnt more from my patients over the years, and my own personal life, than I have from any scholastic arena, and I just plain wanted to pay back to all of us no matter what our backgrounds or education or finances: pay back in a big way through this arena of books, press articles, TV, and news.

"I have studied religions globally, from Judaism, Catholicism, and the Qur'an, to shamanism, etc., and I have lived in many parts of the world. I have studied many ethnic and culturally diverse ways of being, and it has left me feeling very spiritual, very energy-based in my thoughts and beliefs, and I guess some might say I'm truly spiritual.

It was during one of several spiritual retreats that I really asked myself some big questions. What was my calling? How should I be, in myself? How should I help spread the knowledge I have gained? And the answer came to me: I was to pay back to everybody that needed my help; to people that may not access a psychologist but may read news articles and books, or even listen to audiobooks. I guess I found my path.

"I invested an awful lot of my personal money in to my book *Learning How To Leave*. I was in an extremely abusive relationship myself at the time, so I personally knew how tough this was.

Learning How To Leave has now helped thousands and thousands of people worldwide, and I still, to this day, receive beautiful notes and comments from people far and wide. I couldn't ask for more. This is so rewarding.

"Then I launched *Raw Facts from Real Parents*. I had brought up my daughter mostly single-handedly because her mother was very dysfunctional and absent at times. Writing *Raw Facts from Real Parents* was an accumulation of the wealth of knowledge I received from parents accessing my help and bringing to me their own coping mechanisms; their own ideas of how to move forward, and their own resolutions for their children. It's a really amazing book. But more importantly, writing this book helped heal me and accept being an 'OK enough' father. I'm very tough on myself and I had a lot to work through, and I have to say writing this book was a gift. It helped me understand my strengths, weaknesses and how to resolve deep, dark challenges.

And so, to complete the series, I started writing *Weathering Relationships: Making Up, Moving On*, a book about relationship makeups and breakups. This book was based around a new model I developed from research I conducted recently. I challenged very prominent models for grief that did not quite work when thinking about a relationship breakup, and I also looked at models that were purporting to provide healthy ways to make up. But I wasn't sure why someone would want to read another relationship book rather than just looking it up on Google.

So, in 2023, I went on a long retreat in Scotland, and I thought long and hard about what I could do with all this knowledge. I asked the higher power, spirit, God, however you want to call it, to give me guidance. That guidance was to be in my truth, to avoid shame, and to deliver an honest, comprehensive, useful, and more importantly, understandable book that all of us can apply to our lives, no matter who we are. Whether we're living in a castle, a trailer park, an apartment in the city, or a tiny cottage on the moors, this is for all of us. If a person says they haven't had a relationship issue, they are either lying or dead.

So, *Weathering Relationships* has been written in my truth, and it covers everything you will need to know about the journey to permanently moving on or successful making up. It covers hard-hitting issues such as domestic violence and suicide, and has provided the fuel for several lectures I've been honored to deliver since then, worldwide.

"Truly being in my truth as I write, as I lecture, as I present, as I work with patients, has led to amazing feedback, with hundreds and hundreds of different kinds of responses from principal psychologists, psychiatrists, lecturers, and professors all around the world. I've got another lecture this coming summer, in America, and the audience is purported to be around 40,000 delegates. I'm very pleased and honored to be paying back in a big way."

For more information on Michael, visit MPAMind.com

WHY THIS BOOK?

"Execution matters. It's not what you thought to do, it's about what you did."

- Dr. Michael Acton -

Every relationship breakup is different and there is no single route you can take to heal from this experience.

There is something of a shared journey though. Whether we were the one who chose to leave the relationship or our ex left us, we are within a process of huge change.

We have left the familiar road of our former relationship, and we have arrived at an unfamiliar crossroads shrouded in fog. We're directionless, we can't see an exit, and we're scared and feeling vulnerable. We don't know where to go from here. This can be one of the most lonely, confusing, lost, and terrifying times of our lives, so we go around in circles and circles. And sometimes this is very necessary, because as we're going around in circles, we're looking at options. We're looking at where we are and where we've been. Sometimes we need confusion. We need to be lost and hurting. We need that process to take hold before we can move. But when we do move, we have to make informed decisions.

If our partnership ended in a storm, there may still be debris strewn around us, or things may seem eerily quiet. We are struggling, though, and hurting. This is to be expected. If we've been telling ourselves and everyone else that our relationship breakup is plain sailing and we are fine, then we're either lying or we weren't in a romantic relationship and in love anyway - in which case we wouldn't be here right now reading this book!

Shame holds us back. Shame is a good person's way of protecting others and protecting one's own reputation and wellbeing, but at the same time, if we are not honest with people about what we've gone through and what we are going through now, then we can't expect to receive the right kind of responses from them.

So, whether we're leaving our ex behind in our rearview mirror, or we've been shunted by our ex and we're now foraging for understanding, I can personally promise you that there is an exit that leads to healing. But first we have to slow down, we have to get our bearings, and we have to assess what our options are.

We have to be in our truth at this point. If we're creating a drama. If we're creating a story that's not real. If we are doing things to retaliate to something our ex is doing. If we are being or saying or believing something that we're not (e.g., we're not hurting, we are hurting, etc.), then we're in big trouble.

The purpose of this book is to help you do just this, but you have to do more than read it. We have to navigate this crossroads in life that we decided or were forced to negotiate and find the turning that fits us personally.

You will need to stand firm in front of a mirror and really look at yourself. You will need to hold your breaking relationship up in front of that mirror and see it fully in its truth before you even think of what your next move is. If we are not in our truth, how can we know where to go?

Whatever direction we take now, it has to be for the good of our family unit and our own personal wellbeing. Anything we do at this point that is fake, or in response to something else, or not in our truth will hurt us. We will not be on the right course.

Don't fret. If you're not on the right track, we can work it out. We can come back, revisit this part of the work, and redo it all to be in our truth

So, if you are reading this and recognize you have gone off on the wrong trajectory because you haven't been in your truth, we can get you back.

Now's the time. reset now. Stand in front of that mirror and look at who you are, what you've done, and what's been done to you. Then hold the relationship up to the mirror and look at it for what it really is before you make any decisions.

After all this contemplation and reflection, will we move on and leave the relationship in our rearview mirror?

After all this truth and negotiation with self, will we choose the successful reunion route, and if we were to, what does that mean to us? What do we want to see?

Remember and be mindful: we cannot change other people.

Psychology needs to do better!
We should all have a safe place where we can go to get help with our pain and confusion during a relationship breakup, but sadly, there is

not the resource, nor the understanding at times, to work with this experience effectively.

The field of psychology is evolving all the time. Us psychologists that are long in the tooth often cringe at the interventions we once made (e.g., conversion therapy, CBT skill sets, addiction models, abstinence models, etc.)

Another point we need to understand is that every human is unique. We all react and respond in different ways, and we all experience differently, so it is very difficult for a field like mine, psychology and therapy, to really hold each individual. We have to go with models that sometimes don't express everything we need. Most of the work is between two people - or more, if it's a family or couple - in a room where we share experiences, ideas, and realities. We get to the truth and what heals and actualizes somebody (i.e., gets them to a more peaceful, stable, and aware state). Safety is paramount.

Our training needs to adapt to our clinical reality. I've worked in many different settings: public hospitals, private and nonprofit realms, agencies, and I am now a global consultant. I've been supervised and I have supervisees, and we have supervision to make sure we are doing the best for other people and staying safe ourselves. I've been a student through many degrees. Sadly, I have experienced faculty/ theory-led psychology as a system of interconnected agendas (i.e., they're more about challenging the theory than about the people being helped).

As with conversion therapy back in the day, psychologists and therapists, both those in public health and those in private practice, live in fear that their contracts will be reviewed if they step out of line. Yes, my colleagues today are on a yearly contract at times, and if they do not follow guidelines whether they believe in them or not, whether they're for the welfare of their patient or not, whether they put the clinician or psychologist themselves in danger or not, they have a mortgage to pay, and if they don't follow the guidelines, they don't get rehired. Yes, this happens.

Decisions are made by shareholders, drug companies, politicians, admin staff, top-heavy management, and sometimes people just chasing the money. Some of us who swim against the tide are surviving terribly cruel bullying by - yes, you've got it - fellow psychologists who are our peers, line managers, contractors, practice owners, etc. This situation has even been picked up by writers such as Murray (2006) who have highlighted the need to focus on issues of ethical decision making in psychological research and I, for one, wholeheartedly agree.

We all need things to grab hold of. I've designed the two models in this book: the 'Acton Post-relationship Experience Model (APREM)' and the 'Acton Model for Gatekeepers of Domestic Violence (SOS DV8)' as a response to being tired of trying to make theoretical models fit practice with real people. Very few people work at the chalkface (i.e., work with people) their whole lives. I've got 30 plus years of clinical experience. Very few people have that experience and are then able to contribute to the field. I have done that now.

I have worked on my own experiences and those of the patients that have seen me over the years. I have come up with some very practical, solid, experiential, real ways of managing, understanding and resolving difficult post-relationship experiences. In addition, the 'Acton Model for Gatekeepers of Domestic Violence (SOS DV8)' provides a clear, rule-based guide for intervening appropriately and safeguarding abusees of domestic violence.

My own personal experiences, both as a student and practitioner, have provided me with very little reassurance as to what approach I should use and how to practice with our vulnerable patients: my field of psychology failed me and my patients more often than it supported me - hence I joined the British Association for Counselling & Psychotherapy (BACP) where I found a caring and supportive environment with a grounding in clinical practice.

In the world of psychology, sometimes it's who you know, not what you know. Friends help friends publish and gain research grants, and it's that nucleus, that "old boys' club." Of course, the people in those clubs would disagree with me wholeheartedly. Why wouldn't they? But when we're struggling at the chalkface trying to help people, and things don't mesh, we have to be in our truth. And this book is about being in our truth.

Academics spend very little time going out into the field and doing 'bottom-up processing.' That means finding out what's happening at ground zero, with people working, and feeding that back into models and understanding of the field. It is usually a 'top-down process' where people are challenging theories. And this is very important work, but the application needs to be there and that's what is sometimes missing

It's not what school, college, or university we go to that matters. It's what we do with the knowledge and how we use our vision, passion, and determination. What is our intention when studying? To make a difference must be the ultimate goal for all students and academics.

Even psychologists experiencing clinical reality as sole practitioners don't have full agency to practice as they would like. We have to work to keep the money coming in, so there is a pressure to prolong therapy rather than pursue strategies that promote fast healing. We often don't have the time to develop appropriate models or put forward novel ideas, but time is something I now have because I am semi-retired. I'm paying it forward, and that has been my calling for the past ten years.

The environment is incredibly challenging, unpredictable, fast-paced, and demanding. Those that do propose new paradigms and models often have minimal experience in the field. The results are mostly useless and at worst incredibly dangerous. Matt Wotton and Graham Johnston (2022) criticized the undermining of the profession by 'therapy fads' in *Therapy Today*.

Most talking therapies will help patients become unstuck, but those therapists that don't follow the principles of what works best in practice (Fonagy & Roth, 2006) or who don't use clinical supervision effectively, can leave patients even more stuck and even drive them deeper into despair and hopelessness, which is extremely dangerous.

This book is based not only on my personal life and experience of the world and my professional engagement with my amazing patients, who have brought me a wealth of knowledge, but also my scholastic learning. I'm hoping that all of this, pulled together in this one book, will help you understand yourself, your relationships and how to be healthy in them, whether you are going to make up or move on. But more importantly, my hope is that this book will hold you during the process so you feel comfortable, safe, and above all, understood.

There are also various forms of bias and discrimination that those seeking help come across due to their gender, ethnicity, sexuality, or even their social class (Birdsall, 2021).

Why am I bringing this up now? Mainly because it directly affects people in our situation: people that are looking for help, people that are struggling.

These institutional and practical straitjackets restrict our development, distort our priorities, slow our healing process and can even cause us harm, so beware: if you do seek therapy, make sure you check out what the therapist does, what situation they're in, and where they are. And don't forget, there's a lot of free therapy available now provided by specialist agencies. Your best bet is to Google and see what's out there for you in your local area.

One major result is that relationship breakups (and botched makeups) are ignored and have become a hidden crisis lacking true representation in my field. We stop appreciating how deadly serious and painful relationship breakup is, how blood-stained separated couples are, and how we, as therapists, can most effectively help people get through this quagmire of despair.

The number of times I've heard on news reports people saying things like, "Jimmy was doing fine. He was just about to get engaged," or "Mary was great, we don't know why she suddenly terminated herself. She was having difficulties in her relationship, but she was a very happy girl." Well, hey! Let's look at that.

Of course, all therapists will always be present to listen, but listening on its own can leave a person feeling more hopeless and lost than ever if there is no intention to support and guide them. We have to provide active help at times. There is a time to listen, be supportive, and let someone purge, but we do need to have active listening. We do need to know what to do.

We don't have to fully understand why focusing on certain therapeutic strategies and skills is effective. Nevertheless, the work has to be grounded in sound theory and clinical evidence. Otherwise, we could be leading those we are trying to help into dangerous waters. And yes, sometimes medication will form part of a treatment plan, something that is not always recognized or supported by therapists. But I, for one, working in trauma, have seen great benefits of short-term use of SSRIs. However, the GPs/family doctors who usually provide the SSRIs sometimes prescribe the cheapest form of SSRI rather than the most appropriate.

So, to help patients navigate this under-researched area of - what I call the post-relationship experience - I used to turn to models of grief, while also borrowing from other models (PTSD, trauma, obsessions, identity remodeling, etc.) It would have helped me - in my practice and during my supervision sessions - if I had a sound relationship breakup model to refer to.

My model, the 'Acton Post-relationship Experience Model' is premiered in this book, and this is what we're going to be using to work on our post-relationship experience.

As we walk together, side by side, through this book, I will be standing beside you and we will navigate this crossroads together. We will weigh up different options. We will look at hazards. We will notice where we are stuck. We will see where we are going in circles or moving too fast. It's like baking: we have to have the right temperature, ingredients, and timing. Throughout what we're about to experience together, I explain everything in an easy and understandable form. The whole purpose of me writing this book is to help us.

Relationships are one of the most complex, painful and beautiful phenomena of human life. They are a living essence; without care, they die or become destructive. So, why is it then, that a clinician such as myself, after 30 plus years of specializing in relationship work, cannot find a single easily accessible guidebook to navigating the makeup and moving on of relationships?

It is this lack of information that's the reason I have devoted the past ten years of my career to writing about this very topic: relationships in their various forms: parenting, leaving toxic relationships, and now, how to move on or make up in a healthy way. This is my gift to you.

I am a firm believer that this book should be part of every school curriculum around the western world. It would help prevent abuse, suffering, and poor decision making. The models I present in the next chapters are experientially-led, but I welcome the input and reviews of academics.

Hold on, this will be a bumpy ride!
Our goal is to recover from this initial storm, and a relationship breakup is a massive storm.

We can prepare for it, or it can hit us from far left field. We may feel relief before we are hit or we can be hit and then feel relieved afterwards. Everyone is an individual. However, unless we have zero feeling and empathy, the storm will hit us.

If you are experiencing this right now, you are not going mad. Take it from me: this is to be expected.

We have to locate the best decisions for ourselves, and they are covered by layer upon layer of doubt, worry, ego, challenge, fight, and all the other things that happen in a relationship breakup. We can't make a decision in crisis. We can't decide on what's for dinner when the kitchen is on fire.

So, we are going to walk side by side until we can find the best way to one of two outcomes:

- Peaceful closure and successfully moving on. It's important to include moving on because we could have peaceful closure and just sit there. But the best way forward is to have a peaceful closure and to move on to living the best life possible for us.
- Successful reunion, a makeup. However, in my 30 years of relationship work, no one has ever been prepared for what it means to renegotiate that contract. How did we do it before? What were the pitfalls and bumps? What didn't work? What did work? What can we not do again? Throw in the mix all those contextual things that complicate a reunion: there could have been an affair or a death. If we are going to take that route towards a reunion, a way of spending the rest of our lives together, we need the practical steps in this book to work out how we're going to do that successfully, healthily, beautifully, and safely.

For our journey, I had to find a new way of doing things. What I had been working with clinically over the years I had made up myself, so

I did some research to back up my methods. And my goodness me, two and two really did make four, it was great, and I'm sharing it with you here.

We need to take a closer look at what a relationship breakup is before we go on to how best to resolve it and move on or make up.

In our personal experience, a breakup is very individual. If we can understand what our breakup is to us, we can work out what options we have going forward. Our breakup may be a relief. It may be an opportunity. It may be the most desperately unhappy feeling ever.

We have to understand what this experience is for us first. And then we can decide either,

- It's bad but I really do love this person and they seem to love me, so I want to do something with that, or
- It's been dead or unhealthy for a long time. I just want to feel peaceful. I just can't do this anymore. I'm not getting what I want from this relationship and I never will. They'll never change.

When we really look at a breakup, we can either see that there's something to make up with or there's something to leave permanently. And that takes time.

Defining a breakup
Divorce. Sudden separation. Ghosting after several dates.

Breakups come in many forms and every one is unique, but there are common themes. Regardless of the length or type of relationship that has ended, breakups hurt and require time - and work - to heal. After a long-term relationship, breakups can also involve additional pains and stresses: the end of shared friendships, child custody issues, property and financial concerns, etc.

Breakups are a common cause of mental health concerns, with many people experiencing suicidal thoughts, depression, and even post-traumatic stress. There can be co-morbidities. This means that there are several things going on at the same time. So, as well as the breakup, there may be coping mechanisms such as substance abuse; obsessive-compulsive disorder (OCD), or inappropriate loyalty, where the person cannot let go of their ex because they are just not wired that way, etc.

When we are going through a breakup, we know that we need help in some way. We often know that something may help us better, but it's not apparent to many of us what that may be. Some people can't afford therapy. Some people never experience therapy. Some people may have grown up learning that therapy is for people that can't cope or are 'sissies' or weak people. In short, face-to-face therapy is not for everyone, hence this book. This is therapy in a book.

When going through a breakup, our pain makes others uncomfortable, which leaves us feeling isolated. But it can also be a gift. It can be a gift of a shift, a restart, and how we can do things differently. Relationship breakup can also be one of life's levelers, bringing people together. It's not all doom and gloom.

Relationship breakups don't happen by accident. Relationship breakups happen because something is not working. We either choose to act on this or we have change forced upon us: someone breaks up with us or we break up with them. There are elements that can push the grief-like pain of loss into something more severe - even deadly. And people do not receive adequate care for this. We're here to change all that!

The biochemistry of a breakup

To you and me, this means what happens to the body, mind, spirit, energy...all the parts of us.

If we focus too heavily on the psychology - i.e., being in our heads - of a breakup, we can forget embodied aspects of the post-relationship experience. It is important to remember that our bodies are enmeshed with our mind and soul. This relationship is, in my opinion, best expressed through polyvagal theory (see the diagram on the previous page).

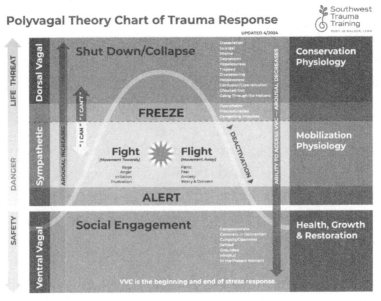

Simply put for you and me to understand, this mechanism explains the shock reaction of breakup, and don't forget that when we break up with somebody, our whole system goes into shock. Drink plenty of water. Our anxiety will go through the roof, we will be tense, we will be in a war-like situation, the 'fight or flight' will come in, we can feel hopeless, we can feel reckless. That is why it is so important, at this point, to not make any knee-jerk reactions. I will get more into that later, but I repeat: do not make any knee-jerk reactions. But hold on to the polyvagal theory because it's something that's great for a pub quiz.

Before you found yourself at the crossroads, there was a watershed moment. Either you decided to leave, and you were done, or your ex dropped a bombshell on you, and said, "I am leaving." Either way, the investment in our relationship has suddenly been torn away. This likely precipitated a severe storm in our lives. The storm, and the debris it kicks up, leaves us feeling very vulnerable, lost, alone, desperate, confused, angry...a myriad of emotions. This is to be expected, and this is because the loss of anything we're attached to is felt like a threat to our survival. We feel like we can't cope, we can't survive, we're not going to make it. And our sympathetic nervous system (SNS) will activate. Yes, that's the part of the nervous system that says, 'Shock, horror!' This is the fight or flight mechanism with which we are all familiar. We either get aggressive and fight and push through or we run away.

John Archer (quoted in Waters, 2011) explained, "Grief - in its most basic form - represents an alarm reaction set off by a deficit signal in the behavioral system underlying attachment." The stress hormones released by the SNS leads to inter-related psychological and physical symptoms. So, we psychologically experience anger, rage, fear, panic, anxiety, etc. It's our whole survival system going on alert.

And don't forget there are physical symptoms including a racing heart, high blood pressure, dry mouth, sweating, and yes, stomach problems, constipation, diarrhea, loss of appetite, overeating, binge drinking, etc. These are all normal, but we have to be aware of them because if we have this 'fight or flight' SNS mechanism activated and we're not aware of it, or we don't understand it, then we can get into big trouble. The fear, the shock, the rage...all of these things have to be understood in order to be managed. Otherwise we can be like a firecracker. We never know when we're going to go off.

This biological reaction to separation makes it more comfortable to stay together. That's why we find it so difficult to leave. We think, 'Oh yes, I'm going to leave this relationship.' However, then we think, 'Do you know what, I'm going to miss all that familiar comforting stuff,' so we stay. It's not until we get to the point where we realize, 'There's no glue to keep me here,' or, 'I'm better off without this,' or, 'I'm going to weather this,' that we do leave. And maybe that's the same for the people that leave us.

To our ancestors, this also provided an evolutionary benefit because staying together increased the chances of survival. "Loss threatens our sense of safety, mastery and control," says Murray." (2016, p.134). And control is the driver for our feeling safe. If we're not in control, we feel very vulnerable. And guess what: eating disorders, addictions and suicide ideation, threats and attempts are all ways of getting back control in life.

Whatever your situation is right now, please promise me that you will be safe. If you have any of these experiences going on, such as suicidal ideation, call your local, free helpline for suicide. If local

help is not available, just use Google. You can get any online help globally now. Just tap into the resources available to you. And if you can't read or write or you haven't got access to a device, ask someone you trust to help you. The most important thing at this moment in time, with all this upheaval, distortion, fear, stress, and shock, is to have other humans with us.

Returning to polyvagal theory, in severe cases of stress, there is a simultaneous activation of the dorsal vagal complex (DVC) which, in many ways, produces symptoms opposite to that of the SNS. It corresponds to trauma-related symptoms such as numbness, depression, dissociation, and suicidal ideation. In this situation, the heart rate and blood pressure can slow, and the person may become withdrawn. This is extremely dangerous. If you feel yourself withdrawing from society, canceling plans, and saying 'no' to things, it's so important to start saying 'yes' to anything. If you can't do this alone, find somebody that you can do things with. Committing to social engagement can help prevent this escalation of our defensive responses.

And if you are in a situation where you really don't have anybody because of family pressures, commitments or work, walk in nature every day, even if it's only for half an hour. Be fed by something. Feel something is your ally. Never feel alone.

It is important that we keep our biochemical mechanisms in check. What ever happens to our body impacts on our mind and vice versa. This may be your primary opportunity to do things differently. Maybe you haven't been living a healthy lifestyle. Maybe you were already experiencing negative symptoms before the breakup. It's time to take care of ourselves. It's time to parent ourselves. It's time to come home to ourselves. It's time to be with ourselves.

Sometimes, we can become lost inside a relationship that hasn't been good for us. Leaving that relationship, or being left, is a good time to reconnect with ourselves and befriend ourselves again. We may feel relief after leaving an ex-partner or when an ex-partner leaves us, but that's not all you will feel. There will be a myriad of feelings, experiences, and thoughts that we will need to navigate and work on together.

Before we even start with the exercises in Part I of this book, we will need to allow ourselves time, compassion, and space for us to heal. We might consider taking some time off work, even booking a short holiday or changing up our routine and taking that daily walk in nature or along the beach, and maybe taking this book with us for these quiet moments. Every small step is a step in the right direction.

Understanding our choices
Regardless of who ended our relationship, we have arrived at this very unfamiliar place. It's shrouded in confusion and the unknown.

We will also see this familiar road in our rearview mirror, and we may start to consider the possibility of turning around and going back. It will be that pull to make everything 'as was', the familiar, something we feel safe with even though it might not have been good for us. Despite all the problems back there in that relationship, all the disappointments, struggles, and whatever was going on for us - and don't forget it's both of us; there are two people in a relationship - sometimes we really want to go back. It's amazing the tricks our mind can play on us because sometimes we can think, 'Do you know what? That pain wasn't too bad back then. This is much worse.' Anyone who has given birth or been severely injured (e.g., in a car crash), will tell you that the human body is amazing at stopping or lessening that pain. It is part of survival, and sometimes we believe that the pain in our rearview mirror was not as bad as the pain we feel now.

You left (or were left) for a good reason, and if you were helped to leave because of our ex-partner's behavior, it may behoove us to be strong, stay left and experience what we are doing and feeling in the present time. Sometimes the grass seen in the rearview mirror can look greener, but mostly it isn't. If your relationship broke up, things weren't going right. Whatever they were, it wasn't healthy or safe.

Don't forget that all relationship breakups are shared experiences. Whenever we leave the familiar roads of a former relationship, we are like refugees struggling to make our way in a strange land. It affects our idea of the world and life; of our past and future; our friendship groups; when we have dinner; our Friday slob night in front of the movies; of who does the washing up and puts the washing out on the line. Our ideas of everything to do with work, community, family, domestic situations, vacations, etc. are all in a strange land now. This is weathering the storm at its finest.

Whatever communication there is with our ex - it may be zero; it may be threatening and 'stalker-like;' it may be aggressive; it may be minimal, focused on courts and children - we need to be stable and steadfast with ourselves, in our truth. We may find ourselves feeling increasingly anxious, but we have to think about what was then, what is now, and what could be in the future.

And keep in mind: the only ceilings on what we can be and do in our future are those that we put there. Take the ceiling off and think, 'If a miracle happened now, what would I want to see my life as?

How would I like to see me in that life? What kind of job, family, lover, and home would I want?" Because sometimes after a breakup or trauma we want the simple things: a calm and quiet place to be. Or sometimes after a really boring life, we want some fun, excitement, and dancing. You would be amazed at how many people have told me that they gave up all of their hobbies and interests just to keep a relationship going.

We need to find out and remember what makes us happy, and to revisit those things. Hold them dear again. Re-experience them.

Coming up is Part I of this book, and I'm going to explain to you how we have to eradicate our fake stories. Fake stories distract us. They give us returns that aren't real for us.

Whatever our age; whether we're 20, 40, 60, or 90, we won't get what we deserve until we can slow down, focus and really be in our truth while asking, 'What do we want? What works for us?'

Once we start seeing clearly what's in front of us because we've been in our truth, we are taking back control and we're working out what *our* journey is going forward.

Decisions, decisions, decisions...

There are only two exits we can take at this point: make up or move on. However, sometimes we decide to move on, then some miracle happens and - bang - we're on the make up trail. Likewise, sometimes we're going along the makeup trail and it still doesn't quite work, so we eventually decide to take the 'moving on' trail.

After we decide on our future, whether it's moving on or making up, we will have another bunch of decisions to make. How can we healthily close down what we had, and move on without any destructive hooks and anchors that might stop us getting what we want. Or how can we be with the person we have decided to be with in a healthier, happier way.

Every romcom movie you could ever watch plays on the dramatic tension between the make up and move on routes. Is she, isn't she? Will they, won't they?

From Romeo and Juliet to West Side Story to Under the Tuscan Sun, Hollywood romances are making a fortune through the same tried and tested formula. Yes, we're very interested in this because it's part of our lives. We can all relate to it. These movies present a relationship, they engineer a breakup, and then they take the viewer on a ride towards either a happy reunion or a permanent breakup. The details of the breakup (how, why, and when it happened) are all factors in how the story plays out. Simple but powerful - and extremely human - this is why they're successful.

So, our choices are:

1. Moving on: a permanent breakup. We are completely healed and are indifferent to (i.e., no longer emotionally involved with) our ex.

2. A successful makeup. We have renegotiated the terms of our relationship and we are both committed to making it work, both being the operative word - make certain of that.

Our choice is simple, but the work required to make the right decision will take every ounce of our being. It's counterintuive to leave and stay left; consider this carefully. It's against our very being.

Our goal for Part I of this book is to take the turning that is best suited to us in our truth and our situation right now. Our decision does not have to be binding at this stage. We can oscillate in fantasy, thoughts, conversations with friends, in therapy, and in any other way. Working outside of absolutes is always wise and can bring us comfort, so don't use the word 'definite.' Maybe start using language such as, "Well, if I were to move on permanently and leave this behind me, what would this mean for me?" or "If I were to work towards getting them back, what would that look like? What's the truth of that? What's getting in my way? Is it worth it?"

The way you use this book is completely up to you. However, it is my strong advice to read it all. After completing Part I, if you're thinking of moving on (Part III), read the making up part (Part II) first, especially where I go through every single step of evaluating how a relationship truly was and how it could have been. It will be helpful to you.
Similarly, if you are thinking about making up, and that's your choice, read the 'moving on' part. It may give you some ideas about how you can individually grow because breaking up often causes an emotional and cognitive growth spurt: it can shake things up and make us think anew.

Successful moving on is to feel kindly indifferent about your ex.

To successfully make up is to find new teamwork, a newfound love, and make new agreements. For our new relationship to be healthy, we need to find a way to be committed to the commitment - not just to each other.

What I'm saying here is that reading the whole book is very important, and sometimes when we're going along the 'moving on' route, miracles happen; that's what Hollywood is all about. This can happen in real life too. Sometimes, there is a cathartic moment for our ex or for us and we do make different decisions.

Likewise, if we decide we are going to go along the make up route, things may happen that lead us to think, 'You know what: this isn't what I want. You haven't changed. You talk the talk but you don't walk the walk.'

Being open to both possibilities is the best policy at this stage of the game. Just be mindful of both options, and start walking through one door and see how it feels. Test it out.

Either way, your ultimate destination is peace, safety, and an opportunity to grow. That's the gift of this book. You have just decided to grow, to think, to see, to learn, whether that means moving on or making up.

Disclaimer: *This is not an exhaustive book about relationship breakup and rehabilitation. It combines my 'Acton Post-relationship Experience Model,' contributions from respected colleagues and peers, and my personal pick of the most helpful relationship ideas I've picked up over more than 30 years of clinical work across every imaginable situation. I cannot be held liable for any negative impact perceived to have been caused by anything I have written or omitted in this work. The content of this book is intended for informational purposes only and is not a substitute for professional medical or psychological advice. If you or someone you know is experiencing mental health issues, please seek professional help immediately.*

This book contains discussions of suicide and self-harm that may be distressing to some readers. If you are struggling, please reach out to a mental health professional or a trusted individual. References:

Acton. M. (2022). *Raw facts from real parents.* Life Logic Publishing

Acton. M. (2021). *Learning how to leave.* Life Logic Publishing

Birdsall, R. (2021). Class and counseling. *Therapy Today.* Dec 21-Jan 22, 32:10, pp 42-45

Murray, J. (2016). *Understanding loss: A guide for caring for those facing adversity.* Routledge/Taylor & Francis Group

Fonagy, P. and Roth, A. (2006). *What works for whom (2nd ed.).* Guilford Press

Johnston, G, and Wotton, M. (2022). We need more faith that therapy works. *Therapy Today.* March

Waters, H. (2011, November 11). *Culturing science: the evolution of grief.* Scientific American. https://blogs.scientificamerican.com/culturing-science/the-evolution-of-grief-both-biological-and-cultural-in-the-21st-century/

PART I: A CATEGORY FIVE STORM

CHAPTER 1

HOW ARE WE GOING TO DO THIS? FOLLOW ME!

"(We) never change things by fighting existing reality. To change something, build a new model that makes the existing model obsolete."
- Buckminster Fuller -

Now, sorry about this, but this one chapter is a bit technical because some people are reading this for research and academic purposes, and if I'm truly honest, sometimes we have to be technical to get the information across to you. After all, it is the research that I, and many thousands of people like me, have conducted over the years that help us in many ways.

New foundations for support
The supports designed to help us lead our best lives evolve all the time. Sometimes they slowly develop and at other times there is a big shift.

For example, eye correction - using glasses - which we now take for granted, was once a huge evolutionary step forward. Without glasses, what percentage of the population would be disadvantaged and unable to operate at so many levels because they wouldn't be able to see?

So, my work on this model has been focused on improving the supports that we can draw upon to achieve healthy relationships.

Ideas of relationships and how we should best work within them have only crudely evolved, and they haven't yet caught up with the 21st Century (i.e., today's idea of a world of social media and intercultural experiences). As I explained in the introduction, one area where we are still failing to support people is in the relationship breakup arena. It's time to take a quantum leap forward in managing this often devastating scenario, hence me talking you through this now.

During my futile and very costly search for existing relationship breakup models, I came across the following suggestion - or appeal - from the founders of the dual process model of coping, Margaret Stroebe and Henk Schut. Now, these people are academics, but they have given an amazing wealth of knowledge to the field that has helped us work with patients, so heed what they say:

"That is perhaps a major next step for researchers to take: to work toward developing a theory that explains the process of dealing with loss and ongoing life... ." (Stroebe, Schut & Boerner, 2017).
I would argue that us focusing on developing a new theory, where we try to fit grieving people into a top-down model, is yet another way to promote the status quo and distance the field of psychology from us, the people it is trying to help.

So, I decided to turn this idea on its head. Rather than creating a new theory, guess what I did? Yes, you guessed it. I wanted to ground my research in established theories whilst taking a purely empirical approach - that means an approach looking at what I've experienced during my working life - to build a foundation for a new relationship breakup model.

My own evidence base would be more than 30 years of working in the field plus my own personal experiences of relationship breakup. And boy, have I had them. Hence my interest in this field.

I wanted to uncover what people were really dealing with during a breakup. In short, I wanted to build a practical, workable idea and model from the ground up (i.e., what people have really experienced in the world) to feed what we do to best help people.

But first, I had to find out how therapists like me are working with patients. How are they looking after patients? What are they drawing upon as resources to help patients work through their post-relationship experiences?

I drew a blank: outdated maps, outdated ideas that would belong more in the 50s and 20s than in the 21st Century
Imagine we get so distorted by our relationship breakup we don't know where we are, we've got no idea where we're going, and we've got no-one there to support us. We've got no phone, no Google, no GPS system, nothing. We can't see any signs. We can't reason with anything. So what do we do? How do we move forward to relationship make up or move on without becoming overwhelmed and taking the wrong turn?

Lots of people snap back to the safety of a dysfunctional relationship, or just a relationship they weren't happy in. Why is that?

We might look at the many thousands of books out there on relationship wellness and health, but unfortunately, most of these books are churning over the old stuff I've been talking about: old ideas and grief models that don't really apply to the 21st Century and what we do with relationships. In other words, whatever we have accessed up until now has been reflecting on what it was like for the Bronte sisters or during the Second World War or in the 1920s. Nothing out there is looking at what it's like to be instantly connected through Facebook, other social media and emails; to be wrapped up in laws about child protection and I could go on and on. It's very complex now, much more complex than ever before.

Hence we are flailing around, not knowing whether to run back to the safe and familiar or run forward, move on and find a new life for ourselves. The crux of it is, we're looking for something familiar and safe; but familiar and safe might not be the right decision for us.

So, how do we best understand managing a post-relationship experience? Well, in the absence of a specific relationship breakup model, therapists (e.g., Potter, 2022) will often refer to a grief model (e.g., Kubler-Ross and Kessler), treating relationship loss as a kind of 'disenfranchised grief,' a term from social learning theories of grief meaning that a loss isn't validated by society (Doka, 2008).

When someone dies, we have a funeral. There is a body, mostly. People get together and commemorate the passing of that person, and with their passing, there is no shame connected; the person is dead. There's support; there's the truth: the person's dead, and unless we're watching some sort of horror movie, that person doesn't come back and haunt us, play tricks on us, run off with somebody else, do things on social media to annoy us, hold on to our money in the bank account, etc. It doesn't happen.

I have to admit I've used the Kubler-Ross grief model in sessions myself (there was nothing else I could do, I did the best I could at the time) and relationship breakup is certainly an unrecognized loss. People often treat it like a storm in a teacup. After all, following a death you would never (or very rarely) have someone say, "She wasn't worth it," or, "Get over it!" or, "Life's too short to dwell on it." To hear these comments after a breakup is terribly isolating. The post-relationship experience is as unique as the individual. Even a breakup during the honeymoon period - after a couple of intensive months or even weeks - can be more devastating to one person than another who is leaving, or being left after, a 35 year relationship. We can't hope to address this if we only acknowledge pain that is socially acceptable.

So, I have used the Kubler-Ross model brilliantly in the past. It does help, but it's not enough.

Relationship breakup is also referred to as 'ambiguous loss.' The term's creator, Pauline Boss, Ph.D., emeritus professor of family therapy at the University of Minnesota, explains, "Complete closure after loss is an unrealistic expectation — and it's impossible when a loss remains indeterminate." She includes having a loved one 'go missing' as an example of ambiguous loss, and she also talks about the amorphous quality of psychological ambiguous loss, where we're not sure exactly *what* we have lost. You can read more about this in Skinner's online article (2021).

So, in a nutshell, what she is talking about is being ghosted. When somebody disappears, we are left with a million questions.

Without denying the reality of this type of loss (disenfranchised and ambiguous loss), I believe that relationship breakup has been chained too closely to the usual grief experience (i.e., dead people) by researchers. For example, Morris and Reiber (2011) coined the term post-relationship grief (PRG). This naturally pushes therapists and patients towards grief models as they seek to manage the pain. But is there really any evidence that we, the people experiencing a post-relationship experience - you reading this and me writing it - can treat our relationship breakup in the same way as grief for dead people? I believe absolutely not. You may be feeling comforted by reading this because we do feel very alone until something is explained to us, so hopefully just this little paragraph right here is bringing you a sense of comfort. I do hope so. That's why I'm writing it.

Through my vast clinical work, over three decades plus, I knew that this grief model (i.e., the Kubler-Ross grief model) was not enough to help my patients navigate relationship breakup. In fact, it turns out that grief models in general have no credible evidence base (Downe-Wamboldt & Tamlyn, 1997). In other words, they are made up without being proven, yet they have been routinely taught as part of the academic curriculae. So, when we are at university and studying to be psychologists and therapists, we're taught that these are things that we should follow and believe in and run with even though there is no validation that they work.

It's difficult doing my job. It's difficult for anyone in my field doing my job that really cares about patients. Sometimes we feel insecure. Yes, your therapist, psychologist, or psychiatrist will feel insecure working with you because sometimes we feel that there is nothing we can do. We have to go through this and feel it, and even though it's so desperate in so many ways, we feel useless. And when we go through this as clinicians working with patients, what we tend to do is grab a model nearby, or a theory or way of working, to make us feel less impotent. People do go into shock. People do get angry and rageful. They get depressed, full of regret sometimes, wishing they had handled things differently.

But comparing these experiences with grief after a death is like comparing the swimming experiences of a recreational swimmer and an Olympic athlete. Sure, we can say that both were dry at the start, both jumped in and got wet, both swam, and both dried themselves off afterwards. But this does not describe the personal experiences of the swimmers at all. What was their purpose of going swimming that day? Clearly, one wanted to win a medal and the other was just enjoying the water. And with their different objectives, how did they propel themselves through the water? How did it feel for them as they dried off? Was it a successful day for them?

For decades and decades, I found the grief model by Kubler-Ross very useful in helping patients to normalize their grief and understand that it is OK to feel strong, painful emotions. But only through my very recent research, carried out a couple of years ago, have I truly understood what exactly drives grief models. They're inaccurate, they're not precise, and they fail to address many issues faced by us, those people experiencing a breakup. They don't take into consideration contextual issues or the history of a person, their childhood, how they are with feeling battered, bruised, and hurt. There's so much missing. There are, of course, similarities to the grief experience when we do break up from a relationship. We may deny the relationship has ended. Has that happened to you? We may feel resentment towards our former partners or pray to a higher power for help to bring them back (some even go as far as creating love spells!) It's important to understand that unresolved, ambiguous loss, that has been complicated and compounded by previous relationship disappointments, our childhood, etc. leads into the mire of depression. We may doubt we are lovable at all. And feeling isolated, rejected, a failure - all these feelings we encounter during the post-relationship experience - will all feed our darkest ideas about ourselves.

We even experience a version of 'anticipatory grief' when we're considering leaving a relationship, or when we sense that our partner is about to leave. We feel panic, excitement, dread, remorse, fear. After all, if we leave, we're hurting the person we love or loved. If we are left, we're losing the person we loved. We may be going through the motions of being in a partnership without feeling loved at all because we realize that our partner has never stepped up and never will. They may tell us that they love us, but their actions may say otherwise. We may realize that the relationship we're in isn't going to work. We're simply not getting what we want from the relationship. We start to try and understand what our world would be without this person in it.

Simply put, whether we leave or were left, there are grave costs to our very core of what it is to be human: loving, kind, thoughtful, connected and wanted. Want is probably the biggest word here.

Nevertheless, after me carrying out a massive amount of literature research and interpreting what has happened with my own patients in my own practice (through confidential interpretative phenomenological analysis [IPA] on a small sample of patients), I found that grief models were like those old paper road maps. Useful to a point but missing a lot of key information. I was shocked at the themes that emerged from me looking over hours and hours of case notes. I already had an idea of what was going on, but it was exciting to go back over the work and see themes emerge that presented a coherent idea of shared experiences. And it's this useful knowledge that I'm going to discuss with you next.

What are we experiencing - as in grief - in the post-relationship experience?

Worden was an amazing person in the field of attachment and grief. His whole world was about belonging, not belonging, and what happened around that. He studied children and adults from around the world and from all walks of life. I was inspired while reading Worden's (1991) account of a group training exercise where he observed and pulled out amazing information about the trainees' grief experiences. He showed me that I needed to ground the model that I was developing for post-relationship experience, in the real world using clinical data. It was Worden that helped me to decide to conduct an interpretative phenomenological analysis (IPA) on a sample of my patient notes. IPA is a very established method for extracting rich qualitative (psychological, interpretative, and idiographic) data from the people you are studying. Simply put, I studied all my notes, all the things my patients had said over years and years of work, and themes emerged - themes that shocked me but that I also knew very well from working in the field for 30 years.

And these themes will help you understand what you are going through, and what it is to successfully recover from a breakup.

We need to make it clear how I came up with my results, so bear with me, the next couple of pages will be a bit dense:

To be eligible for my study, a patient must have experienced a relationship break-up which had contributed to them seeking counseling. An initial short-list of 30 eligible patients was drawn up and, due to time constraints, the list was reduced to six for the analysis sample: three who had been left by their ex and three who had chosen to leave the relationship. To avoid any risk of unintentional disclosure, patients were referred to as simply Patient A, Patient B, etc.

To minimize the risk of bias, an independent researcher went through my notes, pulling out themes representing the Kubler-Ross and Kessler model for grief from death (Denial, Anger, Bargaining, Depression, Acceptance, and Meaning). Where patient statements were not covered by any of the Kubler-Ross and Kessler stages, we would discuss a suitable theme to record the statement under. Themes were later merged and organized under superordinate themes where appropriate (i.e., we were trying to find commonalities between the words, ideas, and feelings that came up for my patients during their work with me.)

I found that while themes correlating with the stages of Anger, Depression, and Bargaining were shared in common between my patients and the grief after death model, there were few themes that correlated with the Acceptance and Meaning stages of the death model, especially with those patients who had been left by their partners.

Interpreting themes correlated with the Denial stage was complicated by the ambiguous loss of the partner. In addition, numerous themes emerged that lay outside of the Kubler-Ross model (I do hope I'm sounding intelligent - this is my research lingo.)

These findings reinforced my idea and conviction that the Kubler-Ross model is not suitable for us experiencing the post-relationship experience. I started to work on building a new, two-pronged model of post-relationship navigation with successful reconciliation and successful separation as the two healing outcomes. Further research helped me to clarify the tasks that patients and therapists would need to work through to achieve these outcomes.

This book you are reading now bears the fruits of that labor. It is information such as this, that is taken straight from the horse's mouth, so to speak (i.e., people like you and me that experience relationship breakups) that can help the healing process. It can help us understand what the experience is, and this can help us all help each other in recovery. And if we help each other in recovery, we will start to make the right decisions for us going forward

What is denial at this stage?
Death is a finish. An end. An absolute done deal. It's non-negotiable. We can never recover our relationship with someone that's dead. We *have to* negotiate a new reality for us without them. Yes, we can be in shock. We can wake up thinking, 'Oh my gosh, they've actually

gone.' Any person reading this who has lost someone dear to them will know the death experience. It does play tricks with the mind. Shock is a way of pausing a human so they can start to recover.

The biggest challenge for the old grief models is that the hope for a relationship coming back together again is possible and therefore is not denial. After a breakup, the person we've lost isn't generally cut out of our lives to the same degree. Rather than a finish, a relationship breakup is acted out between two people. There is an ending, at some point, but it's not clear cut. It is a dynamic dance between those people.

As you reading this will know well, our ex starts to fade out like a polaroid picture in reverse. It's not humanly possible to wipe a memory, so whilst we're holding on to that image, there is a chance that we could get back with them if they're still alive. Even if someone gets married or moves on with another partner, there is still a chance that they could leave that person and come back to us. Again, Hollywood is full of it.

One piece of research, cited in WorldMetrics (2024), found that 87 per cent of partners do return to a relationship following a breakup. Wow! (these aren't necessarily successful reunions - but it does happen).

Following a breakup, we are often plagued with what could have been and, crucially, *what still could be*. Such stalling, oscillating, and going around and around means that there is rarely a complete and lasting acceptance of the loss - and this did come out in my study, although I must stress that the small sample size makes it impossible to draw definite conclusions. Hands up, I'll admit it. It clearly leads more research from people with more time on their hands (nudge, nudge academic, scholastic colleagues of mine.)

However my findings are hugely useful for us. The above revelations point clearly to the one main reason why grief models are insufficient for navigating our relationship breakups. The elephant in the room. Our former partner is still alive! They have agency and mind and the ability to do things. And they can influence us in so many ways - consciously, subconsciously, directly, indirectly, deliberately, accidentally, and maliciously.

So, while the pain of relationship breakup is sometimes described and may feel a little bit like grief (after all, there is no equivalent to a family/socially validated funeral gathering with its opportunity for support and release; no 'memorialized spaces' to carry out acts of commemoration - i.e., we didn't bury somebody), looking to grief models is an unreliable way to heal ourselves from that loss.

I've personally disregarded the term post-relationship grief (PRG) and I've coined the expression - yes, this is an Acton first - post-relationship experience (PRE) when creating my model. I own it because it explains the breakup experience better, and anyone reading this will attest that going through this is not always a grief but, by goodness, it is an experience. I like post-relationship experience because it doesn't put a ceiling on what we're doing. It doesn't blinker us into one idea of what it's like. It opens it up to be this unique experience that we each individually move through. Some of this book will nail what you're feeling. When reading other parts, you might think, 'Well, that didn't really happen to me.' That's what the term post-relationship experience does for us. It gives us the ability to move through recovery and choices at our own pace, honoring our own unique experience. But it will be a model and a way that holds us at the same time.

Finally, I can now present to you a new way of gliding, dancing, jogging, running, navigating through this amazing storm called relationship breakup in a thoughtful, caring, supported way that takes account of how you're feeling and what you're experiencing. The ultimate goal is to be in peace and live an amazing life.

The 'Acton Post-relationship Experience Model (APREM)'
Please jump forward to **A Category Five Storm: Chapter 2** (page 57) if you want to skip this highly technical, scientific bit that needs to be here for my colleagues reading this and scholars that are going to challenge my model, which I would welcome very much because tweaking will never hurt. Bring it on!

So, for those of you that want to learn a little bit about this - or to be impressed by my big words - the next couple of pages are going to be intense.

While this model is empirically based, and can be adapted to fit all forms of post-relationship experience, it is nonetheless anchored by established psychological theories.

For example, there is recognition that the importance of belonging, from Maslow's hierarchy of needs (1943), helps to explain why rejecting or being rejected from your closest relationship has such an impact. In fact, Mears (2022) refers to breakup as 'failed belonging.'

The three most commonly cited types of grief models are task-based, stage-based and dual process. The 'Acton Post-relationship Experience Model' is largely task-based but incorporates some elements of staging.

It can also be understood through the frame of dual processing. According to dual process theories of loss (e.g., Stroebe and Schut, 2010, and Rando's 6R model, Rando, 1993), people bounce between loss focus (working on grief, intrusive thoughts, avoiding others, and experiencing sadness) and restoration focus (managing changes, doing new things, distracting oneself, suppressing grief, experiencing happiness, meeting new people, and creating new roles). People can flip from restoration focus to loss focus without warning, but they still may be making good progress with their healing and coping skills.

'Acton Post-relationship Experience Model': Underlying Structure

My model is structured as three separate but interlinked task-based stages of healing. Task-based theories of grieving, from Freud to Worden, commonly focus on four areas: accepting the reality of the loss, recovery work, adjusting to life without the former partner and finding healthy ways of connecting with them. All of the tasks presented in the 'Acton Post-relationship Experience Model' model can be allocated to one of these four areas, although the fourth area is more complex than would be found in any grief model because both parties have agency in a relationship breakup. I will reiterate that all tasks I've included in the model - and this book - are grounded in clinical practice rather than purely academic theory.

I have divided the tasks into three separate stages which reflect three overarching contexts of the post-relationship experience:

The first stage, which every patient must go through, is the 'Category Five Storm' stage. Seen through the dual process model lens, most of this work will be loss-oriented: focused on fully understanding and processing what you have lost. The patient will need to work through all of the tasks set out in the chapters of Part I before moving on to either the 'Making Up' stage (Part II) or the 'Moving On' stage (Part III). Each of these stages present further tasks that the patient must work through in order to find healing.

Most of the tasks in parts II and III are restoration-oriented, but since the patient is unlikely to have perfectly completed the tasks of Part I, they may need to revisit some of this loss-oriented work.

Aside from the three stages mentioned already, I have also incorporated a separate stage-based model of loss as one of the tasks in Part III because relationship breakup does include stages of denial, anger, bargaining, emptiness, and sadness. Understand that there is no simple progress from one stage to the next. You might find yourself cycling between these emotions several times. Acceptance is not included although this is the end destination of anyone traveling the breakup route.

A note for fellow therapists and academics
Our new psychological models of grief or loss often spring from academia and are based on theories generated from faculty-led research projects. Such theories often rest on scant evidence, and the models they spawn may only be suitable for certain populations

or types of loss. This often results in clinicians working at ground zero trying to fit their patients to the model rather than the other way around.

But there is no textbook-type breakup. Every loss is as unique as the relationship dynamic the couple had; like islands of pain in a shared human experience. As Murray (2016) says, the starting point for understanding grief may be in science, but the endpoint is in an individual experience. It is these varied experiences that we as clinicians work with. For a start, there is the possible effect of cumulative breakups or losses. The duration, intensity, and method of healing is different each time.

What I am intending to do in this study is to give a voice to the people that have experienced relationship breakups, and go from those experiences to inform better practice.

Evidence-based models can be even worse than theory-based models in focusing on specific populations or types of breakup. What's more, there can be a conflict of interests when those collecting the evidence are driven by commercial or ideological motivations. There needs to be some grounding in theory to protect clinicians and safeguard our patients.

Since the foundations of the 'Acton Post-relationship Experience Model' are in established, widely accepted psychological theories, professionals using it can securely hold their patients and safeguard their wellbeing while allowing them to free-fall into their authentic experience.

The evidence to support the efficacy of working through the various tasks comes from over 30 years of clinical experience not a short-term study bank-rolled by a pharmaceutical company or a post-treatment survey following a six week online course.

Nevertheless, I recommend that you, as I do, regularly refer to both your 'internal supervisor' and attend supervision as you work through the various tasks with your patients. As stated by Casement (1985), "Part of the work of internal supervision is to assess which could best serve the interests of the patient and of the therapeutic process."

If you are working with young people experiencing a relationship breakup, note that, just like with grief, adolescents can experience relationship breakup differently to adults. They may display seemingly random outbursts of anger, sadness, or excitement. They may seem to have accepted the loss and then return to anger and distress. It is helpful to consider such behaviors as being due to their limited life experience rather than poor reasoning skills. (Murray, 2016, p.134). Young people need time, space, and support. We can help our youth avoid self-blame and source security from other relationships in their lives.

For more guidance, read:
Casement, P. (1985). *On Learning from the Patient,* p.42. Tavistock/ Routledge Publications.

Murray, J. (2016). *Understanding loss: A guide for caring for those facing adversity.* Routledge/Taylor & Francis Group

Rando, T. A., Nezu, C. M., Nezu, A. M., and Weiss, M. J. (1993). *Treatment of Complicated Mourning.* Research Press Publishers.

Worden, J.W. (1991). *Grief Counselling and Grief Therapy (3rd ed.).* p. 141. Brunner-Routledge.

References:
Casement, P. (1985). *On Learning from the Patient*, p.42. Tavistock/Routledge Publications.

Doka, K. (2008). Disenfranchised grief in historical and cultural perspective. In M. S. Stroebe, R. O., Edwards, K. M., Palmer, K. M., Lindemann, K. G., and Gidycz, C. A. (2018). Is the end really the end? Prevalence and correlates of college women's intentions to return to an abusive relationship. *Violence Against Women.* 24(2), 207–222.

Downe-Wamboldt, B., and Tamlyn, D. (1997). An international survey of death education trends in faculties of nursing and medicine. *Death Studies.* Mar-Apr; 21(2):177-88.

Maslow A. H. (1943). A theory of human motivation. *Psychological Review.* 50(4): 370–96.
Mears, D. (2022). Choosing Life or Death. *Therapy Today.* Jul/Aug, pp 38-41)

Morris, C. E., and Reiber, C. (2011). Frequency, intensity and expression of post-relationship grief. *EvoS Journal: The Journal of the Evolutionary Studies Consortium.* 3, 1–11.

Murray, J. (2016). *Understanding loss: A guide for caring for those facing adversity.* Routledge/Taylor & Francis Group

Potter, M. (2022). Spinal injury - finding strength for an unplanned future. *The Psychologist.* April

Rando, T. A., Nezu, C. M., Nezu, A. M., and Weiss, M. J. (1993). *Treatment of Complicated Mourning.* Research Press Publishers.

Skinner, Q. (2021, November 18). *The sixth stage of grief.* Life Time. https://experiencelife.lifetime.life/article/the-sixth-stage-of-grief/

Stroebe, M. (2008). Cautioning Health-Care Professionals: Bereaved Persons Are Misguided Through the Stages of Grief. *OMEGA - Journal of Death and Dying.* 74(4), 455–473.

Stroebe, M. and Schut, H. (2010). The Dual Process Model of Coping with Bereavement: A Decade On. *OMEGA - Journal of Death and Dying.* 61(4), 273-290.

Worden, J.W. (1991). *Grief Counselling and Grief Therapy (3rd ed.).* p. 141. Brunner-Routledge.

WorldMetrics (2024). https://worldmetrics.org/reconciliation-after-separation-statistics/

PART I: A CATEGORY FIVE STORM

CHAPTER 2

HONESTLY? MY PATIENTS' AND MY OWN PERSONAL TRAILS OF DESTRUCTION INFORMED WHAT YOU ARE ABOUT TO READ

Four case studies wind their way through this book. These true stories are a mixture of personal experiences from my life and situations that my patients have presented to me,

Due to confidentiality and the risk of lawsuits and upsetting people, I've changed the names and places in the following case studies, while truthfully describing the events themselves.

I have also inserted snippets of these case studies throughout the book where I felt they would help us to understand the processes and experiences discussed.

Emily and Laura

Nurse Laura met Emily at a convent on an HIV/AIDS course run by the NHS. Laura was with Ava at the time, an Adlerian psychologist and viola player. She studied in Southampton and lived in London, while Ava lived in Manchester. The relationship ended and Laura hooked up with Emily before realizing that she still had feelings for Ava, so she went back and was seeing both women for a couple of weeks.

Laura realized this was destroying her, and one night she saw Emily standing by the bedroom window and thought, "It has to be you."

So, she broke off the relationship with Ava - it was an emotionally violent, sad, and horrible ending. Laura often wonders what it would have been like if she had chosen Ava because Emily turned out to be a liar and a violent, unfaithful drunk. They didn't even have sex for four out of five years because Emily was having multiple affairs. In fact, she was sleeping with a tenant in Laura's house while she was working away in the USA.

Laura didn't break, but she bent again and again. She thought Emily would change and conned herself into believing that she was in a relationship with a woman who met her emotional and sexual needs. Laura was doing well in her studies and also making money with property investment, so she bought a house that Emily had found in the auction section of a newspaper. She tried to resolve things by being patient and understanding, but Emily was very demeaning and, as an alcoholic, her first relationship was with drink, followed closely by other men and women.

Laura was studying and working in Southampton during the week, but she and Emily would spend the weekends together. Before Ava, Laura had been married to a man, Oliver, and they had a son together, Liam. Oliver was having problems (and would eventually end up in prison), so Liam would often stay with Laura in Southampton.

One weekend, Laura turned up at the London house early to find Emily's computer opened on her email inbox. She saw an email saying, 'Thanks for last night.' Laura clicked on the email to find photographs of Emily with two other women. When she went through her emails, Laura realized that every second night, she had been attending sex parties. Laura printed out the pictures and handed them to Emily after arranging to meet her for a drink. She told her not to return to their London home because the relationship was over.

When they parted, Laura promised to always look out for Emily, and she paid the deposit on a house for her so that she could get a mortgage. But a year later, Emily called Laura for help.She was in financial trouble and had been squatting in the house, not paying the mortgage, electricity, or gas. Laura gave Emily ten thousand pounds and took over the house. Emily found a new partner, called Isla, and they got married. Isla was a drinker and a cocaine user, but as far as Laura is aware, they are still together.

Laura learnt that sometimes we make wrong decisions in life. She wonders whether she should have stayed with Ava. She also realized that Emily wasn't stimulating - intellectually or in any other way - and that she had really gone for a woman that wasn't available.Her family were not available when she was growing up, so she went for the safe option where she was the caregiver, and the emotional and financial support.

Laura also realized that she had been in trauma throughout the relationship because there was always a weekly or daily drama to navigate. She also suffered a blow to her ability to trust because she was always the last to know. People kept on dropping hints by asking, "Have you seen Emily? What's Emily doing?"

Reflecting on her experiences, Laura realizes that having a partner who was emotionally absent, cruel, violent, and aggressive felt comfortable and familiar because it reminded her of the environment she grew up in.

David and James

Therapist James met IT expert David online. David was very professional, and a very powerful man in the corporate world, and he absolutely adored James. James found David very attractive and felt it was incredible to be loved, and the sex was great, too. They were a normal couple in many ways. But soon, it came about that David was tied to his mother's apron strings, and there were some other things that didn't make sense to James, although he did his best to ignore them.

David and James both traveled the world for work, and while James was staying in their Canadian home, David was in London with James' brother, enjoying a meal at Fortnum & Mason. David bought two bottles of champagne as he was leaving, and said he was going to have dinner with Noah and Mia, a couple with whom they did everything.

James didn't hear from David for a day which was unusual for their relationship: David normally called six to eight times a day! James tried to call, but he couldn't get hold of David. His phone was off, and this was before the era of text and smartphones. So, after speaking to his brother, James called Noah and Mia at home the following day, asking them, "How was dinner last night?"

"What are you talking about?" said Noah, "We haven't seen David since you left several weeks ago." James returned from America and confronted David. The couple had a stand-up fight, screaming at each other, with David denying he was having an affair but unable to explain where he had been and why he had lied to James' brother. James had endured previous unfaithful partners and had previously told David that he would be gone if he even smelt another man, or did anything untoward or deceiving. So, when David went to Wales for a business trip, James moved out. David called James two days later and said, "I'm at the airport, why don't you pick me up, and we can go for dinner." James said, "I've left you." David burst into tears in the middle of Cardiff airport, professing his love, but James stood his ground and said, "I'm sorry. I don't know what went on, but I can't stay with you."

James felt very vulnerable and alone because he didn't really have family or friends. He agreed to meet David for lunch at a hotel. During the conversation, David revealed that a friend, Ethan, who was a magistrate judge in a child court, had been arrested on child rape charges. That set alarm bells ringing. James recalled that David had always had a 'funny thing' for the teenage boy that cleaned their car. He also recalled that David had recently got rid of his main computer. Having been abused as a child, James was in turmoil, confused, not knowing what to think or do. Were Ethan and James that different? James loved David, and they had shared a normal life together, but there was something creepy about David's attitude towards children. Sometimes when they had sex, David would say things such as, "Come on, boy!" which made James feel sick. But he ignored it because he didn't want to acknowledge what it might mean. He realizes now that he ignored a lot to survive that relationship - and he almost didn't make it.

After lunch at the hotel, James walked home and killed himself by taking an overdose. He spoke to the Samaritans for two hours as he took the pills. He was rushed to the hospital, and his brother was told that James was dying. James even remembers dying several times. But after the most incredibly painful journey, he survived. He remembers David being there, telling him that he loved him and wanted to be with him, but after he was discharged, James took a cab to David's house only to find out he was away. James recalls David vomiting on the other end of the phone, but can't remember much else.

James was seriously ill at the time, and it took every ounce of strength in his body to recover. At times, he wished he hadn't survived because the pain was so intense. Survival seemed cruel. He moved to Western Australia to heal. He dived in the oceans and drove his Jeep in the Outback, heedless of snakes, spiders, crocodiles, or sharks. He had a beautiful time and his motto was, "If I'm taken, I'm taken." The feeling of being spiritually connected with the world healed him. He spent time with shamans, and it changed his life. He had always been spiritual. He could see and hear things that other people couldn't; he knew when people were dying; and he could feel what was happening in somebody's life without the language to express it. It was this that helped him to become a successful therapist. His time with the shamans, in Australia and, later, America rekindled his spiritual life.

Twenty years on and James is in a different place. He is glad he survived and he has now forgiven David. But he has learned that there are some imperfections he can't accept, such as the attraction of a grown man to a child.

Matt and Sarah
Interior designer Sarah lived and owned a house in Canada and had an apartment in Newcastle, UK, but she was alone and worried about her finances. She was dating a few guys but nothing was clicking.

Her daughter, Sophia, had left Canada to return to England, saying she loved the lifestyle but it was too far away from her father Lucas (Sarah's ex), who was living with cancer. Lucas called Sarah one day and told her, "I'm dying. My cancer is going to go to the brain." Sarah said he could call her at any time. She read cyclist Lance Armstrong's book and flew over to support Lucas through his chemotherapy and surgery, and to say goodbye.

But when Lucas called Sarah some years later, she realized that his cancer hadn't been terminal. It had all been one big betrayal. Sarah felt very vulnerable and decided to move to New York. It was where she had started her career, and she felt happy and comfortable there. She soon met a guy called Matt online, but back then there was no video chat, so they spoke on the phone with only each other's profile photos to go on.

Matt was from New Jersey, and their first meeting was a bad omen. As Sarah flew into Newark airport, the airplane's hydraulics broke and there was almost a crash landing. She lost all of her luggage because it was soaked with hydraulic fuel, so she had to claim for that. When she met Matt, she didn't find him attractive at all. His manner and appearance was nothing like his profile picture and their phone chat had suggested. But she was stuck for now, so she went to dinner with Matt and his friends, whom she found very nice. She accused herself of being too judgemental, and decided to stay the night with him. They had sex and the day after that she moved in, but she realized, after a couple of months, that all was not what it seemed. Matt came from a very affluent background but his father and him were owned by the banks. Feeling sorry for him, Sarah stayed. Besides, they had a really wild life because he was from old money, so they would often be invited to restaurant and bar launches. She recalls one time where there was a caged lion outside a nightclub being fed raw meat as they walked in on the red carpet. The couple were photographed by magazines and newspapers, and Sarah loved the bling and fun of the celebrity lifestyle.

At home, things were not quite so upbeat. She never quite trusted Matt. She often found him watching porn, and then her fears were confirmed when she discovered he had been going to sex clubs and even having unsafe sex with other women whilst they were dating.

Matt promised that he would be faithful going forward, and Sarah believed him. Then Sophie had a baby and went into meltdown and almost died. She was trying to kill herself by self-harming. So, Sarah rented out the house she was renovating in New York and returned to England to take care of her daughter, planning to spend a few months there. She rented a house with a studio flat in Newcastle and was joined there by Matt and his father, Frank. But Sarah soon realized that this wasn't going to be a quick fix. She had to be there permanently for her daughter. She explained this to Matt but, of course, he had no money, and Frank was an alcoholic with a liver transplant. So, Frank went to live with his brother in California, and Matt stayed in Newcastle, England.

Sarah had been ready to end the relationship, but was reassured that he had committed to come to England, while her long-term tenant in New York eased some of her financial worries. But Matt was often very violent and unpredictable. Sarah never knew when he was going to blow up. The final straw came when they were on vacation in California, drinking at a really nice bar on Venice Beach with Matt's friend Ruby. Without warning, Matt turned and started screaming at Sarah. When he grabbed hold of her, Sarah urged the bartender to call security immediately. When security arrived, Matt let go of Sarah, only to find out later that he had been beating up Ruby.

Matt went back to England while Sarah remained in America for four months to help out with Frank's apartment. She also wanted to spend the time rebuilding her design career. She knew she had to leave this guy, and shortly after returning to Newcastle, she ended the relationship and kicked him out. As he was leaving, the truth dawned on Sarah. She didn't love Matt. She didn't want to be with him. She didn't even find him attractive.

Matt went back to the US but it was not quite over. He did return to England, living with a mutual connection whom he was also beating up. Despite Sarah providing all the financial stability, Matt had been telling everybody that she was a gold digger, and that all the money was his because she couldn't get a mortgage. She just couldn't believe that she had been sitting at people's tables, building her life and reputation, while behind her back, Matt had been telling everybody that she was nothing and that everything she had was down to him. She was completely blown away.

It took Sarah two years to get away from Matt, but she did it. And what did she learn? That any of us could be living with a serial killer or a pedophile because she had no idea Matt was living a double life. More positively, she learnt that she doesn't want to be around violence, and she doesn't want to be around someone who doesn't want to work. She wants somebody who has their own money, their own career, and who she can hold an intelligent conversation with.

Most of all, she wants to be with someone who will love her for who she is.

Mary and John

Dentist John was trying to recover from a difficult relationship. He wasn't dating, and he was seeing a psychologist in Glasgow who asked him what kind of partner he wanted to bring into his life.

John said his ideal woman would have an established career and her own money. She would be loving, sexy, and able to hold a proper conversation, not just engage in small talk. His psychologist asked John if there was anybody in his life that was like that.

After thinking about it for some time, John realized that Mary, an attorney he knew from Chicago, was currently single. A couple of years ago, when they were both in relationships, they had enjoyed a boat trip together on a boat she owned. She also had a decent property portfolio, so seemed self-sufficient. They had talked a lot, and John had found her appealing.

So, that night, John was at home with a glass of wine, and he sent Mary an email saying he was going to be in America and that it would be nice to meet up. Mary happened to have a spare seat at a gala and invited John to go with her. John eagerly accepted the invitation. They spoke a couple of times on the phone and got on so well that Mary decided to come to Liverpool a month before John was due to travel to Chicago. She asked him to book a hotel, which cost John £1,000, and although he was surprised that she didn't offer to contribute towards it, he was embarrassed to admit that money was tight due to ongoing renovations to his Glasgow home.

Besides, he felt desperate and lonely. He was setting up a new dental practice, his home was in chaos, and he was struggling with low self-esteem following three unhappy relationships.

Instead of returning to America, Mary accompanied John to Glasgow, and their relationship took off. Convinced he had been to blame for his past failed relationships, John was determined to try harder to make this one work. The new couple agreed that they would spend a month in England followed by a month in America, and that's how their relationship would continue.

When John first flew to Chicago, he was introduced to many people who he presumed were Mary's friends. He realized some time later that they were little more than acquaintances, part of a business group. Mary was staying in a tiny, one-bedroom rental apartment, and John found a note on the bedside table with a 'to do' list that included paying off credit cards. He realized Mary was down on her luck, and he wondered what had happened to all of her properties.

But John was a rescuer, so he thought he could make the situation work. But once John was in America, Mary rarely came to England. So every couple of weeks, John was flying to America and then back to London. He was flying economy, in the cheapest seats, because he was still renovating his house in England.

Although Mary had asked John to move in with her, each time John returned to Chicago, he would find that she had packed away all of his possessions into boxes rather than putting them away in cupboards. John didn't understand, but he tried to ignore it, and eventually they did move in together. But Mary wasn't earning enough money through her private legal work and was unable to secure a full-time job. However, she eventually won a big contract and things improved.

They had moved into a two-bedroom flat, Mary's father helping out with the costs, and John felt they were finally building a comfortable life together.

Then, all of a sudden, Mary told John, "We're over. I need you to pack up your stuff and leave." John just couldn't believe it. He had given up the penthouse he was renting in England, and his house was still not ready, so he had nowhere to go. Mary helped John pack up his boxes and put him on a plane - which John paid for. He was completely lost again.

Mary's dad then took a turn for the worse and she helped move him into a home because he was trying to kill himself. Mary and John did still talk and message one another occasionally, and Mary explained that her father had not been the same since her mother died, despite the fact that he hadn't shown her much love when she was alive. John empathized with Mary's late mother. He had never felt loved by Mary.

While on vacation in Greece, John got a phone call from Mary, suggesting that they take a European cruise and see whether there was a way forward? John was so lost, vulnerable, and lonely that he agreed. While on the boat, John asked Mary whether she thought they would get married. John felt too insecure in America. It cost him a fortune in healthcare and everything else. But Mary said, "I don't think so. Not for now. But let's see how it goes."

Whilst they had been apart, John had put everything into getting his Newcastle house back into a liveable state. He sold his other property and the insurance company finally paid out, so John didn't lose too much money in the process.

But the cruelty from Mary continued, awful and relentless. Mary would punish John by withholding sex, and John continued to pay a fortune for medical care, not realizing that Mary could have supported him with that. She bought him a birthday present - a cruise trip around Italy - but insisted John pay for the airplane tickets, even though she knew he had little money at the time. John's daughter, Sam, was going through difficulties and he was trying to manage her while building his dental practice, working 60 hours a week, traveling, and going out almost every night to networking events that Mary was involved with.

John didn't know what was going on. He was hit by a car and had spine surgery. Then he had more surgery following a high velocity car crash. And he just thought at this point, 'There must be something terribly wrong with me.' And that belief meant that he continued to stay with Mary, but he hated his life. He was so lonely, he cried almost every morning. He was packing his bags several times a week and then unpacking them without Mary knowing. Then one day, as he stood in the kitchen after another really cruel act from Mary, he looked up to the sky and said, "Higher power, I don't like being judgemental. I don't like being angry. I don't like being jealous of other people. I don't want to be this way. Help me change." And sure enough, things started to change.

First, John realized that Mary was never going to change. This was it. She couldn't be any different. John moved into a new place in Scotland, and he had to force Mary to transfer four hundred thousand dollars from the joint pot of money they had built up together. She had promised she would transfer it to him so that he could cover the delay in selling his old property. Even then, she transferred the money just one day before the deadline.

The day before moving in, John was shopping online for toilet rolls and stuff, but Mary sucked out all of the excitement, saying. "Why are you doing that? You can't afford it. You don't have any money." John looked at her and thought, 'We've made all that money. I've got a half million pound house I'm selling. Why would you ruin it now, lying in bed at night when we move in tomorrow?' Every bit of air exited his body.

They moved into the new house, but it was a horrible experience for John. They didn't have sex, they stayed in the guest room, some of the furniture didn't turn up, and Mary really wasn't involved in the process. In fact, she was going to a four-day conference in New York a couple of days later. Mary asked if John wanted to go. "I can't," said John. "We have all this stuff to do here." When Mary sent John the tickets, he noticed they were for three weeks. She was going to leave John to do everything again. He thought, "I'm not doing this anymore," and then, at the same time, John's brother and sister-in-law sat down with John and told him that they were sorry for crossing a line, but they refused to make any more excuses for Mary. The situation was so wrong on every level.

John left Mary at that moment, although he did go back to America to care for their sick dog. When he arrived, Mary had deducted money from her half of a credit card bill, explaining it as interest charged from the money she transferred to England. John was in shock, but he stood his ground. "How can you charge interest on money that's ours?" He said, "What are you doing?" Mary never mentioned it or charged him interest again, but John knew he was done. He returned to the UK as the new kitchen was being installed, and he studied some dentistry courses just to get away and think about what was going on.

Mary had previously said that she would never marry John. Just before they had meant to get married, she had set up trust documents, but they were all in her favor. John had signed everything over to her and had never seen the documents she signed. That's when John realized that it was all a con and had left.

But whilst John was in the UK, Mary called every day. She had realized he had left, so she started to promise John the world, even promising that she would marry him. They spoke, one night, for two and a half hours. Mary said that John was the love of her life and that she wouldn't be able to live without him. So, again John flew all the way back to America, with all the documents to get married, thinking Mary had changed. But when John suggested they get married on a boat - Mary was planning to visit the Antarctic - he caught a sneer in Mary's face or perhaps her soul. He didn't want to see it because he was so excited.

When John got back to Chicago, their house was a mess, and he had to stay in a motel. Mary had lied to him about everything. Christmas Day was awful. So, in a restaurant on Boxing Day, John stood up and asked Mary, "How much are you worth net?" Mary replied, "840," and John said, "Then you've been doing something terribly wrong because you were worth three and a half million several years ago. So, either you're lying then, you're lying now, you've got gambling problem again or something's going wrong. But even now, at this moment in our lives, you cannot tell me the truth." Mary asked whether John was intending to pay the four hundred thousand back, and John said, "No, I won't. I want control over a quarter of what we own. I've said that in therapy, I've said that in writing. That's five hundred thousand, so I need a hundred thousand from you in order to move forward."

Once more, Mary asked him, "So, you're not going to transfer that four hundred thousand back?"
"Absolutely not," said John, standing up. "I'm worth more than this." All of a sudden, he had seen it clearly for what it was: a big con. "You can't go now," Mary said. It was a three mile walk home in the rain. "I'm going to," John replied. "But first I'm going to call my brother and tell him the truth." For the first time, John saw Mary's face turn white with shock. She knew that was him done.

John walked back in the tropical rain, and guess what? Mary drove past him. John had a terrible road ahead of him. He got on a plane, two days later. Mary was tracking his flights and called him but cut the phone off before he could answer. John thought about calling her back, but he now knew that there was not enough glue to keep him in the relationship. He stayed on that plane. It was a really rough journey, but John knew he needed to be in his truth.

John used to lie about his exes, but he decided that this time he was going to be honest with people and tell them exactly what had happened. He made that decision because despite being really worried about telling his brother the truth, he received nothing but love, understanding, and compassion. "Get on a plane now. Go," he had said. And that gave John the courage to be in his truth.

John turned himself inside out over the next year or so, and yes, ideas of suicide came and went. He dated a few people, and nothing gelled, but the most important thing was that he became spiritual, he was in his truth, the energy changed, and he manifested a new life. And he would never change it.
He asked for abundance, and he got it. He sees a bigger purpose in life. He's not struggling anymore. He's got immense knowledge. His

career is taking a new turn, and he is the most peaceful and happy he has ever been.

The biggest things he had to do were to forgive; understand that he is enough; accept his imperfections; accept the imperfections of others; choose his battles wisely; love people; be kind to people no matter what their position; be kind to himself, and move on, be in nature, and enjoy every bit of the Earth: the raindrops, the mist, the smell of moss, the sound of streams.

John: I told my GP that my wife had rather than we had broken up. Instead of hearing the usual, "Sorry about that, plenty more fish in the sea," etc. I got the exact amount of compassion I needed.

PART I: A CATEGORY FIVE STORM

CHAPTER 3

WE WILL WALK THIS TOGETHER: HOPE

"We spend our entire lives in our heads: let's make it a nice, healthy place to be."
- Dr. Michael Acton -

Trigger Warning
The following chapter discusses suicide in detail. Please proceed with caution and consider skipping this section if you find this topic distressing.

We must start talking about suicide when it comes to relationships
In my introduction, I said there were only two possible destinations we can head for after a relationship breakup.

However, there are those destinations that nobody dares to talk about: those that lead to death - either of the self or of the partner. Those roads avoid the work of breaking up or making up altogether, but they deliver only grief for the survivors of suicide and homicide.

Most people would be shocked if they knew how many people took their own lives as a direct or indirect result of a relationship breakup. It's never been studied academically or by the press. I hope this serves as a push for someone out there to heed, take note, and to make this study a priority. I personally am sick and tired of losing good and beautiful souls in the struggle of post-relationship experience battles.

In comparison, the number of people, including children, who commit suicide following a bereavement is minuscule. Where is the conversation about this? Where are the angry protests? Why is so much blood spilled behind closed doors?

One big factor in suicide is the feeling of being rejected. Another is profound isolation. Another is feeling abandoned and unworthy.

We must avoid looking at the length of a relationship as an indicator of a suicide risk. While we may be able to understand that the loss of a life partner and a bitter divorce can tip some people over the edge, the ending of a short-term relationship can be just as dangerous, if not more. The intensity of some relationships, even those that are in their first few weeks, can be so high that breakup is destructive and traumatic. Trauma increases the risk of suicide, as indicated by the polyvagal theory diagram.

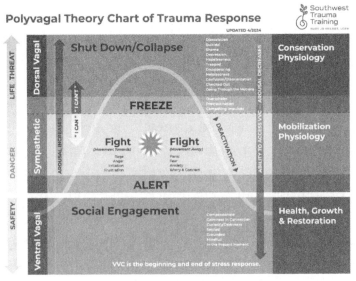

If you're reading this and any part of you is thinking about suicide, please reach out immediately to your local services. Everywhere now has services, but now, with the internet, you can tap into any service anywhere in the world. Talk to somebody. Please, I beg you.

Glimmers of hope

The risk of suicide can be reduced with appropriate professional help, and there are some promising success stories. Halpin's article in a recent issue of BACP's *Therapy Today* highlighted the early positive effects on male suicide reduction coming from James' Place, a community-based therapy center. Even something as seemingly trivial as helping men work through exercise cards with probing questions is saving lives. Connection saves lives. Warmth from other human beings saves lives. Understanding saves lives.

This article stressed the importance of patients acting as 'trusted supporters' for the service, spreading the word to their suffering peers. If this book serves to help you to heal and move forward, then I am truly successful, and please recommend or pass this book on to others experiencing this painful post-relationship experience.

Although relationship breakups happen, of course, irrespective of gender, sexuality, etc., women, on the whole, are more comfortable buying books about relationships than men. Unfortunately, many men avoid such resources because they feel ashamed for needing help. Death is a high price to pay for shame.

With appropriate support, it's possible to channel the drive to kill ourselves into a symbolic act. Therapist and social worker Katherine Best, cited in Mears (2022) explores symbolic suicide (the killing of

our shame, social mask, or false beliefs, etc.)
In all my years working, my worst experiences are when I hear of someone that has killed themselves and they didn't have anyone to hold their hand during the worst time of their experience here on Earth. I personally hold out my hand to all people that are contemplating or planning suicide.

In order to help us understand the importance of being open about feeling hopeless in our post-relationship experience, I have borrowed the help from a very dear colleague, Dr. Diana Kaufman, to contribute to this chapter. Diana and her campaign helps us to understand the healing and the opportunities available that can help us get through the tough times and make the best of this time on Earth. I'm going to pass you over now to Diana, and thank you Diana for helping us.

Love. It makes the world go round. For many it can make the world stop.

Please allow me to introduce myself. My name is Diane Kaufman, MD. I am the founder/director of the Hold On Campaign for Suicide Prevention that uses the power of art to connect, express, and heal (www.holdoncampaign.org). I am a poet, artist, humanism-medicine-awardee, and as of June 30, 2023, a retired child psychiatrist. In 2019, I received the Frank L. Babbott award from the SUNY-Downstate Medical Center's Alumni Association in recognition of my distinguished service to the general community and medical profession. I am dedicated to transforming trauma and despair into life affirming creativity. And how did that happen?

Because I am a suicide attempt and suicide loss survivor who has Bipolar II Disorder. I understand the deadly reality of suicide.

And love? "What's love got to do with it?" to quote from the classic song performed by Tina Turner. Love of life, love for life, and our passion for living and enduring its suffering (call it our life force) is nurtured, strengthened, damaged, or even destroyed by our experiences of love.

I once wrote a poem titled, *Now I Know*. It's from a poetry self-help book I wrote for the residents of Integrity House, an alcohol and substance abuse residential treatment program in Newark, New Jersey. I started volunteering there after I was divorced. I was seeking connection; the opportunity to show care for another in need. I began by facilitating a women's creativity group and wanted to also start a writing group for men and women. In the interim time, while I was deciding whether or not to do two groups or just the one writing group, I had the idea for the poetry book. The poems I chose were ones I'd already written in response to people and events in my life, and these poems also had universal themes. Next to each of the fifteen poems, I wrote a writing prompt inspired by that particular poem's content. I titled the book, *Cracking Up and Back Again: Transformation Through Poetry*, and later renamed it, *15 Poems to Healing & Recovery*, when I added an *Arts Medicine Transformation Curriculum*.

Now I Know
Now I know
It was because I saw your heart
You were wide open
And I looked inside
There it was

A red sparkling jewel
It was beating
It was weeping
It was bursting with love
To share
And feel
And I know
You must have seen
And known
That inside me
There is a heart
Too
Now I know

And here is the writing prompt that accompanied the poem:

"We all want to love and be loved. Life may have hardened our skins and even hardened our hearts, but true love is what we still desire. Often we think it is someone else loving us that will release us. That may be so, but the deepest and most powerful love is the love within our very own heart. Whatever you choose to call it: soul, spirit, higher power of God within, it is this inner love that sets us free and gives welcome and freedom to all we meet. How open or closed is your heart? What made it so? What kind of heart do you want to have?"

We are all woven tapestries of lived experiences. It is only on the other side of the tapestry do we see the multitude of strands, the knots, and all the dynamic and conflicted intricacies that have struggled and may still be struggling to resolve the tension, to reconcile, and make us whole.

Dr. Michael Acton

When I was in medical school, I attempted suicide by taking an overdose of prescribed medication. My intent was to be kill myself. This was no cry for help. Poetry that I'd written (I still have that poetry diary) clearly show a person in worsening mental health, increasing despair and hopelessness, recurrent thoughts of suicide, an upswing into what may have been hypomania, and then a plunge into suicidal despair. I was also involved in an unhealthy relationship at that time. This is the poem I wrote before my suicide attempt:

I'm ugly
I'm worthless
I'm nothing
You can't love who I am
No one can love who I am
No one has ever loved who I am
If I show you who I am
I will have to kill myself
Because being dead will be the
Only way I can hide once more.

"Love" is repeated over and over again. The inability to be loved, to have love, to be worthy of love. This "deprivation of love" was one of the igniting dark flames of my wanting to extinguish myself in combination with the yet to be diagnosed Bipolar II Disorder. The poem's declarations were entirely false, but I could not comprehend that fact. They were the heart-felt and mind-thought distortions of a troubled sense of self and other. I believed the poem's words and message to be absolutely true. So much so that they justified suicide. I felt there was no one to whom I could safely turn. It was, or so it felt to me, only death that could understood my pain. It offered solace and release from pain that I believed would go on forever in the midst of mental anguish. In a strange way, death had become my lover.

It was luck that saved my life. My fantasy was taking the pills, falling asleep, and not waking up. But instead of going into blissful sleep, I became nauseous and felt so sick. I began vomiting. When I began to vomit blood, and it was quite clear I was not going to die, I sought help. I ended up receiving treatment in a hospital emergency room (NG tube and charcoal, maybe ipecac as well, but I don't remember) and was medically admitted for a few days. Once medically stable, I recall being asked if I wanted to be transferred to the psychiatric unit. I responded with a definite "no." This was my reasoning: I was no longer having suicidal thoughts, I wanted to forget the suicide attempt had ever happened, and as soon as possible I wanted to resume my life and role as a medical student to be "normal" again.

Perhaps there was a part of me that would have welcomed a psychiatric admission, as an acknowledgement of what had brought me to this crisis, but I declined the offer. Mostly, I was asking and answering this question: "How can I ever become a psychiatrist if I tried to kill myself and am a patient on a psych unit?" The answer was obvious: you "can't become" a psychiatrist if you've attempted suicide and were admitted. The "admission" in the full sense of that word, would make everything that happened all too real. I was discharged home and followed up with outpatient treatment. I still to this day, though, believe I would have been admitted voluntarily to the psychiatric unit if I'd responded, "yes."

"Best to forget and move on" is what I must have been thinking. But lessons unlearned have a way of repeating themselves. My father-in-law died by self-inflicted gunshot. My adult female patient who suffered from chronic pain took her own life. My adult male patient wrote a series of suicide letters but then had decided not to kill himself. He later gave me the suicide letter he'd written for me. In it he "thanked me" for my help but he was traveling towards death and could not stop himself. Thank God he changed his mind and chose life instead. And there is more...

My teenage patient C. hanged herself the day after our Friday psychiatric appointment. She spoke of being bullied but denied having thoughts of suicide. Indeed, her mother and I had remarked to each other with a smile how well we thought she was doing. Upon learning C. had died, but with the cause of death not yet revealed, my first thought in trying to make sense of what had happened, was that my physically healthy patient must have died from a cardiac arrest from ADHD medication. Not suicide. But it tragically was. I believe it was an impulsive act. I attended her funeral. The mother continued to bring her two sons to see me for their psychiatric care. More than a year later, I wrote a "poetic progress note" about the last time I saw C. The poem, *What Makes Us* (as in to live or die) was "brought to life" by two actors. Later I renamed it, *13 Reasons Why Not*. The video ends with the suicide prevention number and the words, "You don't have to kill yourself to stop the pain."

In August 2019, S., who was my friend and former mental health colleague (a psychiatric nurse practitioner), died by suicide. I used to think I would send family members to see S. if they needed help. So caring and excellent were her skills as a mental health provider. I found out on Facebook about her death. Recently divorced and no longer able to work due to the severity of her mental illness, she was being supervised by a family member who had come to live with her. S., who was the loving mother of two sets of young twins, found the car keys that were hidden from her. She drove to the bridge and jumped off. Depression, like an invasive cancer, devoured the person she once was.

A week or two later and still that month, I was walking down Lovejoy Street near my home, going to Starbucks. I noticed a tree with branches coming off its trunk in what I thought was an unusual location. I took a photo of the tree and spontaneously wrote these words: "Just like this tree. We all yearn to grow. Hope lives. Shame kills. Everyday is suicide prevention day. Take care of yourself and may you grow ever stronger in your love."

There it is again. The word, "love." I sent the photo and my words to artist Amanda Meador and asked her to create a poster. Initially, Mandy's image of the tree had no earth surrounding the roots. The roots were just dangling down and exposed. I told Mandy to "ground" the tree and to add a few flowers to the earth. Good for the tree and good for people. This is how the *Just Like This Tree* suicide prevention poster, that also became an art card with resources on the back of the card, was born. I've had the image enlarged to 7 feet tall and I bring it to NAMI (National Alliance on Mental Illness) Walks events. It always draws attention because of its direct communication on suicide, its beauty, and life-affirming message.

Dr. Michael Acton

In my grief I had turned once more to the power of art to express, connect, and heal. Art allowed me to be witnessed in my mourning. This was also the start of *Creative Life Lines*, a series of posters that reach out with compassion and creativity to help save lives.

This is the truth that all of us share. All who love will one day grieve. And grief's healing calls upon us to rise up from the darkness and love once more. There are many kinds of losses. Physical death. Physical illness. Pain. Ongoing disability. Betrayal, Violence. Abuse. Loss of trust. Moral injury. The loss of relationships. Loss of employment. Loss of financial stability. Loss of dreams. Loss of hope.

Are these losses, these "living deaths" witnessed, validated, honored, grieved, and mourned by ourselves and others?

Can suicide be a grief that was not able to be mourned?

Here's a poem by 26-year-old Katelyn. Her husband, Raymond, has graciously given permission for it to be shared in the hope that it can help save lives. He found this poem in Katelyn's poetry journal. The same journal which she'd asked him not to read when she was alive.

Suicide
Such a simple word
Such an easy definition
Such a permanent choice
Such hard,
Drastic,
And painful reasons.
Would you believe me if I told you I wanted to commit suicide?

Would you still
talk to me?
Or would you treat me like you would every other person who has
done it?
Ignore them.
Make fun of them.
Say they were stupid and selfish,
For feeling the way they do?
Thinking the way they are?
Hurting the way they do?
Is it really selfish to kill yourself when you are thoroughly convinced
that everyone hates you and they all want you to die?
Is it stupid to truly kill yourself after constantly being bullied for a
long time?
Have you thought of this?
Do you still feel the same?
Such hard questions to answer.
Such hard feelings to ignore.
The answer gnaws at you,
No. No. NO.
If *you* felt like *this*,
What would *you* do?
Pain isn't something you can ignore.
Pain isn't something you can end so simply,
Is it?
Such a thing to think about.
Such a thing to contemplate.
But there is always a question going through your mind.
Who would care?
Would you?
Think about it.

I asked Raymond how he would have responded to Katelyn's outcry if he'd been allowed to read her poem while she was still alive. This is an excerpt from his response:

"When have I ever ignored you, pookins? You were my whole world. Even though you actually went through with it, I could still never call you stupid or selfish. On the contrary, you did it cuz you thought the world would be better off without you. It's not; it's far, far darker and colder without you in it. You touched so many lives in the short time you spent on this earth. So many lives that are still missing you to this day. So many who blame themselves for your disappearance. I've come to the acceptance that I'll never be able to get past the guilt. The guilt I know you felt so strongly when your father committed. And even more so when your only brother followed in his footsteps. I didn't fully comprehend the level of grief you were enduring until I lost you. Now I understand but now it's too late... ."

"So to answer your question, I would care! Of course I would care! Now I'm left to wonder what I ever did to make you feel otherwise. If only you'd heard the sincerity in my words when I said how much I would care if you left me. Your mother would care. Your pets would care. Our dog, Zeeba, still waits at the door for you to come home. You know how much separation anxiety she already had. Your friends, your family. They all care. I guess you had time to think about it. I just wish you woulda made a different decision because my life will never be the same without you."

William Shakespeare with acumen spoke of grief's needs in these four lines:

Give sorrow words.
The grief that does not speak
Whispers the oe'r-fraught heart,
and bids it break

Yes, we need to speak. We also need to be heard. To be heard by a part of ourselves that recognizes we need help. To be heard by caring friends and family. Our lives have value no matter what our disturbed mind is telling us. We need to speak our pain aloud and allow ourselves to be heard. We deserve compassion and mental health treatment designed to best address our unique needs, be that medication, therapy, and/or hospitalization. Most importantly, but rarely if ever documented in any treatment plan, we need love.

Art is a means of expression. The poem, the drawing, the dance, and the song safely contain thought and emotion. Art alone, however, without the ability to also keep ourselves safe from harm, will not save our lives. Internal change and external change are possible. Problems can be solved. We can learn to endure what seems unbearable because thoughts and feelings come and go. They are not permanent. Yet all of this is to no avail if we act on our suicidal thoughts. To quote the words on the Hold On Campaign for Suicide Prevention's bracelet: "Hold On. Don't Give Up. Call 988. Save Your Life."

I wrote a lyric years ago when I was taking songwriting lessons with The Prophet X. He suggested I choose a word and create off of that. I decided upon the word, "door," with all its symbolic meanings. The song was titled, *Passionate Miracle*. In contributing to this book's chapter, I revisited that song and was able to comprehend it in a new way. The song is now renamed, *Love's Freedom Song: How to*

Dr. Michael Acton

Live & Love Beyond Heartbreak. It is on my Arts Medicine for Hope & Healing YouTube channel. Here are the song's verses, chorus and bridge:

Verse 1

I've been here so many times before
Standing in front of another closed door
Fighting doesn't feel so good anymore
And my heart is tired of keeping score
But nothing changes if it stays the same
Yesterday repeated is but a fool's game
But if today I gave life my all
Faith in love will knock down that wall

Chorus

Break through the wall and go to the door
Passionate miracle
I've been waiting for
I've been waiting for
Spirit of love is stronger than all my pain
When the door opens
I will be alive again
Alive again
I will be alive again

Verse 2

Holding on to heartbreak strengthens my fears
Inside my loneliness only tears
Without love in my life I'll lose my mind

To love again I must leave the past behind
It's not easy but who said it would be
To stop the blame, regret, what ifs, and maybes
This moment now is the right place and time
Be brave and take hold of the key

Bridge
I pause in the moment feel my breath
The door beckons open what else is left
To live in shadows or be seen in the light
Each morning I answer the questions of life
Life brought me heartache and so much more
My heart has suffered but still it can soar
I ask who am I and what will life be
Will I stay imprisoned or will I be free

Love's spirit, the true meaning of love in word and deed, releases us from heartbreak so that we may live and love again. In the words of 1 Corinthians 13-7, "Love always protects, always trusts, always hopes, always perseveres." This unconditional love helps restore wholeness to heart and mind felt brokenness.

My hope and prayer for all are the words of the *Just Like This Tree* poster: "Everyday is suicide prevention day. Take care of yourself and may you grow ever stronger in your love."

Thank you Diana for your support and help with this. If your contribution helps just one person, then we are truly grateful to you forever for you helping us.

Suicide intervention strategies: the missing question

This next part is me trying to help, in some way, to curb and understand suicide better, and it highlights how ridiculous at times the government are with ways to improve outcomes - not just in suicide but also crime, mental health, equality, etc.

We always have to understand that there is always hope, there is always tomorrow. It doesn't matter what pain we feel now, there is the ability to move forward, but unless we understand where suicidal ideation comes from, we can't really do much about it.

So, in 2023, the UK Government launched a new tool to help empower suicide prevention planners, of which I am one. Named near to real-time suspected suicide surveillance (nRTSSS), the tool aims to rapidly highlight trends in suicide by looking at factors such as age, gender, time of year, and suicide method.

As always, the real underlying question of 'why' is completely overlooked. I was bold enough to reach out to Maria Caulfield MP, who was then Parliamentary Under-Secretary of State for Mental Health and Women's Health Strategy, with the following plea:

Dear Maria,
Would you agree that understanding how people got to the point of killing themselves is critical to driving down suicide rates in the UK? The imminent launch of your government's national suspected suicide surveillance system is an amazing step forward, but I urge you to add 'reason for suicide' to the reporting remit. Adding this metric to those of age, gender and method will help professionals like myself to provide more targeted interventions. In my experience, relationship breakdown

is one of the biggest risk factors for completed suicide. If these data bear this out, it can form the evidence base for educational programs addressing domestic violence, narcissistic abuse, boundary-forming and other relationship-focused issues.
Best wishes,
Michael

Shock, horror! I did not hear back from her. If you agree, I urge you to reach out to the government and add your voice to mine, maybe write your own letter to the new Under-Secretary, Baroness Gillian Merron. You never know: your letter may save lives.

John: *When I left Mary, it sent me right back to my childhood. Why didn't anyone go out looking for me when I left home? Why didn't he fight to save this relationship?*

If you're feeling like you want to end your life, it's important to tell someone.

Help and support is available right now if you need it. You do not have to struggle with difficult feelings alone.

Crisis Helplines
UK: Samaritans - 116 123
US: National Suicide Prevention Lifeline - 988
Australia: Lifeline - 13 11 14
Elsewhere: Check your local resources and get immediate help.
For more guidance, read:
Burke, S. (2021). *In my defense - life after suicide.* Independently published.

Kaufman, D. (2016). *15 poems to healing & recovery.* CreateSpace.

O' Connor, R. (2021). *When it's darkest: why people die by suicide and what we can do to prevent it.* Ebury Digital.

References:
Halpin, Z. (2022). Working with the ultimate crisis. *Therapy Today.* Dec 21/Jan 22, 32:10, pp 34-36)

Mears, D. (2022). Choosing Life or Death. *Therapy Today.* Jul/Aug, pp 38-41)

*"Whatever you do,
as long as you operate
with honesty, integrity
and intelligence,
the universe will
have your back. Always.*

- Ella Patrice, LaWhimsy -

PART I: A CATEGORY FIVE STORM

CHAPTER 4

BEING IN OUR TRUTH FREES US

> **Tasks for us to complete:** From this chapter onwards, we will be working on one or more numbered tasks. These will be clearly explained in the main text and then summarized at the end of each chapter under the 'In A Nutshell' section.

A clean, transparent viewpoint on our lives is symbolic of being in our truth. Yes, there might be lots of distractions, uncertainty, fear, and a whole myriad of other emotions, but it doesn't help if we can't see clearly. When we are in shock or trauma, we try to ease this by thinking of stories or fighting or defending, and with these actions come distortions. And it's very normal to have these for a little while, so if you have felt angry and rageful or made up a story or been dramatic about something to escape something else, don't beat yourself up. You did the best you could at the time. But continuing in that vein will not help you.

We do eventually have to come to reasoning. What is our truth, really? What did happen, really? We can't get inside our ex's head, so we don't really know what they're thinking, feeling, or doing. The only person we can be in our truth with is ourselves. But we play tricks on ourselves, we distort and fabricate things, we embroider upon our truth.

Our next step is really looking into that mirror, clearly, maybe for the first time in our lives. And it might feel embarrassing or frightening. But if we do the work, stay with the feelings and work out why we're feeling them, we're on our way to an amazing future.

It's fast approaching that time when we have to decide whether we're going to move on or make up. In fact, we've got to work out whether making up is actually possible, and that can be heart-breaking and gut-wrenching to think about. But is our ex available? Are we available? Is making up a reality? It may very well be, but we have to check that.

Moving on: do we really want to move on? Do we have enough faith to step into the unknown? What is that? What does it look like? What do we want to bring in?

Shining a 500,000 Watt light on ourselves is the only way to dispel our fantasies

In the book *On Grief and Grieving*, Kubler Ross and Kessler advise that telling our story, in detail, is primal to the healing process, but in post-relationship experience, as in bereavement, the tales we tell are unreliable at best.

For example, it is very common to romanticize an unhealthy relationship, to think about all the good bits, how beautiful, sexy, and cozy it was. This only makes it harder and more painful to deal with the breakup. As Brad Brenner, Ph.D. posted on Therapygroupdc. com, "Getting over your ex requires taking them off the pedestal and de-idealizing both them and the relationship."

As Brenner goes on to say, this is especially so if we had a troubled relationship, if we struggled with intimacy issues, or if we experienced infidelity and deceit. It's essential for us to take a step back and to rethink and reanalyze our relationship.

What is helpful at this point is to start journaling (see the tasks at the end of this chapter). What I tell people to do is open up a Notes section in their phone. Name it anything you want, for example 'Michael,' blame me! And just start putting your truth in there, and see how it feels. Just baby steps. One truth at a time. Challenge yourself by doing this.

To get to the truth, you need to put the story of your relationship under the microscope and shine a 500,000W lightbulb on it. But before you start, it's worth understanding where all that dirt and grime - the falsehoods - came from. Why do we construct fantasies in the first place?

It's essential that we fill in the gaps in our memories of what happened in our own story of life. We can only recall under half of what actually happened. We make up the rest with fantasy. Fact. And we can recall just 20% of traumatic experiences - even worse. We have to put *something* in there, so we cherry pick the facts and ideas that position us as the person acting correctly. We are so skilled at this process that we can even put our own head on our ex-partner's shoulders and believe that they are thinking and feeling things that they weren't.

You are a unique individual. So is your ex. It is very harmful to put on them your empathy, your ideas, your thoughts. They're a different person to you, even though you might have thought that you were the same. This is part of the separating out process, which is difficult.

Here's an example:

The factual situation. You put some washing on the line, reminding your partner to bring it inside if it starts raining. Your partner was on a phone call to their boss, and the radio was on very loud, so they didn't hear you. You picked up the children from school and got talking to a demanding friend who asked for a lift home. You agreed but felt annoyed as this friend is always asking for favors and never reciprocates. In the meantime, your partner goes out to sort out a problem at work. You arrive home, still feeling put out, only to find that your partner has gone out and the washing is still on the line in the pouring rain.

Your authentic recollection. You put some washing on the line, You picked up the children from school and came back to find your partner gone and the washing out in the pouring rain.

Your story. You put some washing on the line, reminding your partner to bring it inside if it starts raining. They decided to ignore you and just go out. You picked up the children from school and when you came home the washing was still on the line in the pouring rain. You felt annoyed because you do everything around the house.

This story paints you as the dutiful, responsible parent and invents thoughts and attitudes for your partner. As you will imagine, this perception, created by our false stories, are highly likely to lead to arguments.

Important to note: If you are a codependent in a relationship with a narcissist, you might switch this and paint *yourself* as the flawed one.

As with the previous example, you put yourself in your partner's head, but you imagine them feeling and acting *as you would have* in their situation. In other words, you invent kind and honorable motives for your partner's behaviors, no matter how despicable and selfish those behaviors are.

Either way, we need to stay out of our partner's head when re-telling our story. We need to own it!

Avoiding rational analysis and simply accepting our fabrications will not help us make the right choices. It will take us to a place that loops us right back to the same place we started. We will be in an endless loop.

For example, in my clinical experience, regret is often the most prominent feeling for both those who leave and those who have been left. Justifying their decision to leave or finding meaning in being left often takes center stage of their breakup drama.

We have to micro-analyze our scripts to avoid falling for delusions such as one-sided blame. In every breakup, we're both to blame. Hard though that may sound, it's the truth. We need to break down and negotiate hard with our fantasies, weeding out our lies and working out which parts of our story are real.

There's an excellent book called *Mind Over Mood* by Dennis Greenberger and Christine Padesky (2016). I actually trained with Christine, and this book is an amazing practical guide to sorting out our own head in situations like this. It's an amazing workbook. I suggest you order it immediately.

Brooding vs self-awareness

Repeating ideas of what happened - i.e., 'narrative re-enactment' - is not the same as challenging them. It keeps us stuck in blame and shame. So, how can we fix our stories and grow? What can we do?

It's essential, and by getting in touch with our conscience, asking questions, and playing with different ideas we can find our way forward

Sometimes with a patient, I ask them, "What would your father say to you about this situation if he were here with us right now?" Sometimes I'm even daring enough to say, "What if your ex were sitting in that chair right now. What would they say to what you just said? Would they agree?" It's a gestalt method of 'open chair' where we can bring different people in and ask them, "What would your view be?" If we can do enough significant others that know the situation, we can get quite a rounded form of what did take place.

When we're insecure, we hold on to our ideas, our blame, and our shame. It's the only way to survive. It works in the short term but is destructive in the long-term,

Here are some questions I recommend asking yourself:

- What was my part in this breakup?
- Is the grass greener outside of this relationship? What are the positives?
- Who are truly my friends and who are my foes in this story?
- Why did they leave? Do I truly know? or, Was I right to leave then? Was that the best time for me?

- Should I have stayed? Was there anything else I could have done to make this relationship work?
- Considering everything, was that the most opportune time to end this relationship?
- Do I really want them back? If they were sitting in the seat opposite me now looking at me, is that what I want?
- What did my ex do right? What did I do right?
- What did I do wrong? What did my ex do wrong?

Write these questions and the answers in your journal on your phone. Start to anchor everything there. Start to treat that as your notes section for this book.

If we've had several breakups because we've had several marriages or relationships, this might be evidence that we keep on attracting the same type of person, probably because we're familiar to that type from our childhood or from some kind of training that took place in our lives. Keep in mind that repeating these patterns is not a reason to blame ourselves.

By this time, we might be starting to get some ideas about how we can bring clarity to our situation, but reading this is not enough to drive real and lasting change. For this, we will need to work through all of the tasks in this part of the book.

Let's get started:

Task 1: Start a journal
If you haven't already, start your journal now. Make this journal your best friend. Write everything in it, even the dark secrets you wouldn't

ordinarily tell anybody. Don't forget to title it 'Michael' or something else so that if somebody does steal your phone or if it gets lost, then they will think that I'm the crazy one, not you.

Task 2: Take a history of your relationship and its breakup

We call this a timeline. So, if you've got an old piece of wallpaper or a notepad, start by writing down the year you were born and the current year. Then start going through all the relationships you've had, significant deaths, significant breakups, exciting times, terrible times... . Start getting a picture of your process and your journey to be here. This is a way of getting a candid history.

Can counseling help?

Counseling is an amazing way of finding support and helping anchor you in these storms right now. It's important you choose your therapist well. The counselor has to be appropriately trained to work with you. A few of the disciplines that I would look for include Transactional Analysis; it's relationship based, about dynamics in our world, for example the Drama Triangle. I would look at psychodynamics which is about relationships again, about past, present, and what we're doing out there in the real world.

Be careful because unfortunately, the reality is that somebody can do a four week course and call themselves a therapist or counselor. There's no protection over the title. It's best if you go through one of the recognized bodies such as the psychological societies or the social work sections of therapeutic licensing organizations in certain countries; but make sure that the people have got training. And I would say for relationship work, it needs to be an experienced person, someone who has been working in the field for at least five years. The person really should be systemically trained so that they work with the systems of a person in context, which you will need. The best thing to do these days, if you're really unsure, is to Google it. There are subsidized agencies in the global nonprofit sector, so Google 'relationship help counseling.' But be careful because a lot of places pay huge funds to be first or second in your search engine results. So, if you're going to have a look, make sure you allow yourself a good half hour to cruise through all the pages, have a look at what's available and go from there

Therapy can also help you to open up about those horrible experiences that never seem to make it to the pages of many self-help guides to coping with loss. Finding your truth is vital but not as easy as such two-dimensional guides would have you think. You may have to be honest about conflicts such as both loving your partner and hating them; enjoying being free of abuse and yet missing them and feeling unsafe without them in your life.

The rewards of successfully addressing our stories can be unbelievable, even in traumatic breakups. Sue Wright published an extract from her book *The Change Process in Psychotherapy During Troubling Times*, in *Therapy Today*. She and trauma specialist Liz Rolls discussed how reworking patients' narratives can help us heal from traumatic loss. Rolls says, 'One of the features that push us into being traumatized is loss of control.' By actively adjusting our narratives, we regain some of this control.

So, again, let's rethink our stories.
Reframing your relationship story can also help us to find or rediscover purpose and value in life, something that logotherapy founder Victor

Frankl claimed was critical for survival. For example, by us reframing our stories and identity as a motivated parent rather than a rejected partner, we can start plotting a hopeful path forward (aka 'a mobilized strategy') - whether we decide to take the moving on or making up route. In Rolls' language, we can 'inoculate' ourselves from trauma and meaninglessness. Simply said, we need to be kind and real with ourselves and re-check in with our stories.

Now, hear me, hear me, hear me. I need to emphasize that we have to be in our truth when reframing. Otherwise, we could con ourselves even further by convincing ourselves that we are, for example, a motivated parent when, in fact, we are looking to hurt our partner by winning our kids' love.

We have to look at all parts of ourselves in the post-relationship experience. We're very good at justifying things to ourselves that aren't morally right, for example things that will bring us pleasure because we're hurting the person that has hurt us. When it comes to the post-relationship experience and anything to do with our ex and being in our truth, we must understand that this a transaction. Nothing more, nothing less.

Now consider this carefully: if we are suffering from true clinical depression, anxiety, PTSD, addictions, etc. that may be distorting our stories, we may not be in the right place to do this exercise? We need to find a stepping stone towards being able to do these exercises in real time, and that may mean having an ally do these exercises with you: a friend, a therapist, an online help group. If you're not stable or healthy enough, mentally or physically, you might need to ask for additional help to fulfill this.

Now, we've really looked at ourselves in the mirror. I'm now going to lead you into the second part of this truth exercise which is where we look at the truth around social media, hooks (these are the things that keep us attacjed to our ex, or our ex attached to us), and other unhealthy activities which we are manipulating or being manipulated by.

Big question: could we be addicted to our ex?
Breaking an addiction and ending a relationship are very similar, believe me. Both really tough cookies to smash. If we have been left by a partner, it's like having cake in the fridge that you cannot eat anymore. Its very existence tortures us with obsessive thoughts about how much we want to or must taste it.

If we were the leaver in the relationship, we may have to deal with the responsibility that comes with holding the power to go back and have a bite. Should we? Shouldn't we? This can leave us riddled with doubt. There's no perfect way forward. We have to feel and consider our way forward, and the more help we have moving forward, the better.

The transtheoretical Model (TTM), sometimes known as the 'stages of change' model is very useful when working with any type of addiction. There is a diagram of the model on the next page:

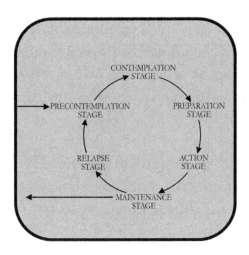

Any kind of change is really tough, and leaving or being left in a relationship is change.

What else have we lost?
Along with the loss of the relationship itself, we need to recognize other elements of life that have been lost or changed out of recognition as the world 'that is' becomes the world 'that was.' Sad but true.

These include:
- Our identity (our role and self-esteem.)
- Our world view on things (how we feel about each other and relationships in general. This might be very marred at this point.)
- Friends and family members (Who stayed? Who disappeared? Who were only interested in you 'as a couple'? Who took your side? Who took their side?)
- Our 'assumptive world' (All of those securities and future hopes and dreams - what might have been and a dash of 'what ifs')

Christopher Hall MAPS, Director of the Australian Centre for Grief and Bereavement, wrote a beautiful and true quote, "Life's most grievous losses disconnect us from our sense of who we are and can set in train an effortful process of not only re-learning ourselves but also the world." Simply said, we have to look at and experience everything differently, and build our confidence to do this well. We have to go out there and make it happen.

What have we retained - or gained - at this point?
We may have been dispossessed by the breakup, but what do we still have going forward? What do we have more of than before? Freedom? Self-respect? Time with family? It's helpful at this point to make a list: what did I lose, and what did I gain? It's good to do this in your journal so you can refer back to it.

In the next chapter, we will explore the Danish concept of *hygge*. This is a powerful feeling of security and belonging that, when lost, can leave us feeling bereft. It is the feeling we may get when we're making a coffee in the morning, we look outside, we see the sun rise, and it's that perfect moment of peace. You may find that peace in another way: walking in nature, having a shower or bath...it's a very deep, complete feeling of everything being right in the world *right now, at this moment in time.* And the reason we stay in a relationship for so long when it's really counterproductive is the familiarity we get from that feeling of *hygge*. It's that deep set feeling of being in the right place and safe. A moment of 'everything's OK.'

Following a breakup, we can start to rebuild *hygge* in our lives by drawing up a list of people with whom we want to nurture friendships. Like the 'home' setting on our satnav, a list of 'our people' can provide a calm feeling of security to bridge the gap between intimate relationships.

John: I had to revisit my value and belief system and decide where I was going to invest. Over the last year, I had been introduced to a lot of people who were not 'my people'. I would have lunch or go to a party with them but they were not part of my tribe. But I've got ten people in my life that I love and care for and want to invest in. That has made my birthday year special because I now have people that I can spend valuable time with. I feel loved, respected and supported.

In the next chapter, we will be delving deeper into our stories. In preparation, I would like us to carry out the following task:

Recognizing (and resisting) unhealthy, damaging hooks and binds: Part 1
When we are rebuilding our lives following a breakup, we are like an untethered balloon in a storm. Hooks lie in wait for us, ready to rip into the canvas or catch our lines, pulling us back to where we started from.

There are many ways, both conscious and unconscious, that we get hooked back into thinking about our exes or even reliving dangerous things. This first part looks at the hooks that we recognize (i.e., those conscious hooks and binds that are at the front of our minds most of the time.)

Some of the most momentous, dangerous, shifting moments can be when:

- Well-meaning friends and family start talking about your ex, mentioning what they're doing now, or bringing to the forefront a photograph.
- Hearing a favorite song that pulls up all those nice moments related to that song.
- We see a social media update from our ex. Social media is an amazing way to connect with people, but it's also a dangerous place to be when we're trying to recover from an ex relationship.

Sometimes we are our own worst enemy and we hook ourselves into our ex's life and con ourselves that they are doing the hooking. Yes, this is what makes us human. We can convince ourselves that two plus two equals five. It's a human trait. Animals don't do that - not to my knowledge.

Task 3: In your journal, jot down what these hooks are and whether it's you or your ex bringing these hooks in. It's very important to do this because we have to untangle it. How can we stay strong the next time we feel the pull of these hooks? How can we stop ourselves creating these hooks? And how can we let these hooks pass through us rather than grab and distort us?

John: There is another agency, soul, so this is not an insular experience. A dead person doesn't post messages on Facebook or kill home security cameras. Serenity is to be patient with what I cannot change, strong with what I can change and wise to know the difference and not waste time.

Denial and bargaining in our breakup
We won't be able to move forward if we are stuck staring into the rearview mirror at what has gone by, so the first hook to address is any lingering thoughts about why your relationship failed.

A very dear auntie of mine in Ireland has always said to me, "That that passes you by is not meant for you." I personally drew comfort from this.

Kubler-Ross and Kessler (2005) explain that refusal to admit that a death has occurred is a form of protective denial (i.e., it's so bad that we try to pretend it didn't happen). My personal experience and scientific research in this field has shown me that this type of mechanism rarely operates in relationship breakups. We are usually painfully aware that a breakup is real and that it is happening to us. However, a combination of our faulty stories and unresolved issues can make it difficult for us to accept that our relationship may have ended *permanently* - hence the storm - and us denying this possibility can hook us and stall us in the road to recovery or to making up. Yes, we might then move into a bargaining phase, trying to sort out what happened and understand why things went so wrong. Why didn't we hold on to the good times and stay? Why couldn't they see the good times and stay with us? Why didn't they look for us? Why didn't they try to help and get together with us? Why didn't we move forward and try to find a resolution? All the 'what ifs.'

It's only when we come to the point when we realize, 'I left for a reason,' or 'Do you know what: I wasn't abandoned. It just didn't work,' that we begin to heal.

I'm not saying we should give up hope of rekindling our relationship. But this first set of exercises is about facts not feelings. Just pretend you're being your own lawyer and putting the facts down on a piece of paper. Take out the emotions. Give up the old stories. Be in your truth. Even if you can't be in your truth with friends and family, be in your truth with your journal and this book and me.

We need to shift back and focus on correcting any faults in our relationship story and accepting - for now - that there are unresolved issues and that our relationship may be over for good. In fact, forget the 'what ifs' and 'maybes,' and let's do an experiment and just pretend it's done forever. Where does that put us? It could be dark. It could be awful, but let's just face that in the mirror. If it's over forever, what are our options. This task is all about cleaning away everything that isn't proven to be true so that we can look out of a clean window and start moving forwards with purpose, free of distractions and distortions.

If we're convincing ourselves that we like strawberry trifle when we really hate it, then we're going to keep on eating strawberry trifle and not liking it and not being fulfilled. It's the same thing if we believe that we liked a relationship or liked certain aspects of a relationship or liked ourselves in the relationship when we didn't. And don't forget, a positive relationship is one where we like who we are in it.

If we're not in our truth, we're kidding ourselves, and we're not going to have a good future because we won't really be going after what we want.

A UK relationship nonprofit Relate (2018), where I had the honor of being trained for a part of my career, and actually being part of their training, reveal how their therapists often work with patients that feel stuck going over and over what happened in their last relationship, whilst often blaming themselves for messing it up. Does this sound familiar?

I'm giving you permission right now to stop beating yourself up about your brooding. What's done is done. However, we can only move on from what's done if we are looking at the truth of it. Just understand that only once this cycle is broken will we have the freedom to move carefully towards our future. Only then can we identify and make the right turn for us going forward.

Don't worry, being in our truth is probably the most difficult thing for a human because we make up stories to protect ourselves and others. And this is fine when it is functional. It's not fine when we're making up stories to ourselves and others that hinder us getting what we want out of life. And don't forget, this isn't a dress rehearsal. This is our life now.

Common things that people have said to me when they're going through work is that they are tired of wasting time; they're tired of being hooked, they want to move on, and they're tired of being tired.

How do we let go of our need to know?
William Worden, who is a world guru for grief, attachment and belonging said very famously that 'successful grieving' is learning to live without the answers. These words could not be more appropriate to relationship breakup. Even after micro-analyzing our stories of our relationships, going over and over them, we may be left with unanswered questions, especially regarding what happened, what was done to us, what we did to our ex, and what was behind all of that. What were the motivations? We will never know. Even if we hog-tied and gagged our ex and put truth drugs in them, we will only get their version of what their experience was.

If we are no longer communicating with our ex, we may never get any answers whatsoever. And guess what: we have to learn a way to be OK with this. It does get easier. This too shall pass is a favorite saying of mine. But think about it. We have questions without answers. Maybe it's best to leave it there.

"Can't get you out of my head" (Dennis & Davis, 2000)
Kylie Minogue certainly was spot on when she sang about the struggles of getting her ex out of her head. We may think we know our ex-partners, but we don't. If we don't know ourselves very well, and we're not in our own truth, how the heck can we expect to know our ex-partners and be in their truth? Whenever we think we know what they're thinking, feeling, or doing, we are only projecting *our ideas* onto their shoulders. Just as we have been changed by the breakup experience - and we changed immediately, it rocks our world - and also through the work we are doing on ourselves (i.e., reading this book, walking with me, challenging ourselves, rebuilding,) they will be changing too. Maybe not in the same direction as us. Maybe they're just finding a replacement. Maybe they're repeating patterns. Maybe they haven't stepped back and thought, 'Well, it didn't work this way. I'm going to do it differently.' They might just be blaming everything on you.

Whatever the case is, you cannot control them, you cannot think for them, and you really don't know what they're doing, how they're feeling, or what their plans are. Only they will know how they're managing their lives. And guess what else: it's now not our business. Our business is us reconnecting with us, becoming whole again, so we can move on, be a whole person, and welcome in what we want in life.

We must be very careful and never judge anyone, especially our ex. We are all in the place we are meant to be at this moment in time. We all progress at different paces. Sometimes, we develop faster than others, and maybe then we will slow down and other people will take over. We are all unique. It's important to remember this, especially when thinking of family and friends. Some of your family and friends may not understand your post-relationship experience. They may not have experienced a breakup themselves, and if they have, their experience will be very different to yours, so they will be wondering why you're not doing everything the same way. Just be mindful, be patient, and accept difference. That's your strength right now. That's your Ace card.

If you were to have trouble separating out who you are from who they are, Cain (2022) has written an article that helps us disengage from over-identification. As Cain puts it, "You never get to see inside their heads, you don't get to choose their behavior, and ultimately you know them only by what they do and what they say. Most of the time, *no matter how large their role in your story,* they're simply offscreen somewhere out there in the world, doing who knows what."

Family relations
Some of our family members and friends won't accept that that our relationship is over, and some may encourage our breakup for their own purposes. Maybe their selfish hope for our reunion (or support for our breakup) must also be seen for what it is: a hook that must be removed before we can make a rational decision on the correct course of action for us.

I can't tell you how many people told me, "Oh, you'll get back together again," because they didn't want to lose the friendship they

114

had with us in coupledom. Likewise, some people may have been jealous of our relationship or even our lifestyle, and they may be very pleased it's over so they can have us back all to themselves. Then you get another set of family and friends that may relish the drama of our relationship breakup because they are 'drama queens.' Whatever the situation is, keep in mind that other people have their own agendas. We have to stay firm, solid, and anchored. And working through this with me is a way of anchoring, of seeing things for how they are, accepting people for being different, and moving forward.

Sarah: I recently considered getting back with Matt and a couple of friends exploded. "Oh my God, don't you dare!" they said. But a part of our relationship was very good.

Social media: friend or foe?

If we were to consider songs on the radio and comments from friends are occasional jabs in the arm, then social media can be an intravenous drip of information that we want, hate, love, are scared of, etc. In today's 'always connected' world, it is so much harder than in previous generations to disconnect ourself from painful reminders of a past relationship: just a simple Instagram or Facebook update about our ex's post-breakup activities can leave us heartbroken or enraged all over again.

It can be particularly painful if an ex starts to see someone else. According to the philosopher and cultural theorist Byung-Chul Han, the apparent narcissism of social media activity could, in fact, be a 'defiant shamelessness' in the face of constant judgement from society (Barford, 2022). In other words, what we may interpret as an ex 'rubbing our noses' in the fact that they've moved on (i.e., quite a narcissistic motive) could actually be a 'screw you' to society at large.

Either way, seeing constant reminders of our ex is highly unlikely to help us make decisions moving forward with a clear head. We may be enraged, we may be defensive, we may be heartbroken. All these different feelings don't give us a clear lane to walk down towards peace. So, ultimately, we must resist the temptation to stalk our ex on social media, and we have to consider they are entitled to stand or fall by their own sword. But a little note to you all: if you're fearing all is fantastic in the world that your ex is showing everybody (and knowing that you're going to be told about it), nothing is perfect in Paradise. Bring yourself comfort in the knowledge that all situations have their highs and lows, ups and downs. And if your ex did move on very fast, and is throwing it around and flaunting it, that's not what a happy, considerate, concerned person does. See it for what it is. And think about it: if we are happy and kind people, we will behave in happy and kind ways. No maliciousness, no judgement, no acts of sabotage. Kind and happy people act as kind and happy people. Hold that close to you at all times. Maybe that could be one of our goals.

As a clinician and a human being, it makes me so angry when I read blanket advice to immediately unfollow or unfriend an ex partner. Most knee-jerk reactions are unwise, and staying connected to our ex can, in some cases, support us in our healing. I go into this in more detail in Part III of this book. Consider carefully that this is not always the case. For example, if our ex was abusive or if we had our own abusive streak, then sometimes a clean break is required.

War: when these hooks are used to wound and kill

Hooks are anything a person can do to keep our attention, whether the bait is fear, envy, longing, anger or something else. A common example of a deliberately threatening, fear-based hook is stalking.

Stalking

In a sample of over 1100 undergraduates, 80% admitted to engaging in unwanted pursuit behaviors (UPBs) - i.e., stalking (Dardis & Gidycz, 2017).

Stalking will be off the radar of any therapist using a grief model to help somebody with their relationship breakup. If a person were stalked, ridiculed, followed, harassed, and even had their kids damaged and manipulated by a ghost, it would be front page news (or more likely, the person would be in a psychiatric institution). Once again, an ex's agency - their ability to think and do - is the biggest difference between coping with a corpse and moving on from a relationship. Be mindful, keeping ourselves safe and disconnecting from hooks is the ultimate goal.

Sarah: *Matt stalked me for a number of years. I would sense it. I would feel someone watching me. I would tell myself that I was imagining it, but it started to escalate, and I did discover that I was being stalked.*
There was one night when I was talking to my sister on the phone. She is very together - twinset and pearls - and I just said, "It feels like someone's watching me." I was in the garden room in my house. My sister immediately said, "Get out of there now. Move. Go to another room." I had never before seen my sister react like that, so I went upstairs, looked out of the window and there was a car parked in the church car park opposite, facing me, with a figure inside watching me. There was no reason to be in that car park.

Matt was also in my airline accounts, he was creating pseudonyms on Facebook, and he was actually driving around, parking up, and watching me in my home. I didn't respond to those hooks until two people posed as real estate agents came to the home to value it. They asked to come in, but I said, "I haven't organized that," and they replied, "Well, we're here to do it." But before they had actually knocked on my door, they had been videoing my garden and through the windows of the house. I told them to leave immediately and called the police, and found out that they were private investigators instructed by Matt. I still didn't throw the ball back, but Matt continued stalking me using slander, saying awful things about me in the community. I only weathered this because I had promised myself I would be dignified, and I had the solid help of my sister. I said to myself that I would only respond to anything if I felt in danger, and in fact, the police did arrest Matt at one point.

Although I didn't react, Matt's stalking had me hooked into his head, into what he was thinking and what his next steps might be. And I really had to spend time working on myself and telling myself that I would only respond, by reporting each incident to the police, even though that got wearing, because the police needed these files just in case something did happen.

Hooks can come from our exes in many different guises. It depends on their MO and their level of desperation as to what they're prepared to do.

John: *When I broke up with Mary, silence was her first hook, followed by finances. After our 10 year relationship, there was zero communication until, a month later, my accountant and I received a fraudulent 1099c (cancellation of debt form) from her regarding a 'loan.' In order to file a 1099c, one has to have the documentation to prove that there is debt owed and that there have been attempts to recover it.*

Well, there was never a loan. I left six hundred thousand dollars in our 'pot' which we had both agreed was mine, but she was angry and starting to do desperate things. That hook could not be ignored because I had to find out what my legal position was, and of course, she is an attorney.

I was also hooked into fear and worry. I reached out to Mary, asking, "Can we mediate this? Is there a way to avoid lawyers and courts because it's a lot of money, and we know the truth, and you have to be in your conscience about what the right thing is to do." I didn't receive any response, but I started thinking, 'If she's using fraud to hurt me, what's her history?' We looked into it and discovered that she had actually been prosecuted for fraud in the past for forging signatures and stealing notary stamps and using them. We also found out that someone with exactly the same full name had been married in the past - when she was 17, to a 15 year old - and there were also a lot of foreclosures. Mary actually walked away from millions of dollars of property debt just a couple of years before we were together. I had never before been made aware of any of this, and it made me feel very insecure about my money.

So, I reached out for a third time. This is the hook because I'm thinking, 'OK, I want my money, but I don't want to hurt you.' And there was still no response. I went to great lengths to include a recorded video alongside my letters because Mary had always said that she hated things in writing. She would never respond to anything in writing. Still no response. And then, just before the third attempt to get my money back and to go into mediation, I found out that she was with another man called John! Mary actually texted her cousin Jane in Houston, someone I had stayed in contact with, saying that her and John would like to visit. Jane reached out to us both and said, "Oh, I can't believe it. It's wonderful you're back together again. We're so pleased."

Mary was able to orchestrate that because, unbeknown to me, she actually had access to my telephone account, and she could see every single telephone number I was dialling. She could see that Jane and I were still on good terms. So, that was her cruel way of letting me know that she was with somebody else. For six hours I was excited, thinking, 'Gosh, she's going to work it out with me. There's still time to change,' but no, it was a cruel trick, and it really broke me. But it released me, too, because it reminded me exactly of why I was right to leave. As for the 1099c, that has now been proven as fraudulent. So, sometimes hooks backfire on people. Every single one of those friends and family members that knew us both have stated categorically that she has not let go of me. There's something about her that will not let go. She needs to pay me and move on, but this is the last hook she's got: she's holding on to the money, and now we're spending a lot of money in legal fees for me to get the money back. For her, it's still a hook. It's still a connection. But I'm at the stage now where hooks don't work.

So, the best thing to do with this kind of hook is to pass it over to your higher power or whatever your faith is, and pass it over to your lawyers to take care of. Do not engage at all with the person trying to hook you.

How can we make hooks a positive?
During our breakup process, we may want to remove all of the hooks that keep us attached to our ex. However, sometimes, when we feel worthless and alone, our ex's behavior can remind us that we still exist to them. However, we have to realize and tell ourselves that our ex has the power to withdraw their hooks at any moment, so it's best not to become dependent on any of them. Weigh up if you need them or not.

John: Finding out that Mary had been checking the security cameras actually helped me to heal. I feel it was a gift from the higher power.

Are we now ready to make a decision moving forward? Move on, make up, and how we do that

How do we know when we are ready to take that leap of faith - and it is a leap of faith. We've been bashed and battered but we have weathered the storm at this stage. Now it's time to bite the bullet and start thinking about decision-making. This can be exciting, painful, rewarding, and hurtful.

Through my own personal experience and clinical practice, I have found that people who are ready to move on become tired of the fake story of their former relationship and of going over and over why things went wrong. This is a good sign. This means we are getting ready to accept that there is no way back to the relationship that we once had, or maybe we're getting to the point where we accept that we could never change our ex, and the only way we would ever consider any kind of make up would be if they prove to us - not tell us - prove to us, without a shadow of a doubt, that they have changed.

John: I am tired of the story. I'm tired of it taking up my time and my friends' time.

I never give up on people, so this has been very hard for me. I had to keep reminding myself why I left. And it wasn't because of our last conversation. It was because of what was broken from the start. It was an ongoing major issue involving a lack of care and breaking important agreements. I never knew where I was or what I could trust.
Something has changed. Today, I took my wedding ring off for the first

time since I left. I feel comfortable about that. I am very proud of myself today. I am in my truth, and if romance comes along, I'm interested. I don't think Mary can change.

Beliefs, values, goals, options: choosing wisely

In order for us to start a new life, we have to reinvent - or at the very least reframe - our existing one.

What does this mean, though? Working on our values, beliefs, and goals is essential due to the profound effect that a breakup has on our world and often what we think of the world - our worldview. We've held up a mirror to ourselves and put our most recent relationship under the microscope. Now, it's essential for us to look at our whole life and previous relationships from a 'drone' perspective. Only from an aerial view can we see where we've been, where we are now, and what the terrain ahead is like.

Task 4: Let's revisit our timeline and really make sure we have completed all the major life events. The first is us being born; then siblings being born; a wonderful wedding we went to; it could have been one of our own children being born; graduating from college; getting our first job in a bakery...whatever it is. Map out what our life was before, during and now, after the breakup. This helps put things in perspective.

Revisiting our values, beliefs, and goals is like a thorough post-breakup triage process. Triage is what happens in emergency rooms when a patient first gets admitted. They look for blood spillage, they look for life-threatening situations, they look for what needs to happen now and what can wait until later. It's looking at the whole thing to ensure the best overall outcome. Triaging our values, beliefs, and goals can help us weigh up what needs emergency patching up (e.g., locking down bank accounts because our ex has access, changing passwords, etc.) and what needs long-term treatment; which opportunities to take and which to pass up. It can help stop us making hasty decisions, such as sleeping around, indulging too much in something, changing career, etc., which can all be great quick fixes to escape loneliness or (in the case of rebound sex) reassure ourselves that we are still attractive, but in the long-run can be detrimental to our wellbeing and safety. Rebound sex is a distraction at best. At worst, it can cause further harm to everyone concerned, especially ourselves.

As Dr. Adrian Needs (2022) states in the title of his article, 'Change must engage a person's senses of identity, meaning, control, and belonging.' So I guess what Adrian is saying is that we need to pace ourselves. We need to think about who we are, what is appropriate for us, what is truly meaningful, what truly nurtures us, and where we can find our people.

It's vital that we look at ourselves in this manner and think about what would best be chosen for us if we were our own best friend and parent (which we are meant to be). How do we choose wisely for ourselves, rather than react to the world or what other people are doing?

Warning: This is a big warning to us. If we don't do this work. If we were to consider moving forward without revisiting what our identity, meaning, belonging, etc. are, and facing our fears, we are in mortal danger of repeating the patterns that don't work for us.

It's like saying, "I love mayonnaise on my sandwiches," when you actually hate mayonnaise. You are going to keep on getting mayonnaise on your sandwiches from everyone, until you actually start saying,

"Do you know what? I don't like mayonnaise." Then people will start delivering what you want, including yourself. Sometimes we want mayonnaise on our sandwiches because it's fashionable. Sometimes we don't want to be awkward by saying, "Hold the mayo!"

When we're in our truth, we get what we want. The energy of our world starts to change. It starts to work with us instead of against us.

What are my guiding stars?

Nobody can decide on our values for us, but it is important to dig deep and unearth what qualities will support us on our road to healthy moving on or makeup.

- If words such as integrity and honesty come up, we will benefit from refusing to drop our moral standards.
- If empathy and compassion surface, we may be able to find a way to reach amicable solutions by appealing to the feelings of others.
- If our core values include courage and duty, battling on for the sake of our children may help us stay the course.
- If faith is important to us, what meaning can we draw from our experiences?

Whatever our unique constellation of personal values, being in our truth, and communicating this in a way that other people will understand, will help to free us from shame and ultimately ensure we receive the support we need.

Most importantly, giving ourselves permission to forgive ourselves and our ex is also key to a healthy breakup, and it is even the precursor to a healthy makeup. When we can say to ourselves, 'I don't need to support myself by trashing somebody else,' we will have come a long way.

It is important, at this time, to understand that we're changing, and that these changes will create changes in our circle of friends, family members, and colleagues. Life is like a bus journey. Some friends, family members and colleagues may get off the bus permanently. Their time with us is over. Not all connections are for life. Some of our connections may step off the bus temporarily until they have had similar experiences to us. Then they might catch the bus again and reconnect with us. Give yourself permission to let go of people, to change your dynamics with them, and to readdress who complements our journey and who takes away from it.

How much power do we have to create?
Nature seems always to bounce back from destruction, often stronger than before. In the aftermath of a flood, fire, or hurricane, seeds start to germinate in fertile ground again. Before long, buds form, and flowers explode into life.
We're not dissimilar. We are part of nature. After the fire or storm, we too can start to grow and flower.

What will our new circumstances naturally create for us? What can we create for ourselves out of the debris left over from our relationship? And what can we leave behind for good? What do we do with all this freedom? We must never put a ceiling on our options. Nothing is beyond our reach.

When we get our story straight with ourselves and others; when we are in our truth; when we know where we are and where we want to go, we can then see what's really happening in our lives and what we want to change. We can manifest the strengths and skills we need in order to develop ourselves and achieve our goals.

Before we go to the next chapter, we have to really think about what's been said so far; write notes in our journal; revisit ourselves; and really work on being in our truth, seeing ourselves clearly and only holding on to stuff that's useful.

The next chapter is going to be a tough one, so we need to make sure we have prepared beforehand by completing all of the tasks in this book so far.

In a nutshell

Task 1: Start a journal

Task 2: Put your recent relationship under the microscope, i.e:
- Who is my ex, really?
- What factors negatively affected our relationship?
- Draw a timeline.
- Can I accept that the relationship may be over for good and that unresolved issues may remain (not saying that we can't make up at some point, but for now it's gone)
- Recognize and avoid constantly bargaining with self (What if? If only?, etc.)
- Let go of our need to know everything. Be open to learning.
- We must get out of our ex's head! We don't really know them.
- Consider professional help for any trauma or relationship addiction that may exist.

Task 3: Recognize and remove obvious hooks
- Reminders from friends and family. Politely ask them that you would prefer not to hear about your ex as you are doing work on

yourself, and if they don't accept your request, maybe distance yourself from them for a while.
- Familiar places, songs, movies.
- Social media - but don't block/unfollow as a knee-jerk.
- Deliberate attacks (see Part III for strategies to protect yourself).

Task 4: Reinvent and/or reframe our lives
- Take a 'drone view' of our lives.
- What have we lost altogether?
- What have we gained?
- Re-evaluate our values, beliefs, and goals - what are my guiding stars?

For more guidance, read:
Greenberger, D. and Padesky, C. A. (2016). *Mind over mood: change how you feel by changing the way you think.* The Guilford Press.

Hill, C. (2019). *How to stop overthinking.* Independently published.

Kubler-Ross, E., and Kessler, D. (2005). *On grief & grieving: finding the meaning of grief through the five stages of loss.* Scribner.

References:
Barford, D. (2022). Narcissism - the therapist's friend? *Therapy Today.* Dec 21/Jan 22, 32:10

Cain, D. (2022). You are always the other person. *Raptitude.* https://www.raptitude.com/2022/07/you-are-always-the-other-person/

Dardis, C. M. and Gidycz, C. A. (2017). The frequency and perceived impact of engaging in in-person and cyber unwanted pursuit after relationship break-up among college men and women. *Sex Roles: A Journal of Research.* 76(1-2), pp 56–72.

Dennis, C. and Davis, R. (2000). Can't get you out of my head [Song]. EMI Music

Greenberger, D. and Padesky, C. A. (2016). *Mind over mood: change how you feel by changing the way you think.* The Guilford Press.

Hall, C. (2011). Beyond Kubler-Ross: recent developments in our understanding of grief and bereavement. *InPsych.* Vol. 33:6 December

Kubler-Ross, E., and Kessler, D. (2005). *On grief & grieving: finding the meaning of grief through the five stages of loss.* Scribner.

Needs, A. (2022). Change must engage a person's senses of identity, meaning, control, and belonging. *The Psychologist.* April.

Relate. (2018). *Getting over a breakup.* https://www.relate.org.uk/getting-over-breakup

Wright, S. (2022). The aftermath of traumatic loss. *Therapy Today.* May, pp 39-42.

PART I: A CATEGORY FIVE STORM

CHAPTER 5

AT THIS POINT, WHAT ARE OUR FEARS AND HOW DO WE OVERCOME THEM?

David Kessler, who worked with Kubler-Ross during the latter part of her career, created the sixth stage of grief from Kubler-Ross's five stages of grief, and in so doing he explained that grief is of the heart, not of the head, and that when we compare people's grief experiences, ours is inevitably the worst (Skinner, 2021).

The work we have so far done together has helped us to stabilize our emotional reactions to things. However, despite the shift in our thoughts - our cognitive way of seeing things - not all parts of our story are visible. What we need to do is really pull out a microscope and have a good look at what we're not seeing.

We will have to plunge into the darkest depths of our broken heart for the rest of the pieces of our story. This is tough. I will walk with you, and I really mean that. Every word I'm speaking to you right now is because I care and understand deeply what this process is all about, and it's tough. It is digging really deep into our broken heart and our lost hopes. This is where we can find the greatest healing, but first we must come face to face with our worst fears Communicating these fears - and other ineffable feelings - will be more challenging than what we've had to express so far because the heart speaks a different language to the head.

An idea as to why I stayed in toxic and very unhealthy and dangerous relationships, was my fear of abandonment, of not belonging to somebody, and of not being wanted or good enough.

It would be an idea for you now to start thinking about this, and to jot anything that comes to mind in your journal. As a reference, put the page number of this book and list your ideas under 'My Worst Fears.' What are the worst pains you feel with your heartbreak? What are the darkest spots? What do you feel that you will never be able to get over? I also wonder why you stayed in a relationship that wasn't working for you.

Meeting the shadows of our soul
All of us lock away parts of ourselves we don't want to accept or think about. It's quite natural. This is a way of us protecting ourselves. This can become manifested as something Jung called the shadow, an ominous presence that stalks our dreams and prompts us into destructive actions.

Yes, most of what we do is driven by our worst fears and our most wanted needs in life.

Since everyone has a shadow, this part of the work is not about finding out what's wrong with us but is about understanding what happened to us and what doesn't work.

A colleague of mine Plagaro (2022) explains this shift very succinctly as, "A subtle difference of meaning that moves the therapist from the expert view...to 'I'm going to try to understand what's happened to you and work with you to seek a solution.' "

That's what I'm doing with you in this book.

Simply put, we can all be ruthless. We all have this internal dialogue of being unloveable or wronged or selfish or bad or evil. Our ex is better off without us, we're better off without them. Blame, blame, blame. It's an internal storm. It all gets messed up.

When we catch ourselves judging ourselves or somebody else, that's a sure sign of a shadow. The biggest thing for me growing up was if somebody had a tattoo, they were from a dockyard or a sex worker. Nowadays, that's not the case, but each time I see a tattoo, I can see that hovering somewhere in the background. I think tattoos are very attractive. I think they're very personal. I've got nothing against them, but that old thing haunts me. I can see it's still there. That's a shadow. It is an idea that tattoos are for troublemakers or people that would be looked down upon as I was growing up, not by me but by the society of the time. That's still with me, and I've worked on it.

Projection
The biggest thing a human does to another is projection. By projection I mean that if we're very insecure ourselves, we might see insecurity in our ex. But they might not be insecure at all; they might just be an arrogant prick. We either think they feel the same way as us or we want them to feel our own insecurities so we project it onto them so they own it and we don't. It's safer for us to do this. This is a natural human thing to do. If you're doing this, it's not wrong. It's not helpful, but it's not wrong because we all do it.

The purpose of facing our shadows is to stop doing certain things that don't work for us. Projection is a way of protecting ourselves, it's a human instinct, but if it doesn't work, then we need to fix it. So, projecting stuff onto our ex is a massive no-no because it says more about us than them, although we all have destructive impulses.

The role of sex

You will probably need to reconfigure your sex life to find a safe way of being with sex as a single person. It depends on the content of sex and intimacy in the former relationship, but if you were having sex with your ex, that's something that's missing now. Sex can be an amazingly powerful push and drive that's an itch we want to scratch, so it's very helpful to learn how to pleasure ourselves or to find a way of understanding that intimate sex will come back with the right person.

If we're used to a volatile relationship that includes passionate makeup sex - some of the most amazing sex a person could know - that's not going to happen if we're now out of a relationship. Keep in mind that to go and get hookup sex, even between consenting adults, can be detrimental to them or you. Just be mindful to be safe at all times.

Shame

The biggest thing that hides our truth and steers us wrong is the feeling of shame. In my own personal journey, the last time I broke up with someone, I decided not to be in my shame anymore.

In previous relationships, I was always dignified about all wrongdoings and things that didn't work for me. But my last relationship was fraught with cruelty, damage, manipulation, coercive control, indignity, and humiliation. When I left, I decided to be in my truth. I told somebody very dear to me the truth, and I was amazed at the response I received. I got the love, care, concern, and support that fitted my experience of the relationship. And with that one experience of being in my truth, and not letting shame make up a story to protect my ex and myself, I was rewarded with amazing warmth.

Dr. Michael Acton

Unresolved business from past shock and trauma
Intense pangs of grief, angry outbursts or knee-jerk withdrawal at inconvenient times usually mean that something is going on that we're not aware of. We're not all cut from the same cookie-cutter, and our responses depend on many different factors: how much we were loved as children, how much trauma we've experienced in our lives, substance use and withdrawal. Either way, we have to revisit why it is that we feel this way. Why do we seem to struggle more than other people with this issue or situation. Can we unveil clues from our past? Was there trauma or childhood abandonment? Never underestimate how our past experiences help form our present day reactions. It's important to uncover these roots in therapy, or maybe it's a good place to cover this in your journal. Why did I react that way? is a good question at this point in our work. Over-reactions are a key to where we need to focus our work.

Other feelings to be aware of
Other feelings that can trigger us and stop us from being in our truth are guilt, regret, anger (that can turn into abuse), pity, betrayal, disempowerment, and doubt.

Guilt can be the strongest of all emotions to work with, especially in therapy, but shame hides a multitude of sins, and it is the shame that keeps us asking for mayonnaise when we don't like it. It's very important to be in our truth at this stage.

How can our sense of belonging and attaching to people help us now?

The work we're doing in this book right now together has largely been informed by my own personal experience; scholastic learning at university; professional courses; the wonderful, rich knowledge that my patients have brought to me over the years, and also by colleagues such as Ainsworth, Bowlby, and Maslow. All of the above form the cornerstones of the 'Acton Post-relationship Experience Model', helping us to overcome the forces that can prevent us from making clear decisions. For example, these theories can help explain some of the less rational responses we experience following a breakup - those knee-jerk over-reactions.

For us to belong to a group is a very primal, basic human need. It used to be purely for survival. However, being rejected from a group causes scars. When our connection with a partner is severed - even when we do the cutting - this often triggers ingrained feelings of being unwanted, unloved, and abandoned, even cheated. Rebuilding our sense of belonging requires a massive adjustment.

Returning briefly to the stories we tell ourselves, if we're feeling lonely, it might help us to reframe being 'alone' as being 'with self' for the purpose of rebuilding our lives. This is not cheating ourselves; this is re-framing it. Lonely has connotations of desperate and unwanted. Being with our self has connotations of a nice comfy night in sitting next to a fire, watching TV, or reading a book. It's an evening in with ourselves.

This kind of thought re-framing prevents us slipping into a downward spiral of loneliness and isolation (see Part III, Chapter 8).

Even if we're in the most happy, healthy, abundant family, it's our nature to feel slightly rejected, lonely and isolated at times. But after a relationship breakup, this can intensify and make us feel desperate. So, next time you find yourself on your own at night time for dinner, turn it into something special. Think of a way that we could celebrate the peace, what it's like to revisit and be with ourselves.

There's a wonderful book by Thema Bryant, a colleague of mine, called Homecoming (Bryant, 2022), and the whole book is about pulling in parts of our lives we've split off, that felt bad or unwanted or dangerous for us, and how we bring all these things in to make ourselves feel whole again, so we want to be with ourselves. We get permission to be comfortable being with ourselves.

Our goal is to make ourselves sustainable - to run the course, to become a survivor. Sustainability is vital because any fear of us not surviving can rapidly lead to hopelessness, an inability to work therapeutically, and even suicide.

The feeling of being left behind by our ex, even though it may not be the truth, is probably the loneliest feeling a person can have. They're off having all the fun. They've mended. They've moved on. But hold dear to yourself, and understand what is keeping you moving forward and what's not holding you back.

Be mindful, you can't judge. You don't know what's really going on. You never will. Bring the focus fully back to self. Stop wasting time on what 'may be' happening. Remember: no-one's life or journey is perfect.

Michael: I had nothing and no one when I nearly died at 16. I had my aunt and cousins but not my parents, etc. I lived only to get to the UK and be told by my mother the next day, "I wish you had died there." Less than a year later, I had run away and was living in a car. My parents never came looking for me. That was my first experience of being left, and it was worse than death because I was left alone with the most tormenting thoughts and painful feelings.

Two types of mourning: future and past

If someone is dead, it is often believed that we only mourn the future because the past has ended. In fact, we mourn both the past (what was) and the future (what could have been).

When moving on from a relationship, we also mourn both the future and the past. We not only lose the person we were with in that relationship, but also who we were in that relationship. We become someone new who never fully belonged in that story.

John: Our best times were always when we were in public. The intimacy wasn't there though. I was constantly being rejected. I'm now grieving that we're done.

If we were a survivor of suicide, our grieving might combine aspects of both bereavement and relationship loss. We have to come to terms with the fact that the person was not taken from us. Instead, that person chose to leave us. In a way, they rejected and abandoned us.

Dealing with the psychache (psyche ache) of breakup

Let's not kid ourselves. There is often a profound emotional, spiritual, and social pain that comes with relationship breakups.

Edwin Schneidman, an American suicidologist, coined a name for it: psychache (Mears, 2022).

Several tools have been designed to measure emotional and psychological pain, including Shneidman's own Psychological Pain Assessment Scale (PPAS) See the diagram on the next page and the associated article by Baryshnikov and Isometsa (2022) for more details.

Keep in mind: although we can use these models, diagrams, and scales, every journey to emotional recovery is different.

So, what does affect our recovery journey?
A major factor that impacts us is the timing of the breakup. Was it after just having a child? Was it in the 'honeymoon period,' that first few months of a relationship? Was it after 60 years of devoted love?

If a breakup isn't too impactful in someone's life, we wouldn't need this book. Here, I'm only looking at what can negatively impact a recovery journey. Some people do break up, and it's the right thing to do at that time for both parties, and they seemingly don't have too much of a struggle. We're only looking here at an average breakup that has a massive impact on our understanding of life and our future.

Another factor that affects how we recover from a breakup is our role in the relationship because if one of us did all of the cooking, washing, and cleaning, and the other did all of the bills, etc., that's going to leave a massive hole, and it's going to create a new learning or relearning experience, which can lead to anxiety. There can be loose ends to tie up and a need to become independent in certain areas.

Name	Description	Assessment of psychological pain			Reference
		Current	Lifetime tendency	Tolerability	
Psychological Pain Assessment Scale (PPAS)	Includes a definition of psychache and the Thematic Apperception Test (responders are presented with 10 pictures and asked to rate psychache experienced by the main heroes); assesses intensity of current and lifetime worst psychache on a scale from 1 to 9, and feelings prominent in the worst pain; and requests the method used in a suicide attempt and a rating of lethality from "very low" to "close to dying"	Yes	Yes	No	(39)
Orbach and Mikulincer Mental Pain (OMMP)	A self-rating 5-point Likert-scale with 44 items, including nine factors: a) irreversibility, b) loss of control, c) narcissist wound, d) emotional flooding, e) freezing, f) self-estrangement, g) confusion, h) social distancing, i) emptiness; conceptualizes psychological pain as a perception of negative feeling	Yes	No	Yes	(31)
Psychache Scale (PAS)	A 13-item scale, with each item coded with a 5-point Likert score	No	Yes	Yes	(44)
Visual Analog Scale for Psychache	A visual analog scale from 0 to 10 on psychological pain currently and during the last 15 days	Yes	No	No	(54)
Mee-Bunney Psychological Pain Assessment Scale (MBPPAS)	A 10-item self-report scale with 5-point Likert items, assessing both frequency and intensity of psychological pain	Yes	Yes	Yes	(58)
Psychic Pain Scale (PPS)	A 20-item scale based on Maltsberger's theory of suicidality. The PPS assesses frequency of a range of negative affects on a 5-point Likert scale; two factors: affective deluge and loss of control	N.d.[1]	N.d.	N.d.	(80)
Unbearable psychache Scale (UP3)	A 3-item scale, derived from the PAS, for rating the unbearableness of psychological pain	Not directly	No	Yes	(62)
Mental Pain Questionnaire (MPQ)	Assesses psychological pain "in the past weeks" with 10 items and yes/no responses	Yes	No	No	(81)

[1] = Not defined.

Of course, one of the primary factors that can affect recovery is if the breakup were an unexpected blow, like a sudden death. It could be that you found your ex with somebody else, or they could have all of a sudden said, "It's not working, goodbye," they walk out of the door and you never see them again. That creates massive trauma and shock, like being hit by a train, and that clearly requires more recovery.

So, just consider how your relationship dissolved. Was it gradual? Was it sudden for one of you but planned by the other (e.g., did you pack and unpack your suitcases several times without anybody knowing?) Did you separate beforehand for several months? Was the writing on the wall for a long time?

Another factor is conflict in the relationship. Was there domestic violence and coercive control? If so, it's not only the breakup you need to recover from. How badly damaged were you from toxic, unhealthy behavior in the relationship?

Leaving vs being abandoned

While feelings of regret are common in both leavers and those who left, there are important differences too.

If we left the relationship, we may feel the weight of that responsibility. This can heighten feelings of guilt and we will feel that anything bad that happens to us, our ex, our children, or anybody else affected by the breakup is our fault. We may need to regularly return to our justifications for leaving the relationship (i.e., convincing ourselves it was the right move).

If we were left, our pain may crystallize around feelings of being powerless or having been abandoned. In this case, going back over the specifics of our relationship breakup, while letting go of unknown factors, can help us to rationalize our loss. We mustn't beat ourselves up about what happened in the relationship. That was then; this is now. We need to work on accepting hard facts while protecting our self-esteem. Our partner may have lost interest or found satisfaction elsewhere but that is their journey. We have a different path and that doesn't have to mean more rejection.

If we were left, we are also more likely to have experienced shock if the breakup came suddenly. It is very important at this time to drink lots and lots of water because it helps the body to handle shock; don't forget the mind and body are interlinked. Also, we need to give ourselves time and permission to unfold from it.

And then there's the shock...

Relationship breakup is always somebody's choice, and that deliberate severance leads to one of the major characteristics of the post-relationship experience: severe shock for one or both parties. As explained in the introduction (polyvagal theory), intense shock can lead to symptoms such as dissociation and depression. Flashbacks, nightmares, and intrusive thoughts are also possible. We might even deliberately provoke our ex into pushing our hot buttons so that we can overcome numbness and experience grief symptoms (DeGroot and Carmack, 2022).

Traumatic relationship loss is akin to complicated grief, and working through our current breakup may very well bring back previous trauma. We may need professional help with a PTSD trained therapist to unwrap this. The gift is that the previous trauma may help unravel any negative coping mechanisms that are holding us back from overcoming our shadows.

If we feel we have made no progress after a year, we may be experiencing a 'complicated breakup.' This is the timeframe for diagnosis of prolonged grief disorder (PGD) in the ICD-11 (World Health Organization, 2022) and DSM-5 (2013). Many relationships ended during the COVID-19 pandemic, and it is not a huge leap to make to suggest that the correlation between COVID deaths and prolonged grief disorder (Jackson, 2022) would be mirrored by COVID breakups and recovery complications.

Important: If you feel that you need professional support for the symptoms of relationship breakup trauma, look for therapists who have been trained in trauma-informed practice or post-traumatic stress disorder (PTSD). They will be sensitive to the risk of retraumatization.

Task 5: Overcoming the shadow
Your next task is to decide on an approach or set of techniques that can work at this level.
Here are some suggestions:
- List the top three things that we dislike about other people. These are usually the things we hate about ourselves.
- List the top three things we are afraid of.
- Look into therapeutic tools that work at a subconscious level, for example:
  ◊ Shapiro's EMDR. A trauma reprocessing technique that's hugely popular now and very effective. (Plagaro, 2022)
  ◊ Hypnosis. To change the unconscious drives that keep us repeating behavior patterns or ruminating on things. Make sure that you get a hypnotist that is qualified and used to your situation.
  ◊ Somatization. Where you work with your body to release stuck trauma.
  ◊ Spiritual approaches. Explore faith-based approaches that resonate with you (shamanism, hands-on healing, etc.)

Task 6: Recognizing (and resisting) hooks and binds: Part 2
This second part on relationship hooks and binds focuses on those that are hidden from our awareness. These include our wired-in instinct to seek human company and the silent but powerful attractive force of familiarity.

Our human desperate need to contact at any cost
If we want proof of the connection instinct in humans, all we have to do is watch the CCTV footage from the aftermath of a disaster. Following an earthquake, bomb attack, or serious accident, most survivors immediately seek the nearest human contact.

The London bombings in the seventies and eighties showed CCTV footage of people really damaged in the bomb blasts, bloodied and missing limbs, all moving towards each other and wanting human touch. This footage taught us a lot about human need.

After a relationship wreck, we see a similar behavior with the 'rebound

Never give up. Your rewards may be closer than you think

relationship,' or the decision to forget all grievances and return to the ex-partner. Both may be dangerous.

But it is not just this primitive human homing instinct that acts to bind us into unhealthy relationships. There is something much more subtle at play.

Revealing our *hygge* drives
Sometimes there are no words in our native language that truly encompass an experience or a feeling. While soul-searching for this

book, I wanted to find a word that encapsulated that warm, cosy feeling of belonging and familiarity that we experience when we are with somebody special.

Eventually, and quite by fluke, I found a Danish word that hit the nail on the head: *hygge*. Wanting to rekindle this feeling of *hygge* can be one of the strongest hooks that keeps us in - or draws us back towards - a familiar but unfulfilling or toxic relationship. People sacrifice a lot to retain *hygge*. Its power is in its subtlety; it's a deeply enmeshed connection that fades into the background during daily life, gently reassuring us, during life's tough moments, that someone is with us, that someone will notice if there's a problem. We are special to somebody. If something were to happen to us, at least this one person would know about it.

It is like coming home to us. When we experience *hygge*, we feel we have a witness to our lives, a caring monitor to our activities, a personal alarm, a safety net, a diving buddy, an identical twin, and a security blanket that we can gently tug on when we feel vulnerable. It is the promise of *hygge* that allows us to enjoy our alone time, safe in the knowledge that our partner will be back before long - or we will at least get a call or text.

Our innate need for human contact combined with the loss of *hygge* is so profound, it pushes many of us to jump into the wrong sack with the wrong person, an urge that can lead to repeating unhealthy relationship patterns.

The key to avoiding this outcome is doing the work in this book. When we have worked on understanding what didn't work for us and the relationship, we can understand whether we attracted somebody who wasn't good for us or things just dissipated, and we went in different directions.

Unless we work on ourselves, we won't know what's going to be healthy and wonderful for us in the future. If we don't work on ourselves, clearly you can see for now that these hidden, behind the shadow drives will ruin everything that comes our way. We must face them and resolve them.

The absence of *hygge* hits us at unexpected times and levels, triggering profound loneliness, penetrating grief, painful thoughts, and a whole plethora of evils tearing our soul apart piece by piece.

John: I've just felt this terrible pang while driving. What if I went off the road. I can't shake this horrible feeling, now, that if I were to have a car accident, there would be nobody really grieving over me. I don't have somebody special to check in on me. I guess this comes from my childhood because I never really had that. Before, Mary would have realized something unusual had happened. She would have raised the alarm. Sure, she would sometimes play games and not call me for a couple of days, but we were both like that. But now I could go days without anyone coming across me. I would be a 'John Doe.' They would find it difficult to find out who I was.

And I was the one that left! She was the first to say we should breakup, but I wrote her the leaving letter - and I left her. I had no choice though. I had lost my self-respect, so I needed to give that familiarity up.

Hygge is an example of what Needs (2022) terms a 'strong attractor state'. In dynamic systems terms, this strong attractor state is triggered by the uncomfortable chaos of our new and unfamiliar situation. For those who have left a relationship, staying suddenly may seem a more comfortable and far less painful option for us. It is similar to the force that compels criminals to re-offend when released from the order of their prison life to the chaos of the streets. Keep in mind that familiarity may not always be our friend.

When to cut our losses
We often justify giving in to the pull of hygge and human contact by telling ourselves that things will get better. Always living in hope, we hold on to a dissatisfying relationship in the hope that things will improve.

When thoughts of leaving cross our minds, we remind ourselves of all the years of emotional investment we have made in making our relationship work. I can't tell you the number of times I packed a suitcase in the morning, only to unpack it before my partner returned in the evening. Sometimes, at the worst times of our relationship, I would do this several times a week. He had no idea that I had done this. I just carried on as if everything was fine because I felt safe in the familiarity. My soul knew that I was unhappy, but my head was going for that usual feeling of hygge, of safety and the familiar, not for what was right for me. *Hygge* was so powerful it made me stay in a very cruel and toxic relationship.

Our truth is, and you'd better believe it, that the longer our unhappiness continues, the more that value is being eroded by the situation. In some cases, this situation is mirrored by financial investments as more of our money becomes tied up in mortgages, savings, car finance, etc.

However, emotional investment is similar to financial investment. You would never invest in stocks and shares or a savings plan that actually gave you back less money than you were putting in. In a toxic and unhealthy relationship that is what happens every time. So, what makes us stay? Yes, it's the *hygge*, that need for familiarity and safety through routine.

If this is the case for you, it is probably time to cut your losses. When we cut our losses, we stop what we were doing in order to prevent a bad situation from becoming worse.

Directors of companies are right to cut their losses, admit they chose the wrong pathway and make a change; it's called pivoting. By adopting the same attitude, we can pivot, cut the losses of a bad relationship and move towards healing and great things. Yes, believe me, the future's amazing. But first, as we're saying, we have to cut all the baggage loose so that we're not tethered to and laden with past loads and past falsehoods. And then we can really fly
Consider this carefully: cutting losses is not the same as saying you should resign yourself to giving up something you have the right to (i.e., money you made together, property, child custody, etc.,) It is the loss of the emotional investment we made in the relationship that we will have to give up. We have to accept losses at times in life, in order to move on to gaining again.

Cutting our losses will help us choose our battles wisely rather than fight for the sake of keeping some sort of connection and belonging alive, no matter what.

See **'In a Nutshell'** for some tasks based on this section.

John: After the exercises I've worked on, I realize now that Mary has lost a great person whereas I have lost an insecure person who was disappointing in so many ways. That realization has given me strength.

From truth to forgiveness
As well as being in our truth, we have to genuinely forgive ourselves and our ex. I'm sure you will agree, this deep shadow work will enable us to recognize an important truth: that good and bad in our relationship never belonged to one person. It was shared between us. From that position of truth, we can take ownership of our future direction and finally exit the turmoil with a clear view ahead.

Forgiveness is ultimately a powerful force for healing and moving on, and we can take a huge step forward by forgiving both ourselves and our ex-partner for the 'bad' that pulled us apart.

Task 7: I'm not becoming all witch-like on you, but sometimes a ritual can help us with forgiveness. We need to think of the top three behaviors that we need to forgive ourselves for. Sometimes we do bad things because we are hurting. We need to forgive ourselves three things that we did in the relationship (and in the post-relationship experience, if that's appropriate). But in addition, we need to think of the top three things that our partner was crap at, dangerous at, or awful at and forgive them. This isn't about accepting cruelty, bad behavior, domestic violence, or deceitful behavior. This is about saying well, it happened, but hey, I forgive you. This is the only way to be free of it. Living in despair and anger or rage only damages us and keeps us stuck. Forgiving is releasing. Choosing battles going forward is very important. But leaving battles that are over behind us is even more important.

Your ritual could involve writing the six behaviors you are forgiving (three of yours, three of your ex's) onto a piece of paper. In pagan times, the most powerful rituals needed to involve water, fire, earth, and air. So, for example, we could burn the paper, put the ashes in a coconut shell, and put the shell in the river while speaking a statement of release. It may sound silly, but these rituals really work, and there's a big resurgence of these rituals worldwide as people try to adapt to the challenges of 21st Century life.

Whatever it is you do: putting a message in a bottle, dancing in a circle, etc., it only works if you absolutely genuinely forgive and release. Maybe now is not your time. Maybe you have to revisit this book. Go back and read this book again from the beginning, or put it away for a few months until you're ready. Unless you go through this book in your truth, in genuine 'task-focused' fashion, you are not going to move forward. But the fact that you have this book, whether you bought it or received it as a gift, is a sign that you need to do some work, move on, and make the best life you possibly can.

Finding deeper levels of meaning
We ended our tasks at the end of the last chapter by re-evaluating our beliefs, values, and goals (i.e., our boundaries). By delving into the depths of your soul, we can access deeper levels of meaning that help us move through painful feelings of rejection, guilt, regret, and abandonment.

Overcoming our shadow is no small step, but if we are unable to find meaning in our loss, we can struggle with lifelong anxiety or depression. Don't get stuck. Don't escape through suicide. And let's forgive, let go. and move on. It's the only way.

In a nutshell
Task 5: Explore therapeutic approaches for deep healing
- EMDR
- Hypnosis
- Somatization
- Spirituality

Task 6: Recognize and practice resisting deep-seated drives for unhealthy connection
- Sleeping around without boundaries, getting involved with toxic friends, excessive partying, burning yourself out at work, etc. Revisit these and consider healthier alternatives for establishing human contact.

- Belonging, familiarity, and hygge: 'Better the Devil you know.' List your 10 special people that can be your new 'home' setting. Also consider who you want to let go of.
- When do we call it a day? Cutting our losses rather than holding on for unattractive returns.

Task 7: Responsibility and forgiveness
- Share responsibility for the good times: think about and celebrate the good times we experienced in our relationship.
- Forgiveness: What are the top three things we need to consider forgiving our ex for? More importantly, what are the top three

things we need to forgive ourselves for? Look at the relationship itself and what has happened since.
- Ritual release: create a ritual to release the six things you are forgiving (e.g., write them on a piece of paper and burn it, let it blow away, send it down the river, etc.)

Many relationship breakups involve domestic violence (DV) and this complicates the journey to moving on or making up.

Before we continue our journey together, I need to check you over. For all I know, this book could be the first you've looked at since your breakup. All first responders, like myself, are potential gatekeepers for domestic violence because what we do and say in these early moments could change our lives. So, the next chapter is going to focus on this area.

Even if domestic violence plays absolutely no part in your breakup, I do recommend we read through these next chapters anyway because one day, you could be the first on the scene of someone's relationship car crash. And to borrow the words of Marya Meyer, CEO of the Women's Fund Miami, "When you do, you don't want to be numb." (Acton, 2023)

For more guidance, read:
Banks, E. (2022). *Who the hell is Abraham Maslow.* Who the Hell is...?

Bryant, T. S. (2022). *Homecoming.* TarcherPerigee.

Krumwiede, A. (2014). *Attachment theory according to John Bowlby and Mary Ainsworth.* GRIN Verlag.

References:

Acton, M. [MPA Mind. (2023, May 31). #MPAMind - Expert panel discussion: 'What Would You Put in #MichaelasLaw ?' #MichaelaHallDay 2023 [Video]. YouTube. https://youtu.be/xR0ROex9TwE?si=7pSyyzbTdpw_ninI].

American Psychiatric Association. (2013). *Diagnostic and statistical manual of mental disorders.*(5th ed.).

Baryshnikov, I. and Isometsa, E. (2022). Psychological pain and suicidal behavior: a review. *Frontiers in Psychiatry.*

Bryant, T. S. (2022). *Homecoming.* TarcherPerigee.

DeGroot, J. M., and Carmack, H. J. (2022). Accidental and purposeful triggers of post-relationship grief. *Journal of Loss and Trauma.* Advance online publication.

Jackson, C. (2022). Navigating complex grief. *Therapy Today.* Jul/Aug, pp 18-22)

Mears, D. (2022). Choosing Life or Death. *Therapy Today.* Jul/Aug, pp 38-41)

Needs, A. (2022). Change must engage a person's senses of identity, meaning, control, and belonging. *The Psychologist.* April.

Plagaro, I. (2022). *Healing the wounds of rejection.* EMDR Therapy Quarterly. https://etq.emdrassociation.org.uk/case-study/healing-the-wounds-of-rejection/

Skinner, Q. (2021, November 18). *The sixth stage of grief.* Life Time. https://experiencelife.lifetime.life/article/the-sixth-stage-of-grief/

World Health Organization. (2022). ICD-11: *International classification of diseases* (11th revision)

"I will be free, always.
I am free.
I will always have warm and loving company.
I do have warm and loving company.
I will bring in abundance.
I do have abundance.
I am safe.
I am confident.
People will always treat me with love.
I am loved.
I will always demand respect.
I am respected.
I am safe."

- Dr. Michael Acton -

PART I: A CATEGORY FIVE STORM

CHAPTER 6

ARE OUR RELATIONSHIPS ABUSIVE? WE MUST CHECK THIS OUT

"Never let anyone get comfortable with disrespecting you."
- Dr. Michael Acton -

Even if you don't believe you are in a situation involving domestic violence or narcissism, it's worth going through this chapter because most relationships have an element of narcissism. If this doesn't appeal to you, pass on to page 197

All first responders to an emergency need a simple rulebook to help them quickly assess the situation, prioritize their actions and intervene appropriately - which always includes listening and providing a reassuring voice.

Domestic violence is a global crisis which will cross most of our paths making us all potential first responders. Sometimes, an emergency intervention will be needed. At other times, being there on the sidelines will be enough.

But how do we know what action is needed and when? To answer that question, I designed an eight-rule model specifically for this purpose: 'Acton's Domestic Violence Model for Gatekeepers.' An adapted version for mental health professionals was launched as a credentialed online course in April 2024 by the Mental Health Academy. You can access the course at:

https://www.mentalhealthacademy.co.uk/credential/domesticviolence/enrol (UK)

https://www.mentalhealthacademy.net/credential/domesticviolence/enroll (USA)

https://www.mentalhealthacademy.com.au/credential/domesticviolence/enrol (Australia)

To follow is a summary of the original version of 'Acton's Domestic Violence Model for Gatekeepers (SOSDV8)'. It is designed to be broadly relevant to any individual and agency that might come into contact with domestic violence.

We could actually be gatekeepers for our own domestic violence. It's amazing how many times I've brought up the domestic violence card with somebody and they've said, "Me? No. Never," before it _does_ turn out to be domestic violence. Please read through this with that mindset. Perhaps imagine that I am running through this rulebook with you and providing you with appropriate advice.

Rule #1. Triaging & Threats

Before anyone can act on domestic violence, they have to recognize it. But domestic violence is very difficult to pin down and it appears in different guises due to context and the unique souls involved.

Academically, there is ongoing debate about defining domestic violence (e.g., see Walker and Gavin, 2011). In the public arena, the Center for Disease Control and Prevention (CDC) in America defines intimate partner violence (IPV) as physical violence, sexual violence, stalking and psychological aggression, which includes 'coercive acts.' This could be from a current or previous intimate partner. But this definition isn't specific enough. What about physical violence in self-defense? Could an abusee be convicted by a court of law for protecting themselves? What about the use of finances or technology to limit or restrict someone's freedom? Would this meet the threshold for psychological aggression or a coercive act?

These contested and vague definitions make it all the more important for us as first responders to ask the question, 'How would we *ourselves* define and recognize domestic violence?' This leads on to further questions:
- Where do we draw the line between harmless but difficult conflict and something more sinister and damaging?
- What is our background? How does this affect our 'barometer' of abuse?
- Is there an existing tool that could be used to identify domestic violence (e.g., the Demographic Health Surveys (DHS) Domestic Violence module?

This framework of 'Acton's Domestic Violence Model for Gatekeepers' aims to take away the personal biases of individual first responders, so they can assess potential domestic violence with clear eyes and open minds. (It can be helpful to think of domestic violence as similar to alcoholism but instead of struggling to free themselves from a substance, an abusee is trapped and controlled by a thinking, acting person. How would that situation show itself in an abusee?

Here are some ways a first responder might detect hidden domestic violence:

- Discrepancies in behavior (being less punctual than usual, swearing more, dressing differently, etc.)
- How the quality of the person's voice changes in response to certain questions (in fluency, tone, pitch, etc.)
- Body language, especially a 'guarding' posture
- Shame in the eyes (often the hardest to conceal sign)
- Gestures and facial expressions
- For experienced therapists, how the person reacts to them and how they react in response (transference and countertransference)
- Tools such as the Pragmatic Protocol (Sobhani-Rad, 2014). These can be useful but are limited
- Avoiding difficult questions about their relationship. Calling this out can be a powerful tool to help an abusee to open up

If the first responder has been abused themselves, an abusee will often unconsciously form a strong alliance with them - even without disclosure on the responder's part.

Either way, first responders to domestic violence must draw on their intuition, which can be thought of as a holistic sense of a situation. If they suspect domestic violence in someone they know well, they might sense a fakeness about the relationship? Is the person putting on a face? Do they often cancel or avoid social events when before they used to be available? Having a hunch is not enough. A first responder must own their intuitive insights and use them to frame appropriate questions. Making the right call is critical because questions are agents of change (Boroff, 2010).

Here are eight powerful questions that are similar to those we use in counseling and therapy to support patients in opening up. They pave the way for applying Rule #3 of 'Acton's Domestic Violence Model for Gatekeepers' - creating a safe space to talk.

- You seem nervous. Is there anything you're not telling me?
- There's something you're not saying. What is it?
- You don't seem happy. What's on your mind?
- What makes you stay in this relationship?
- Are you struggling with anything?
- I feel your heart's not in this relationship. Why is that?
- You don't seem yourself. What's been happening?
- You disappeared there for a moment. Where did you go?

Once the first responder has found out all they can about what's happening, they can move from assessment to action.

PS. First responders are often children. They will need to bring their concerns to the attention of another adult (teacher, parent, grandparent, 'of age' friend, etc.)

PPS. Be wary of tactics that could be used by an abuser to frame themselves as the abusee

Rule #2. Safeguarding Self/Abusee
The number one priority for a gatekeeper of domestic violence is their own personal safety.

Next, they need to assess whether to call the emergency services on behalf of the abusee? They are looking and listening for signs of potential harm to the abusee or someone else. Is the person talking about hopelessness? Are they talking about how they can't go on? Are they talking about their pain? Have they got injury marks on them? Are there children at risk? Does their personal hygiene indicate dangerous self-neglect? If it's someone the responder has known for some time, has there been a major change in the abusees lifestyle, behavior, or social involvement? Have they suspected depression (domestic violence can have similar symptoms)?

I cannot assess you personally through this book, but if you recognize that you are at risk of being a danger to yourself or others, you must get emergency support. Google 'emergency mental health support' or similar in your area and you will find instructions from health services, charities and other organizations.

If your situation is dangerous but not an emergency, you can file a report anonymously. Few people trust the internet (we know IP addresses can be tracked), so the safest way is to put a note through the police station letterbox. This puts the responsibility on to the relevant domestic violence teams. This advice also applies if you are in the position of a first responder to someone else's domestic violence.

Now that we have triaged your domestic violence risk together, we can move on to Rule #3.

Rule #3. Creating Head Space
Once the first responder is satisfied that an emergency intervention is not needed, they can switch to reassuring them that help and safety is available.

They must be empathic and non-judgmental. Now is not the time for criticism or making demands.

Most people reading this book will no longer be living with their abuser, but perhaps you are only contemplating leaving or maybe you have left and returned. Don't be hard on yourself. People often stay in an abusive relationship because they have conflicted feelings. On the one hand, they are desperate to escape the abuse, but on the other, they care for their partner and may even love them.

This is normal, and a first responder can gently explain that it is possible to care for and love someone at the same time as recognizing that they need to leave them. This will enable you to move on to discussing your motivations for staying and for leaving.

Questions that can help clarify and open up this sensitive area include:
- If I were to stay, what needs to change?
- What's changed between when we first met and now?
- What still works from our early relationship? What's missing?

Break down what you are really feeling. For example, if a patient were to confide in me that they were scared, I would be asking them, 'What do you mean by that?'

Domestic violence might have left you feeling worthless and unloveable. Challenge the facts supporting those feelings.

Put yourself in the shoes of your ex as you recall an abusive incident. Put their behavior in the spotlight. For example, if you remember feeling scared of your partner at the time, switch your perspective and imagine how they might have been feeling towards you. Were they angry with you? What would a kind and considerate person do if they knew you were feeling scared or worthless?

Challenge any justifications you are using to defend your abuser. Remember, there is never an excuse for any kind of domestic violence, whether physical, psychological, financial, or sexual.

Another important fact to understand is that you can only ever change yourself, although by changing your own behaviour, you will alter the relationship dynamic (for better or worse).

Your partner will only change for the better if they do work on themselves.

We don't choose to enter abusive relationships. Reviewing how your relationship changed over time can often clarify what went wrong and when. Did you fall for the wrong person? What attracted you to your partner (and vice versa)? When was the first incident of abusive behavior (of any type)? What information does that bring to the table?

If you are still living with your ex, be aware of the potential for escalation of domestic violence should they become aware of your intent to leave. Think about how you would manage this. Don't make a knee-jerk reaction, and read through the rest of this chapter. You might find the chapters that follow supportive as well.

Rule #4. Reality Check - Past, Present, Future
From the gentle explorations of the previous step, it is likely you came across examples of justification and downplaying. Now it's time to slightly harden your stance to help you recognize the abuse for what it is, and to accept that there is never a valid reason for it. Be kind to yourself, but commit to being honest.

In working through Chapters 4 and 5, you will have become aware of the distorted stories you tell yourself and the hidden forces of the unconscious that cloud your vision. Use this approach to challenge conflicting narratives. If your ex really cares for you, why did they refuse to go to the hospital appointment with you? Is that the behavior of a caring partner?

Being honest with yourself will help you to regain your power and strengthen your motivation to stay away from abuse. If this brings up shame, that's OK. If you can learn to manage those feelings, you will build resilience against future abuse.

Some of your relationship dynamic will have its roots in the past. Are there clues in your childhood upbringing and previous relationships that can shed light on how you interact now? Were aspects of your unhealthy relationship normalized by your parents or caregivers? Did one parent's actions negatively affect the family so that you are determined not to follow in their footsteps. For example, did your parents stick together through domestic violence, or did they break up, upsetting the family harmony?

How was your ex abusive to you? Domestic violence is a complex issue, so the more you can break the experience down into specific behaviors and reactions, the easier it will be to understand what is going on without being overwhelmed. For example, you could pick out three scenarios and explore them in depth rather than trying to think about your entire relationship as a whole.

Examine your role in the abusive dynamic. No, this is not 'victim blaming'. It is empowering you to think of yourself as an active 'cause' in your dysfunctional relationship rather than a powerless 'effect'. It in no way condones domestic violence, but it does give you the power to choose to do things differently rather than waiting for a change or an intervention that will probably never come.

Take a third party perspective. What would your best friend advise you to do if they knew everything that was going on in your relationship?

Whether or not you have left the abusive relationship, how do you see your future? What are your hopes and fears? How close or remote are your dreams? In therapy, here is where I would use solution-focused techniques to help my patient find a positive and practical way forward. If I sense avoidance, I will gently push them with, "What are you not telling me?"

Are you hoping that your ex will change their ways so that you can eventually go back to them? Be mindful that the phrase, 'I'm sorry,' is meaningless unless it leads to a real change in behavior. What evidence would be proof of real change? What is the ideal outcome? What would your relationship look like if your ex did do the work?

Doing this work on your own is tough, so it is important to reach out to someone who can hold you through the dark times. You may feel hopeless and even suicidal. This is normal, but you must

seek emergency help if you are at risk of harming yourself or someone else.

Rule #5. Navigating Escape

This chapter applies mainly to those who are living with an abuser, although its content will be invaluable if you need to support a friend or family member to escape domestic violence.

When the abusee reaches the stage where their motivation to leave overcomes their desire to stay, the gatekeeper's role can switch to one of practical support. The first piece of practical advice should always be, "Don't rush into a knee-jerk reaction. Leave at the right time for you."

The abusee's planning needs to be meticulous and rational. In the business world, a SWOT analysis is often made for any new venture, and this can also be applied to escaping abuse. What are the strengths (resources), weaknesses, opportunities, and threats they will need to manage.

Strengths might include a place they can stay and a car of their own. Weaknesses may be a lack of income, settled children, or nobody to help them move in to a new property. They include thoughts and emotions that they may need to work on before they are ready to leave. Threats could be the reaction a partner will have to being left. Are they likely to be violent or to threaten suicide? Are children, parents or pets safe from harm? This needs to be treated seriously. According to Florida's Domestic Abuse Shelter, Inc. (2019), 75% of women who were murdered by an abusive partner were killed as they were leaving or after they had left. Even if there is no physical threat, the abuser's behavior will escalate when they find out the abusee is leaving. What form might this take and how can it be managed?

Opportunities might include an upcoming promotion, giving the abusee more financial security, or a window opening up due to the partner having a holiday abroad. They also include all of those opportunities that the abusee can access as a result of leaving, such as rebuilding former friendships and taking up a new hobby or sport.

A gatekeeper can help the abusee think through their options. What do they need to do to escape? Which local agencies can help? Do they have local support systems in place? Do they have someone else in their life that is safe to talk to? Is this their first attempt at leaving or have they tried before? What went wrong that time?

Preparing a 'safe box' or 'grab bag' can be a gamechanger when leaving an abusive relationship. This could include items such as:

- Cash
- A key to a 'safe space' (friend's house, car, storage unit, etc.)
- Spare credit/debit card
- Spare mobile device and charger
- Form of ID (birth certificate, passport, driving license, etc.)

Explore whether clothes and valuable items such as jewelry and framed photographs could be discreetly moved to a safe location outside of the house before the abusee leaves.

The abusee may not have thought through all of the implications of their decision. Be honest about the downside while providing them with the reassurance they need. For example, there is a risk that someone they confide in could have loyalties to the abuser. Unless there is clear evidence of violence, it is likely that friends and relatives will refuse to believe the abusee and defend the abuser from their accusations. Those who do believe and care for the abusee will respond by rejecting the abuser, thus shattering the fantasy of an idyllic future for the couple. The loss of hope can be devastating for the abusee.

While the abusee may be level headed when discussing their escape, explain that stress hormones are likely to cloud their thinking at the time. Having a list of support numbers to hand (domestic violence hotline, trusted friend's number, etc.) can make a huge difference.

Make sure the abusee has one or more backup plans should Plan A hit a problem. For example, if their car is in the garage, do they have an Uber app and funds to pay their fare.

On a cyber-security level, it is likely that the leaver will need to carry out a security audit on all of their digital accounts, including social media accounts. They may have to revoke access permissions, change passwords and remove devices from shared accounts. By preparing the abusee to face these unpleasant and challenging scenarios, a gatekeeper can help them to build the resilience they will need to 'stay left.'

Rule #6. Staying Strong

Once the abusee has left an abusive relationship, gatekeepers can help the person to work on difficult emotions, and to develop and strengthen the mindset that they are leaving forever. On average, it takes someone seven times to leave an abusive relationship. Yes, seven is the magic number!

In the previous two chapters, you were introduced to the various conscious and unconscious hooks that keep us chained to our ex-partners. Be aware that when a person leaves domestic violence, there are going to be even more hooks attempting to drag them back into danger.

A big one is guilt. Once out of the cauldron, they might feel empathy towards the soul they have left and start wondering whether they have been thoughtless, cruel or overzealous in leaving. They might start making excuses for the abuser's behavior and wondering whether the criticisms the abuser has drip-fed them are true after all.

Then there are the barbs thrown out by the abuser. They will use anything they can to get the hooks in. And keep in mind that they will know exactly how to get under the abusee's skin.

Abusers can and will change the style of abuse, switching between aggressive, blaming and ghosting tactics. They might weaponize credit cards, taxes, technology, social media, or childcare. They could threaten suicide. They might even agree to attend couples therapy, only to use the language and tools of therapy against the abusee.

Understanding an abuser's low emotional intelligence and childish mindset, and comparing their game-playing with how reasonable adults negotiate, is a key skill for the abusee to master.

Gatekeepers can further help by regularly reminding the abusee of their right to refuse a relationship and their commitment to leaving permanently. They can also help the abusee to recognize the hooks: those they impose upon themselves, and those their abuser throws in their direction.

Seduction is another common tactic. If the abuser is apologizing, flattering and making promises, a gatekeeper can play Devil's Advocate with the abusee, asking for evidence of genuine change, which is rare, but can happen. Has the abuser reflected on their abuse? Have they set out a concrete plan of action? Who will support them? Are they likely to stay the course?

The gatekeeper can help the abusee to clarify their dealbreakers. Will the abuser respect their red lines going forward? How can they be sure? Do they really need their abuser? If they had £10m in the bank and a perfect social life, would they be as keen to go back?

Finally, the gatekeeper can help the abusee to stop expending energy in fighting their abuser and instead focus on the challenges (Rule #7) and opportunities (Rule #8) that lie ahead.

Rule #7. Choosing Battles

If an abusee engages in a personal argument with their abuser, they are going to lose, especially if they are a codependent escaping a narcissist. All they will be doing by fighting is aggravating the abuser or giving them the opportunity to find another weak point to hook into.

If an abusee needs to find a practical solution for issues with childcare, finances, housing, car, pets, etc., mediation is the best way forward They can use either a trusted friend or family member or a professional body.

Keeping children and vulnerable adults safe from harm and distress must always be a priority. If there are any concerns about safety, the abusee should go straight to the professional bodies for mediation. Both parties must work together to ensure that children are in a safe environment because child protection units can and will intervene to remove them from danger.

To ensure mediation is conducted in a mature and responsible way, it will help if both parties can act according to their core values and morals.

To keep negotiations on track, it is a good idea for the abusee to set out their top three or four wants and needs (e.g., a fair share of money and childcare, a secure home and the ability to live in peace).

Legal action is a last resort, but it may be inevitable (e.g., if failed mediation leaves the abusee vulnerable to losing their home).

If the courts is the only way to resolve a dispute, a gatekeeper can coach the abusee into working effectively with their lawyers.

This means:
- communicating only via lawyers
- making full disclosure of relevant facts, and
- taking out anything of a personal nature.

This approach will help to minimize legal fees while giving the abusee the best chance of winning the case. It may help to explain to the abusee that determining right and wrong, even in court, is rarely possible, so they may end up not getting what they believe they deserve.

In all disputes, it will help the abusee to focus only on themselves and their needs, recognizing potential triggers and getting completely out of their ex-partner's head. This can be tough, especially if they have been trained for a long time to react to their partner's moves.

If the abuser continues to assault, threaten, stalk, or otherwise terrorize the abusee, contacting the police is the best course of action. The police can also signpost quality domestic violence resources. If the abuser is well-connected in the local area, the abusee may prefer to access regional or national services further afield.

Rule #8. Building Onwards & Upwards

Leaving an abusive relationship can be tougher than any other challenge a person has faced. Before they can achieve a healthy, balanced life, the abusee will need to work through all of the raw grief and trauma of the breakup. They have to let go of their hope for a future with their ex. That is what much of this book is about, especially Chapter 7 of Part III, in which I explore the relationship between breakup and grief.

On top of the doubts and fears inherent in any breakup, there are the combined effects of all the put downs, humiliations and demeaning comments they have been subjected to by their abuser. They have to turn themselves inside out in order to heal. This involves a lot of work, and can take a very long time.

Rather than lamenting the past, this rule is all about supporting the abusee to come home to themselves, reconnect with life and look forwards.

If they are to have another relationship, what kind of person would they be safe to be with? How can they recognize the red flags of abuse and avoid repeating the patterns that led them into their previous toxic relationships? They need to believe that they are attractive, that there are people out there that will love them and want them for who they are and not what they can get from them.

How can they stay strong? Building healthy routines in terms of exercise, sleep, nutrition, and daily structure will play their part. If they have indulged in unhealthy habits since their breakup (overeating, excessive drinking, sleeping around, etc.), tackling this is a good starting point.

Rewards can be motivating. A gatekeeper could encourage the abusee to celebrate milestones (e.g., a week, a month, six months and a year of successful separation).

The onward journey involves redefining the self, setting goals and continuing to build resilience from the foundations set in Rule #6.

The abusee needs to think hard about what they honestly want in life. how have they changed? Where do they want to live? What kind of work or activities do they see themselves doing now?

There are some tried and tested ways of helping people discover their true wants and needs. As a gatekeeper, you could:
• Ask them to tell you what they definitely do not want in their life.
• Ask open questions such as, 'What does hope look like for you?'
• Ask them to imagine their best friend was in charge of their future. What would they create for them?

- Ask them what they admire about their friends' lifestyles and relationships
- Ask them what they would wish for if they could wave a magic wand.

As their self-confidence grows, the abusee can be supported to overcome their fears and open themselves to love and kindness. Then one day, they can ask themselves the question: am I ready to take the ceiling off of my life?

Toxic Tactics

Human language will never encompass the ineffable horror of being trapped within a toxic relationship. But analyzing some of the words we do have at our disposal can help us to see the mechanisms by which we are abused.

In this chapter, I'm inviting you to look deeply into the words that lie at the root of the toxic strategies used by perpetrators - often narcissists - to keep us under control.

Illusions, delusion and disillusionment

Most of us understand what an illusion is. It is something that appears different to what it really is. For example, the visual construction of optical illusions trick the mind into perceiving false colors, perspective and movement.

Illusions can also be intellectual fantasies, and these are more usually termed delusions (e.g., delusions of grandeur). When someone deludes us, they trick us into believing a falsehood. They make fools out of us by telling lies, making false promises, creating confusion and undermining our sense of reality. Delude shares a root with ludicrous (*ludere* is Latin for 'to play'). Deliberately deceiving someone is commonly termed 'gaslighting' today.

We can also be caught up in self-delusion. This is where we create (or co-create) an illusion - and convince ourselves of its truth. Often we do this because it's more comfortable to believe a lie than to accept the truth.

When reality starts to dawn, we experience the loss of that comforting illusion. This is what is meant by relationship 'disillusionment.' Much more profound than simple dissatisfaction, disillusionment includes feelings of
disappointment, regret, hopelessness, and defeat. We realize that the relationship isn't what we want and that we can't fix it.

There is a powerful proverb that can help you escape this hall of mirrors. It is: First, to thine own self be true.

Be yourself; be true to yourself; do not engage in self-deception.

Cruelty and contempt
Cruel people willfully or carelessly inflict suffering onto others. They have no conscience and therefore no remorse.

Arbitrary. Atrocious. Awful. Barbarous. Bitter. Brutal. Callous. Catty. Cold-blooded. Cruel. Crushing. Cutthroat. Despiteful. Draconian. Evil. Grim. Harsh. Hateful. Heartless. Horrible. Hostile. Inhuman. Inhumane. Merciless. Relentless. Ruthless. Sadistic. Scary. Spiteful. Terrifying. Tyrannic. Tyrannical. Unkind. Vicious.

Wicked. Austere. Bestial. Bloodthirsty. Brutish. Butcherly. Demoniac. Depraved. Disagreeable. Devaluing. Fell. Ferocious. Fiendish. Fierce. Hard. Hard-handed. Hard-hearted. Hellish. Implacable. Inexorable. Intemperate. Iron-hearted. Malevolent. Malicious. Malignant. Mean. Monstrous. Nasty. Oppressive. Pernicious. Pitiless. Rancorous. Revengeful. Rough. Rude. Savage. Searing. Severe. Stony-hearted. Taunting. Terrible. Tough. Truculent. Uncivilized. Unfeeling. Unfriendly. Unpleasant. Unrelenting. Vengeful. Vindictive. Virulent.

None of these words have a place in a healthy breakup scenario.

The best way to purge cruelty from your own actions is to embrace the opposite state of being.

Meditate on the following words:

Sweet. Kind. Mild. Moderate. Conscientious. Deferential. Delicate. Eleemosynary. Equable. Fair. Just. Mellow. Soft. Light. Tempered. Idealistic. Indifferent. Modest. Merciful. Gallant. Genteel. Gentle. Tolerant. Beneficent. Generous. Compassionate. Kindhearted. Altruistic. Considerate. Benevolent. Thoughtful. Big-hearted. Empathetic. Gracious. Humane. Moral. Softhearted. Tenderhearted. Caring. Charitable. Chivalrous. Decent. Feeling. Forbearing. Friendly. Giving. Good. Magnanimous. Munificent. Sensitive. Sympathetic. Tender. Warm. Warm-hearted. Forgiving. Helpful. Lenient. Liberal. Nice. Philanthropic. Piteous. Pitying. Pleasant. Polite. Propitious. Public-spirited. Ruthful. Uncruel. Understanding, Benign, Benignant. Good-hearted. Kindly. Loving. Unmalicious. Honorable. Civilized. Courteous. Affable. Amicable. Agreeable. Noble. Accommodating. Easy. Easygoing. Thoughtful

Rather than becoming an inhumanly cruel or wicked 'monster person' yourself, aim to be a good person, an angel, a paragon, a Samaritan but above all a humanitarian.

Cruelty can manifest as contempt in toxic relationships. Contempt is a strong feeling of disliking somebody or something. When it infiltrates a relationship, it can kill the recipient's self-worth.

In narcissistic relationships, contempt is what keeps a codependent in a position of powerlessness. Slowly but surely, the demeaning approach of an abuser will destroy us and dissolve our self-respect. As Caroline Hobdey stated clearly in my discussion panel (MPA Mind, 2023) an abuser's contempt is like a tap that is drip, drip, dripping onto concrete.

Some abusers are so scornful of others in general that they will see themselves as above the law. Even lawyers are not immune to disrespecting the law by using it to serve their interests. Whatever their profession, if someone obstructs the court's ability to fairly administer the law, they will be in 'contempt of court' which is a crime.

Ghosting
If your ex-partner is using ghosting as a way to keep you on the hook, the best thing you can do is to stop wasting mental energy thinking about them.

If they are genuinely ghosting you (rather than getting on with their own lives in a healthy manner), then they will likely be waiting and watching for a reaction. If you're looking happy and healthy on social media - and out in public - they will realize their tactic has failed.

So, turn your thoughts towards yourself and your own needs. If you bump into one another, keep exchanges brief and formal (you don't need to be mean). Look after your physical and mental health. Not only will this make you feel better, it will show your ex that their tactics are futile.

Make sure you are:
- Getting enough sleep
- Eating a healthy, balanced diet
- Exercising regularly
- Drinking plenty of water
- Attending to grooming
- Dressing well
- Being self-assured and projecting confidence

If you are finding this tough, try the following:

- Confide in a close friend. Most people will have been ghosted before, and sharing experiences can be healing. Alternatively, seek a qualified counsellor or psychotherapist
- Write down a list of your strengths and read them to yourself when you're struggling
- Celebrate every success and occasion
- Accept failure graciously
- Smile - even when you don't feel like it
- Use positive, assertive statements ("Let's go out for a coffee," instead of, "I don't suppose you would want to go out somewhere?")
- Take up a new hobby or class
- Embrace new experiences (create a bucket list and make the most of your new found freedom to go through it)

- If appropriate, start dating. Take things slowly and focus on building connections. There's no rush to be exclusive with someone new.

Breadcrumbing - beware!
A common tactic used as part of the ghosting strategy is 'breadcrumbing.' If you stop reaching out to the ghost, they will often throw you a few short messages to tantalize you. Something like, "Hey, how's tricks?" or "Sorry, busy spell. You OK?" Breadcrumbing is designed to keep you hooked, hoping for an explanation or some sort of closure. There will be no substance to the messages - just empty word crumbs.

Compare this with a genuine attempt to re-establish communication. That might go something like, "I'm really sorry I haven't been in touch. Do you have some time this week so we can meet up and talk this through?"

Of course, this could still be an empty gesture, but at least there is a suggestion of a commitment to improving your relationship.

Should you continue to post on social media?
If you are active on social media, the best way to respond to ghosting is to carry on posting at your usual rhythm. If you withdraw from social media altogether, your ex-partner will know they have affected your world. If you post more images and stories than normal, they will know you are trying to make a point.
Continuing to post at your natural cadence has two benefits. First, your ex-partner will realize that you are getting on with your life and their attempts to hook you aren't working.

Second, you will be replacing any painful reminders of your former relationship with fresh pictures and stories, a healthy reminder that you have a rich and varied life.

PS. You may want to unfollow your ex-partner's social media accounts to avoid any temptation to engage. Your ex-partner may well change their social media behavior in a bid for your attention. If you do stay connected, be prepared for happy photos of new romantic interests. Your ex may even deliberately post at certain times or in specific locations that are meaningful to you.

Accept that closure may never come
Just as with bereavement grief, healing requires accepting that there are some things you may never know. Is your ex-partner being deliberately cruel or are they ghosting you out of fear or even misplaced kindness? Accept that you may never know the reasons why they broke off contact. Stop looking for answers and move forward with your life. Better days lie ahead.

"I was the type of person who would cross the ocean for someone who wouldn't even cross the street for me.
I apologized even though I did nothing wrong.
It took me a long time to understand that others didn't make me sad or disappointed.
It was my own misguided belief that everyone has the same heart as me..."

- Jodie Foster -

If only a narcissist could tell the truth
Many relationship breakups (and toxic makeups) are fueled by the narcissism-codependency dynamic that I wrote extensively about in *Learning How To Leave*.

People often wonder how their lives may have been different if they had known how their partner would turn out. What would the narcissist have revealed during that first dinner date if you could have given them a truth serum. Maybe it would go something like this:

Narcissist: Before we go any further, I need to explain that I'm a narcissist.

Codependent: You can't be. You're so nice.

N: Nah, I'm just reading from my playbook. Basically, I know that if you see me as nice and funny, and if I give you plenty of attention and affection, then you will fall in love with me.

C: OK. But why do you need me to fall in love with you?

N: Because then you will stay with me when I start lying, humiliating and gaslighting you.

C: But that sounds like abuse.

N: Oh yes, it is. When I've worn down your self-worth, it will be so much easier for me to control you. You see, I'm deeply insecure. My ego is very fragile and I'm scared of being rejected. That's why I created this fantasy world and put myself at the centre. You, like everyone else, have to be beneath me - and revolve around me. So, it's OK for me to abuse you. I'm sorry about that (actually, I'm not).

C: Well, thank you for the warning. Otherwise we could have formed a trauma bond. I would have been unhappy for years.

N: No problem. It's only fair that you know the rules in advance. By the way, do you struggle with low self-esteem and a lack of boundaries?

C: Absolutely. You're spot on.

N: Damn, I knew it! Plus it's useful that you told me about your previous abuse and neglect. I could have repeated the pattern of abuse and you would have blamed yourself for it. We would have made the perfect toxic match.

C: Yes. I'm just glad you told me this all up front.

N: Well, you're lucky. I'm not usually this honest and transparent on a first date.

The Narcissist's Mantra
"That didn't happen.
And, if it did, it wasn't that bad.
And, if it was, that's not a big deal.
And, if it is, that's not my fault.
And, if it was, I didn't mean it.
And, if I did, you deserved it.

\- Dr. Michael Acton -

For this section of the chapter, the term narcissist refers to the modern definition of someone who has narcissistic personality disorder (NPD), whether diagnosed or not.

Not all cases of domestic abuse involve a narcissist, but anyone who is in a relationship with a narcissist will eventually experience domestic abuse. Here is a brief list of the characteristics of people with NPD:

Lack of empathy
Note; this doesn't mean that narcissists never shed a tear! Non-narcissists cry when watching both happy and sad movies because they are capable of empathy. The narcissist, however, only cries as a method of manipulation or when the world as they know it is about to end (e.g., you are leaving them). In short, they only cry for themselves.

Desire for attention
As I wrote in *Learning How to Leave*, Narcissists don't love themselves. Rather, they love the person they wish they were (in Freudian terms, their ego-ideal). They trick their fragile ego into believing they are that person by demanding admiration, to be treated as someone of importance. This obsession with their ideal self leaves no room for others as individuals. Their personal relationships are therefore superficial and parasitic, maintained for the sole purpose of bolstering their self-esteem.

Sometimes, this craving for attention is not obvious. Covert narcissists have just as powerful a need for attention but achieve it in a passive way. They are often stubborn, resistant to change, and prone to sabotaging the efforts of others.

Charm

Narcissists know how to weaponize social proof. The most skilled are so charming that they cause everyone around them to drop their guard (Frith & Frith, 2022)

Then they can just move on in for the fruit that's most ripe for picking. They will use their charm to elevate their image in the eyes of those around them. This often comes at the expense of their codependent host, as Sarah's next example reveals:

Sarah: I was with Matt for eight years, and in all that time, I thought people understood that I was the one with money, I was the one with properties, and I was the one working. I had no idea, until a year and a half after kicking him out for having sex with somebody in our home, that the whole of the area we were living in thought that Matt had given me a mortgage, that I was poor, and I was a gold digger. He told other people that he was property-rich, and only did a part-time waiting job for six months because he was bored and wanted something of interest. He was so charming and convincing that everyone believed him, even though I was a local professional.

I was living a life, I thought, in truth. In actual fact, the life he was creating for me with everybody was one of a lie. But he was so charming and convincing, everyone believed him. Even when I kicked him out, he was so believable. He said he'd been kind to me by allowing me to stay in the house (even though he had apparently given me the mortgage!) But all the time he was f*****g people in toilets. He was f*****g people at work. And he got fired after six months because of his aggression in the kitchen.

As detailed in *Learning How To Leave*, in order to escape a relationship with a narcissist, we have to be honest about the role we - as codependents - have played in maintaining the relationship.

However, the opposite *does not* apply. In other words, you recognizing the narcissism and escaping the abuse *does not* depend on the narcissist admitting to it. As psychological consultant David McPhee explained in a post on LinkedIn, denying abuse is just another form of emotional abuse, and if you need an admission of guilt before you accept what is happening to you, this is clearly going to be a problem.

If you need external help to leave the relationship, reach out to trusted professionals or agencies, and to relatives whom you trust to keep you safe.

Can a narcissist genuinely change for good? And what are the signs that they are committed to changing?
As emphasized in *Learning How To Leave*, I have never come across anyone with narcissistic personality disorder who was genuinely able to change. This fits with the theory that their disorder is a survival mechanism and that to admit fallibility would be, to them, the equivalent of deliberately grasping a live wire.

However, it is possible that someone with narcissistic tendencies could find the internal resources to change. The three main positive signs to look out for are:
• Admitting that they have narcissistic tendencies
• Attending therapy for multiple sessions. This includes preparing for each session, staying for the entire time and completing homework. Beware! Many narcissists will be happy to turn up

to one or two couples sessions but this is usually to hook their partner back into the relationship and to find new ways to abuse them.
- Taking responsibility for their behaviors (less blaming)

Additional signs include:
- Consistent, positive behaviors, especially those carried out when you're not present and without comment
- Less boasting and fewer lies
- More willingness to share their vulnerability
- Less verbal abuse and humiliation
- Change in their social circle to include more genuine friends and fewer shallow hangers-on. This will be a reflection of their internal shift.

Personal notes from an author and a coach

I come across manybrave souls in my line of work, and I can honestly say that Carolyn and Michelle are not only brave, but they've generously brought forward their infinite wisdom. They have buried their shame, and they're sharing, for the good of others, their struggles in the world.

These are two prime examples of abusees that have recovered, have fought for their rights in the world, and have also moved forward in a healthy fashion from toxic relationships. I know they will help you, the reader, relate to their stories. And if one ounce of what they're talking about helps you in any way, this is a gift from us to you.

I hold both in high regard, and they really are two amazingly accomplished examples of how any living soul in this world can be abused. It can be disastrous for anyone who is kind, thoughtful, and caring to be in the wrong hands. Thank you both so much for helping me reach out to people and give good examples of how to move forward safely.

Carolyn Hobdey: author and Founder of The Broad Room:

'Abused.'

'Victim.'

Even the word 'Survivor' didn't feel like a term I was worthy of.

People who had suffered abuse were not my tribe! Were they??

It took me a long time to accept I had been abused.

Domestic Abuse was something that happened to other people. It involved being hit, concealed bruises, and implausible excuses about walking into doors.

I'm ashamed to say that in my mind it took place in the lower echelons of society.

That wasn't what had happened to me. Yet, as I stood in the wreckage of my life, an acknowledgement began to grow within me that I couldn't deny.

I was an abusee.

Dr. Michael Acton

I was what that looked like.

Insidious emotional manipulation was what abuse looked like.

Affluent households were where it took place.

Of course, the shame of all that took hold. I was an abusee. And I was mortified by that fact.

Surely no one would believe me. Family and friends would laugh if I told them... wouldn't they?

And that's the thing about abuse - whether physical or emotional - it's isolating. Your abuser deliberately isolates you. Your fear of derision isolates you further still.

It's like your abuser locks you in a prison and you put on an extra padlock just to make sure...

Believing myself was the most important step I took in escaping that prison. Naming what I had endured as 'abuse' - however uncomfortable that word made me feel - was huge in numerous ways.

It wasn't a quick-fix switch that I flicked, of course it wasn't. But it was the key to the lock.

It allowed me to begin to forgive myself.

It enabled me to do research to inform myself.

It permitted me to seek help - to tentatively reach out.

That was the important part; it gave me permission.

I won't dress it up. Some people accepted my categorization of what had happened. Several shared their own stories. Others didn't accept it.

I learnt to accept that. Talk of abuse makes others feel uneasy, most especially those who love you; it hurts them to accept your hurt.

What I gained from my self-acceptance was so much greater than what I lost.

I found my tribe. People just like me. Not sad, hopeless victims. Instead, positive, empathetic, strong, and inspirational people. Those who had learnt to laugh again, trust once more, and carve out who they were beyond the abuse.

People who made me feel heard.

Our silence is the thing that holds us in abusive situations and our silence holds others in theirs.

'Speaking up' takes merely one conversation. Start there. Say it out loud. Own it. Stop letting it own you.

Dr. Michael Acton

Michelle Cappelli Gordon: mindset, self-esteem and relationship coach:

Dear Reader,

If you are reading this book, you are likely frustrated and possibly discouraged about your relationship. You may have wondered how you seem to end up with partners who have destructive behavior, who don't acknowledge how they have hurt you, and who don't prioritize your wellbeing. You probably find yourself thinking, what's wrong with me? You may feel ashamed for attracting, remaining with, or going back to this person. But if you are reading this book, you also know that something isn't right, and the mere fact that you are pursuing personal growth information to gain understanding and guidance means that you are willing to learn about how you can approach your relationships differently to improve your situation. I doubt your partner is doing the same because, as we mentioned, they do not prioritize your wellbeing. This dynamic in itself is the answer to the ever-so-common question: should I leave? If your partner doesn't hold your wellbeing as a great priority, no matter how seemingly good some of their efforts may be, it is a destructive partnership. Being in this type of relationship is exhausting due to the amount of energy it requires you to exert in order to survive emotionally, which in turn robs other areas of your life in which you desire to grow and excel. How do I know this? I was once in your shoes. There is good news: you can change this dynamic. It is important to be patient with yourself; there is a reason you are here; it is to discover how and why you are here and to be willing to evolve. Another thing to remember is that those who criticize you for your situation don't know or understand the underlying reasons

193

you are going through this. Don't take their well-intended, naive criticisms to heart. You've probably also been told you could do so much better and that you should just leave; however, without the right help, you'll likely unwittingly allow similar destructiveness in the next relationship. Seek support from a qualified expert to safely explore how your past experiences have impacted your self-concept today. Once you work through things you may not even be aware of, you can begin to know and believe the truth about who you really are - an incredibly valuable person who is worthy of love, appreciation, and respect. You will begin to connect with others despite your past pain, not from it. You have what it takes to transform your life!

Michelle Cappelli Gordon

In a nutshell

Task 8: Read through the eight rules of 'Acton's Domestic Violence Model for Gatekeepers.'
If domestic violence is (or was) part of your relationship, imagine I am the first responder and you are the abusee. Take appropriate action. Note any insights in your journal. You may also want to consider reading my book Learning How To Leave. Go to https://www. amazon.com/dp/B09J1N58TR Even if you have already left, there is some good information on staying left. And if children are involved, please go to my parenting book Raw Facts from Real Parents for help and support. Go to https://www.amazon.com/Raw-Facts-Real-Parents-Children-ebook/dp/B09WF7M5MB

Task 9: Toxic tactics and narcissism
- Reflect on whether you or your ex are using any of the toxic tactics revealed above.
- Reflect on the possible role of narcissistic traits or narcissistic personality disorder (NPD) in your relationship issues.

Somebody with narcissistic personality disorder (NPD) can be recognized by:
- Lack of empathy.
- Need for attention.
- Exaggeration of talents.
- Preoccupation with fantasies of success.
- Belief of being special and above others.

If your ex is truthfully working on reducing their narcissistic tendencies, they will:

- Admit they have such tendencies.
- Attend all therapy sessions on time and do the homework set.
- Engage in fewer blaming behaviors.

For more guidance, read:
Acton. M. (2022). *Raw facts from real parents.* Life Logic Publishing

Acton. M. (2021). *Learning how to leave.* Life Logic Publishing

Hobdey. C. (2022). *De-twat your life.* Ink! By The Author School

References:
Acton. M. (2022). *Raw facts from real parents.* Life Logic Publishing

Acton. M. (2021). *Learning how to leave.* Life Logic Publishing

Boroff, M. (2010). The art of asking questions in a narrative therapy. *Dissertation Abstracts International: Section B: The Sciences and Engineering.* 70(9-B). p5807.

Domestic Abuse Shelter, Inc. (2019) *Definition of domestic violence.* https://domesticabuseshelter.org/domestic-violence

Frith C., and Frith, U. (2022). Reputation matters. *The Psychologist.* June

MPA Mind. (2023, May 31). #MPAMind - Expert panel discussion: 'What Would You Put in #MichaelasLaw ?' #MichaelaHallDay 2023 [Video]. YouTube. https://youtu.be/xR0ROex9TwE?si=7pSyyzbTdpw_ninI

Sobhani-Rad, D. (2014). A review on adult pragmatic assessments. *Iranian journal of neurology.* 13. pp113-118.

Walker, J., and Gavin, H. (2011) Interpretations of domestic violence: defining intimate partner abuse. *The 12th Conference of the International Academy of Investigative Psychology. Crime, Criminalistics & Criminal Psychology: New Directions in Investigative Behavioral Science.* March/April.

DECISION TIME: NOW FOR THE HARD NAVIGATION

We have successfully completed Part I of this book. Now we have to shed, clean out stuff, and morph into our better self. We have to face and challenge ourselves, the reality of what happened, where we are now, and what we want to bring in for the future.

The next section of this book forms two parts. As in the subtitle of the book, Part II is Making Up and Part III is Moving On.

We may jump between these during our post-relationship experience, and that's OK. Sometimes, we might think about moving in one direction and then we don't do it, and that's OK. These are still uncertain times. Weathering relationships is about working out, enduring, moving through, with the target of being peaceful on the other side of the storm.

Consider this carefully: weathering relationships is never a linear process, it's never straightforward. We can be in and out of what we want and feel. We may think the work is done just before something comes back and again haunts us.

Making Up is about healthy relationships and starting again. Ground zero, so to speak. We clear out everything, we do the work, and then what have we got? What do we want going forward? And both parties have to dance the dance, not just talk the talk.

Moving on focuses more on our own development, and if we are not thinking of making up, then, of course, we will take this path.

So, it's best for us to read all of the chapters in *both* Parts II: Making Up and III: Moving On before we make that firm decision about how we move on from here.

"Every second we spend comparing our life to someone else's is a second spent wasting our own."

- Dr. Michael Acton -

PART II

MAKING UP: DOING IT DIFFERENTLY

"Accept people for who they are, not who you want them to be."

- Dr. Michael Acton -

PART II: MAKING UP

CHAPTER 1

LEARNING FROM OLD HABITS

It is important at this stage of our work to question everything and also to be curious. A large part of the work in Part I was us adjusting to our relationship story and being in our truth. This process will have helped us to decide that a successful reunion with your ex is a possibility.

But at this stage, we may not know how much work, if any, our former partner has done on themselves. What is *their* story of your relationship and breakup? Did they find their own way back to us and the make up road, or did we convince them in some way that it would be a good idea, and pull them from their moving on road? Whatever the situation is, we need to be clear and ask these questions.

Just imagine we ping ourselves back in history to the time when we first got together with our ex, wondering if we should be together, live together, maybe get married, etc. We are re-enacting that same situation here, and similar questions will come up.

Are they as committed as we are to doing the tough work required in Part II of this book, what we're talking about now? If we are engaged in any battles with them, will they agree to a truce whilst we focus on the deeper issues of our relationship? Are they willing to accept that it may take months or even years to reach a peaceful and rewarding destination together?

Yes? Good.

Our first step is to compare notes and make sure we are both comfortable with our interpretations of how our relationship unfolded and broke up.

We have to now do a joint revisitation. Are we *broadly* in agreement? If not, there is some preliminary work to do here. We cannot move forward into a new relationship together if one of us is looking to repeat past patterns - especially if this could renew a cycle of abuse. As explained by Stroebe *et al.* (2018), 14 per cent of abusees return to their abuser, often due to social pressures. Although this experimental sample was limited to women in college, I've seen this trend through my clinical work over the last three decades. In addition, the Women's Fund have gathered certain statistics to suggest that this is the case in day to day practice in the 21st Century.

It may help for us to consider the tasks in Part I, Chapters 4 and 5. Can we agree on the facts that led to us breaking up? What was said and by whom and when? Did we fail to meet each other's expectations regarding sex, communication, money, housework, child-rearing, fidelity, family obligations, boat-driving etc? Was there third party interference? Did the relationship fizzle out over time or end in a blazing row? was there a significant life event that caused a rift?

If we were to disagree on the facts, which of us needs to adjust our story? Both of us? Maybe. Has one of us misinterpreted behaviors or catastrophized a minor disagreement? Does our own story and breakup timeline still need work?

In addition, can we identify different sets of 'life rules' or boundaries that may have contributed to our breakup? Perhaps we believe crying is a sign of weakness while our partner values emotional expression as a strength.

In terms of emotions, can we both set aside blame, guilt, and other strong emotions in order to move forward in an open-minded and open-hearted way? We will learn more about working with these emotions in Chapter 7, but for now, can we identify issues from the past that may have caused us to split (e.g., a lack of emotion in our childhood home or an affair in a previous relationship)? Don't worry if you can't, we will also be working with this in later chapters.

How successful can we really be?

Plenty of research has been conducted on the success rates of relationship reunion, but the results vary widely, and cycles of breakup and renewal themselves can impact the ultimate state of a relationship (Dailey *et al.* 2020, Dailey *et al.* 2009, Parsons *et al.*, 2014).

At this point, it's important for me to reiterate that every relationship is unique, so there is no guarantee that your journey will end the same way as anybody else's. Whichever route we take, move on or make up, we never know the outcome until we follow the process. It's as simple as that.

So, what's the glue?

For a relationship to survive, the emotional glue that keeps us together must be stronger than those forces that will inevitably try to drive us apart.

What is behind this glue? It is trust. Trust is important in all areas of life. For example, we need to trust that our tax payments will be used properly to repair potholes and keep our roads in good shape. If we are constantly paying out money to repair our car due to bumpy roads, we will feel angry and let down with those in charge.

It is even more important that we can trust our partner to deliver on their promises and for us to keep to our promises to them, so that the trust goes both ways.

Trust is vital in any relationship, so take your time to evaluate the strength of your mutual trust and, if it's lacking, prioritize re-establishing it because without trust, there won't be enough glue to keep you together in the long run.

Boundaries and ground rules

We've chosen this path, but at this stage of our relationship rehabilitation, we can't necessarily expect to pick up where we left off. In fact, it's dangerous to. To avoid any early conflict, we have to agree on a set of ground rules. These might include, but aren't limited to:

- Living/sleeping arrangements (will we stay in the same house? The same bed? When will we make that move to be together again? will intimacy start?)
- Allocating a weekly time and space to work on our relationship.
- Ending an affair or a new relationship.
- Stopping drinking or gambling.
- Agreeing on whom we will both rely upon as our primary source of external support, whether this be a therapist or a family friend, etc.

- Deciding on a 'safe word' to indicate the need for a time-out, especially if domestic violence is involved (see Chapter 7 for more details on managing time-outs).
- Agreeing to attend professional couples counseling alongside reading this book. An effective therapist will provide a valuable external perspective and a safe place where we can talk through our concerns, thoughts, and feelings. Unlike some helping services, our therapist is there to do more than just listen—they are trained to help identify patterns in our relationship issues, define our goals, clarify what a healthy relationship means to us, and develop and model healthy relationship skills, including those I bring to you in this book.

Note: For issues involving addiction or domestic violence, you will also need specialist support (an effective therapist may advise and refer you appropriately.) Read Part I, Chapter 6 to refresh yourself about the information on domestic violence in relationship breakup.

How it all began

While we will never be able to recreate the magic of 'falling in love,' we may rediscover what it is that first attracted us to one another. Even though romance often seems natural and spontaneous, on one level or another, we chose each other because we synced in some way and met each other's needs.

So, why did we become a couple? What needs did our ex meet? What needs were they able to still fulfill before we broke up? We don't need to go too deep into this at this stage. We will be digging further into this in Chapter 6, but we have to consider it now.

By retelling our story of how our relationship began, we can both move on to the next task in a positive, hopeful state of mind. Even if we can find hardly anything nice to say to one another today, tomorrow may be different. Resentment is our enemy. Resentment is unprocessed anger.

A message of hope to you
Having worked through this first chapter, we may already be feeling overwhelmed by the road ahead. However, many couples find that just one small adjustment in the way they're doing things can create amazing comfort going forward, or turn what was a massive block ahead into smaller, more manageable obstacles. Stepping stones to a healthy relationship is the way ahead. Step by step. Piece by piece.

As long as we are both willing to roll up our sleeves and work without giving up or grabbing on, we have every chance of success.

In a nutshell

Task 1: We must prepare for the path ahead by:
- Calling a truce over any ongoing battles. Remember: resentment is unprocessed anger, and it has no place here.
- Clarifying together the facts and timeline of our breakup. What truly happened?
- Identifying conflicting 'life rules.' What are our deal-breakers?
- Gently exploring past issues that may have contributed to our breakup. We have to explore our differences as well as our similarities.
- Becoming familiar with research on breakup and renewal patterns. Even just Googling this can help us see ourselves more clearly and become aware of any potholes ahead of us.

- Identifying the 'glue' that every successful reunion needs. Be mindful: if there is not enough glue, this is not going to be a successful pathway.
- Setting ground rules is the same as setting healthy boundaries; it's necessary.
- Retelling the story of how our relationship began.

For more guidance, read:
Bee, B. (2024). *Speak your truth.* Independently published

Marshall, A. G. (2011). *How can I ever trust you again?* Bloomsbury Paperbacks

Schmidt, J. (2016). *Energetic boundaries 101.* CreateSpace

References:
Dailey, R. M., Zhong, L., Pett, R., and Varga, S. (2020). Post-dissolution ambivalence, breakup adjustment, and relationship reconciliation. *Journal of Social and Personal Relationships.* 37(5). pp 1604–1625.

Dailey, R. M., Rossetto, K. A., Pfiester, A., and Surra, C. A. (2009). A qualitative analysis of on-again/off-again romantic relationships: "It's up and down, all around". *Journal of Social and Personal Relationships.* 26(4). pp 443–466.

Parsons, A., Knopp, K., Rhoades, G., Markman, H., and Stanley, S. (2014). Let's try this again: the impact of breakups and renewals on dating relationships and marriage [conference session abstract]. *122nd American Psychological Association Annual Convention,* Washington D.C.

Stroebe, M. S., Edwards, R. O., Palmer, K.M., Lindemann, K. G., and Gidycz, C. A. (2018). Is the end really the end? Prevalence and correlates of college women's intentions to return to an abusive relationship. *Violence Against Women.* 24:2, pp 207-222

PART II: MAKING UP

CHAPTER 2

DON'T 'RINSE, REPEAT'

If we don't recognize when something's going wrong, how are we going to know what to do to put it right?

There's an old saying, 'If it ain't broken, why fix it?' We'll reverse that and say, 'If we can't see that something's broken, how can we fix it?' That's what this part is about.

While most of this part of the book will focus on the skills we need to help navigate the making up route of our relationship (i.e., effective communication; meeting each other's needs; coping with emotions; sexual skills; honesty; etc.,) this chapter will help you recognize and deal with the signs that your relationship needs attention. Let us start by looking at our relationship breakup.

Ignorance isn't always bliss
When our relationship first started to go wrong, we may have ignored the signs, pushing difficult feelings down and out of awareness (i.e., going into denial). Sometimes this is the only way we can truly survive a bad relationship or difficulties. Perhaps we went even further by actively dismissing or laughing off our partner's concerns as well as our own. These are common reactions to fear; after all, we were facing the death of our closest relationship and losing control over a major part of our lives.
But ignoring all that was going wrong and challenging us didn't save our relationship then, and it won't save it in the long run.

How do we control being out of control?

Panicking is another common reaction to relationship difficulty, and it's equally unhelpful. Perhaps our sex life was starting to go off the boil or disagreements were becoming more frequent. Sex is the ultimate mirror of communication issues in a relationship. In fact, people don't understand that sex is the most powerful form of communication between two people, revealing our vulnerable, exploratory, and exciting selves.

Rather than feeling these difficult emotions, facing them, understanding them, and working with them so we don't skid out of control, we carry on regardless, overcompensating and causing more harm than good. We're clearly out of control, and rather than getting back on track, by fearing and over-reacting, we're pushing ourselves even more into danger.

This fear can hide behind anger or tears. Did you or your partner yell to force the other to submit, or did you or they burst into tears in a bid for sympathy?

As we will know by now, none of these defense mechanisms ultimately prevented our breakup. In fact, they may have provoked equally unhelpful responses, turning minor skirmishes into an all-out war.

Now, we have another chance. We can try to accept the inevitable ups and downs without reverting to old patterns of defensive and outrageous behavior.

As we master the skills presented later in this book, we will gradually replace those destructive habits with more healthy responses, with consideration and calmness. This will, in turn, help us to acknowledge problems as they arise. We may understand their origins better, and we can then compromise for the sake of our relationship. And let it be known that compromise is the stabilizing effect for all successful long-term relationships, and compromise simply means to give and take fairly.

Excitement versus reality

When we decide to work on making up in a relationship, it can be all-new, glistening, and almost like a repeat of the honeymoon effect. It can be fast, powerful, wonderful, secure, loving, exciting - exactly what created the initial bond between us. But it is not enough to sustain that glue into a long-term relationship. If we are going to go for a healthy, long-term relationship, this is going to require mastering a set of powerful relationship skills, which include:

- Solving conflicts.
- Providing emotional and practical support.
- Negotiating major purchases and life decisions, which involve compromise.
- In some cases, co-parenting.

These skills and more are at the heart of real love.

If one or both of us are hoping to ignore the work and reset our relationship to its initial state, we are destined for disappointment. After that injection of novelty, the cycle will repeat.

Unfortunately, this brand of romantic love, the one we are mainly exposed to through the media, doesn't really exist. Hollywood may be based in reality a lot of the time, but it is fantasy. When that feeling inevitably fades, we feel that the relationship is dying and our future will be loveless. Or we can do something about it. The good news is that this 'in love' feeling is not necessarily gone for good. Once our relationship is on a more realistic footing, it is likely to re-emerge at times, and it will feel all the more special when it does.

Stepping stones to relationship growth

Following a breakup, it is natural to focus on what went wrong and to look at the negative changes you experienced (e.g., less sex, more arguments, betrayal, deceit, lying, etc.) However, if we were to compare our relationship before the breakup with our first few dates, we will probably find evidence that we have developed various skills that have benefited your relationship (for one, we're committed to trying to stay together!)

Let's take a break from reading, and try to find three ways in which our relationship has developed since we first got together. If we are working through this book together with our partner, share your ideas with them. Here are some possibilities:

- Are you more relaxed in each other's company? And what does relaxed look like?
- Do we know more about each other's needs (that will be useful for Chapter 6)? And what are these needs exactly? Don't forget, this only works if we're absolutely transparent and honest.
- Have you found out how to please each other in all essences of an intimate, loving relationship?

If our relationship has improved before, then we can do it again, no holds barred. But it only works in our truth.

So, what is the energy feeling like in our relationship now?
Now we've reflected on our previous relationship warning signs, it's time to focus on the present. How are we feeling about this? Are there notes of disharmony? What is going swimmingly? For instance:

- Is one of us finding the others' expectations a burden, a bit of a task?
- Is there a basic mismatch between our needs? Let's explore what those differences are. It could be fun.
- Has something that first drew us together turned toxic?
- Are there unspoken assumptions that still need to be agreed upon? Who's kidding who?
- Have our needs changed with circumstances, age, and time. What used to be good for us may now not work.
- Do we trust each other, or is there a distrust between us?
- Are our confidence levels similar, or do we suffer from being overly self-critical?

One dangerous warning sign we must heed at this point is where there is one person who is always taking while the other one is always giving, especially if there is cruelty and self-criticism respectively. This could indicate narcissistic abuse.

However, not meeting each other's needs does not necessarily equal deliberate cruelty. Could there be another interpretation? Regardless, this situation will lead to resentment unless we commit to changing through the skills presented in the remainder of this book. Heed my warning: this work must be done in order to move forward together, genuinely and without reservation. It's either all-in or we just give up, and really think about that.

In a nutshell

Task 2: Reflect on how we recognize and react to relationship issues:

- Do we ignore signs and avoid talking?
- Do we laugh at and actively dismiss each other's concerns?
- Do we panic and do whatever it takes to avoid conflict?
- Do we yell or cry to get our own way?
- Can we commit to accepting the ups and downs of this process without resorting to our usual defense mechanisms?
- Find three ways in which our relationship has improved since we first met.
- What signs of disharmony are currently present for us?

For more guidance, read:

Patterson, S. (2019). *The great compromise.* Independently published.

Smolarski, A. (2024) *Cooperative co-parenting for secure kids.* New Harbinger Publications.

Tagoe, B. A. (2023). *20 relationship red flags: understanding relationship warning signs.* Independently published.

PART II: MAKING UP

CHAPTER 3

SO, JUST EXACTLY HOW *DID* WE MESS UP?

Accepting the truth, our truth, is above all our most powerful stance. In this chapter, we're going to zoom in closer to the details surrounding your breakup. By the end of this, we should be able to isolate the internal and external factors that combined to put our relationship off the tracks.

Managing change is one of the most difficult things we can do as a human being.
However, nothing in life is constant, and at the root of every relationship breakup is change, massive change.

We may argue that our relationship died because of stagnation, but in that case, it was our attitude towards our commitment we had to our partner that changed. There was change. What caused that shift? Did we learn something new about our partner that highlighted a mismatch? Or did we become aware of new needs that our partner was unable to meet? It could have even been a flirting attraction to somebody at work or at the grocery store that made us step back and think and look at our own lives.

Let's try to identify that point of change and own our reaction to it. Did we fight the change by attacking our partner? Did we avoid the change by ignoring our feelings or pulling back and locking out our partner? We may have even combined these tactics.
It's important to nail this. It's important to see where it started going wrong.

Developmental and life changes

Relationship changes are often triggered by external factors. These can be broadly divided into developmental changes and life changes. No two people stay the same. Believe it.

Developmental changes are those natural physical and chemical changes that occur through our lifespan. Even our position in the family can affect our relationship style. For example, the first born will often be used to taking responsibility for other people while the youngest member of the family might be indulged or constantly thwarted. In an intimate relationship, they might repeat these ingrained patterns or rebel against them later in life. Children from large families may find it easier to compromise than those who grew up as an 'only child.'

As we get older, our personalities change and our goals evolve. We may want to work more and play less. We may seek more or less commitment in our relationships. The way we approach situations is also likely to change. For example, a teenager may rush towards opportunities whilst an adult may take a more measured approach. Wisdom evolves.

Life events are often closely tied to our personal development. Young adults may leave home, get married, or enter a civil partnership; they might even decide to start a family (see the next section, below).

Other significant changes include career moves or promotions; children leaving home (empty nest syndrome); family illness (physical or mental); redundancy or reaching a career plateau; new caring responsibilities; accidents; affairs; deceits; rape, and bereavement.

Aging adds processes such as the menopause, increasing frailty, reduced fitness, and often age-related diseases such as dementia, arthritis, etc.

Even outwardly positive changes can be too much for a relationship to sustain. Moving in with a partner can trigger an inner conflict between independence and security leading to one partner returning home. Marriage can lead to affairs and excessive socializing if one half of a couple feels trapped. Meeting a new and exciting friend can ignite fears of rejection in an insecure partner. Even a promotion can have unexpected effects: the worker may feel both more confident and more stressed, while the partner might struggle with resentment and might even try to undermine the worker's efforts.

Any one of these things can alter each of our's perspective on life, shift the balance of activities in our relationship, and trigger difficult feelings such as fear, panic, insecurity, anger, guilt, blame, rebelliousness, sadness, regret, anxiety, hopelessness, or depression. No wonder relationships and their homeostasis are one of the most difficult things we have to manage in life.

Was it one or more of these life changes or events that triggered your breakup? Who was involved? What happened, really, truthfully? How did it affect your thoughts and feelings?How did it affect how we related to one another?

In short, what caused our relationship to change, and how did that push us off course?

Keep in mind that depending upon the situation, such as drug abuse, family crisis, bereavement, or all the other things that can happen in life, we may need specific professional support to get us through, either as an individual or as a couple. This is the time to clean things out.

Starting a family

Bringing children into our world is one of the most profound changes we will experience. How that journey begins will deeply affect our relationships. While many couples, of all sexualities and genders, want children, prepare for the changes they will bring, and successfully adapt their lives, this is not always the case.

Pregnancy may be unplanned. One partner might not really want children, or they might discover that they are not prepared for the reality of being a parent.

Then there are those couples who experience fertility issues. Partners might blame themselves or each other for their inability to conceive. There might be a criminal history that stops one of you from adopting or becoming a foster parent. If you are a step-parent, foster parent or adoptive parent, you may face a tough journey as you try to maintain a healthy relationship while coping with a lack of acceptance, trust, and love from children you did not biologically conceive.

Children also bring financial commitments, especially when it comes to higher education, which can put pressure on any relationship. It is also commonplace now for adult children to continue to live in the parental home or to return there later in life. Children with disabilities require extra care and attention which presents unique challenges to a family system.

As parents, it is very important to allocate regular time together, without the children, where you can focus solely on your relationship. Don't forget, the kids will leave. Your relationship with each other is vital and so important. Make sure you water it, nurture it, develop it, and expand it.

Note: My book *Raw Facts From Real Parents* provides bite-sized chunks of practical guidance for parents looking for support on a wide range of parenting issues. And that's for both children and adult children.

Illness, bereavement, and grief

We all deal with bereavement in different ways, and this can challenge a relationship to its very core. One partner may not feel comfortable expressing their feelings, and the other may interpret this as lack of feeling. As they turn to friends and relatives to share their grief, their partner may feel shut out. The death of a child can be particularly devastating for a couple, and they will almost certainly need outside support.

During mid-life, and sometimes earlier, one or both partners may be required to care for their aging parents. This can test a relationship because both partners must adjust their lives to accommodate their new responsibilities. Parenting our parents can be like having children in the house. One partner may resent the time given to an in-law or their own parent, while the other might start worrying about their own mortality, especially where the parent is living with an hereditary illness.

Changes that challenge our values
Some of the most difficult changes to manage for us are those which highlight a rift in our value systems. In such cases, one or both partners can feel betrayed and let down.

A common example is a love affair, where one person deems it acceptable to satisfy their unmet sexual needs with another partner rather than attempt to communicate those needs with their present partner. Even if you seem to have weathered an affair, there will always be an impact on your relationship (e.g., reduced communication, low self-esteem, loss of trust, possessiveness, guilt, poor sex life, resentment, etc.)

Other examples of a value mismatch include:
- Our partner reveals that they don't want children when we want to build a family.
- We discover that our strict parenting style is the polar opposite of our partner's laissez-faire approach.
- Our partner's extravagant spending habits shock us because we were brought up to count every cent.
- One person engages in criminal activity to achieve a goal to the horror of their law-abiding partner.

In such cases, it is wise to resist the urge to punish and to instead focus on why your partner sees things so differently and how you can change your relationship to benefit you both.

The meaning of your breakup
This doesn't always have to be a negative in life, but there is one change that has affected everyone reading this book: it's our

relationship breakup itself. If we really analyze the changes that have impacted our relationship, remember we have to include both partners' reactions to the breakup.

If we were the one who left the relationship, we may be holding on to feelings of guilt that will need addressing. If we were left behind, our anger or relief might prevent us from relating openly. Did we have agreements broken? Have we moved the goalposts? This all needs working through using the skills in the following chapters. We have to find some sort of common ground.

Most of all, we both need to believe that a new start is possible, draw a line under the past, hold hands and walk forward.

Change precedes growth

We will need to talk about what is happening in our lives, how we are all doing, feeling, breathing, and changing. What's impacting us. No place for eggshells here. Adapting to change means compromising, communicating. How can we meet in the middle?

Regardless of the specific change we are going through, understand that it can lead to growth if we accept it, understand its origin, and adapt our relationship accordingly.

Where possible, focus on the interesting and fun aspects of any changes we are navigating. This will help us to maintain hope and become more resilient. It's tough.

In a nutshell
Task 3: Identify internal and external triggers for our breakup:

- Isolate moments of change in our relationship. How did we react to those changes?
- Consider the many developmental and life changes that you experienced as a couple. If possible, swap notes with your partner. How did these changes contribute to your breakup?
- Do we need additional support for challenging life changes? And if so, who, what, and how?
- Have you felt betrayed by your partner's behavior? What differences in your value systems has this revealed? Can you accept these differences in your relationship moving forward?
- How has the breakup itself affected your relationship? And is this permanent?
- Decide whether or not you can move forward in this process. Can you adapt to past, present, and future changes?

For more guidance, read:
Acton. M. (2022). *Raw facts from real parents.* Life Logic Publishing

Christensen, A., and Jacobson, N. S. (2020). *Acceptance and change in couple therapy: a therapist's guide to transforming relationships.* W. W. Norton & Company

Usher, K., and Usher, N. (2024). *A couple's guide to menopause: managing the change together.* Hero

Reference:
Acton. M. (2022). *Raw facts from real parents.* Life Logic Publishing

PART II: MAKING UP

CHAPTER 4

CHANGE IS TOUGH: NO KIDDING

We're done looking backwards. After getting this far, we should know exactly what went wrong last time and how developmental changes and life events drove us off track. Often, the root of our issues is conflicting needs not a deliberate desire to hurt. Challenge the vindictive ideas we may have at this moment.

It should be clear to us at this moment that managing future changes in our relationship is one of the keys to success going forward. This chapter is all about helping you to take back control of the wheel and steer our way through challenges ahead. Pushing forward is so important now.

Not always a big deal, but change is necessary
Some people will turn an upcoming change into a huge and frightening monster that they need to battle, but in many cases, all it takes is for both parties to understand what the change means for each other. That understanding alone can help us navigate the change. It's really simple: we're turning stumbling blocks into stepping stones.

So, how can we communicate? It's important. How can we listen to each other without interrupting? When it's your turn to talk, share both your thoughts and your feelings. Where there are big differences in your reaction to a change, one of you is probably feeling threatened. The other should accept this and not dismiss it. Defensive behavior is tough to be with but not difficult to surmount. Talking about change is not about deciding who's right and who's wrong. There is no right and wrong about feelings. They're things we own for ourselves.

At this point, it's really important to have talk time, and a wonderful thing I ask my patients to do is to have a kitchen timer or a timer on their phone, and they have five minutes talk time each, so that's ten minutes a day.

You sit down somewhere very quiet, you start your timer, and one person just starts talking about their day: their fears, their wants, their wishes, their desires, their dreams, whatever it is. This is not a time to punish each other, it's a time to talk about how we are, in ourselves, at this moment in time. And the other person has to just listen for those five minutes. And then, the timer is moved over to the other person, and they get their five minutes to talk about their true position right now. And don't forget, this only happens if we are absolutely in our truth. This is not a time to attack or be defensive. This is a time to purely communicate to your partner what's going on for you. It's a simple and highly effective tool. Try it.

If we feel defensive or angry, we must recognize that the source of these emotions are deeper than this specific change. Perhaps we have experienced pain from a similar change in the past. Whatever our feelings are, acknowledge them, but don't act upon them. We want our partner to be open and honest, not to close up and stop communicating. You can return at any time to Part I of this book to work through your emotions in your own time.
If your partner becomes angry or upset, tell them that you recognize how they're feeling, but don't be tempted to defend yourself. Again, there is no right and wrong way when it comes to feelings.

Just because we are in a relationship, we are not twins joined at the hip. This is a time to discover how we are different and how that may complement each other. Or it might reveal what adjustments are needed to bring us more in line. It can be fun learning about each other.

From words to action
Now we're all on the same page about what an upcoming change means, we must reflect this understanding onto our ongoing actions. We not only need to talk the talk, but walk the walk.

For example, if we have reassured our partner that their redundancy does not make them useless, ask them for help with something you know they are good at. But also make it clear that a job needs to be found.

If our partner has admitted they are worried our new hobby will leave us less time together, set aside a date night to show them that their fears are unfounded. A date night once every week or two weeks is a superb way to keep a relationship clear, understanding, and healthy . If you're not doing date nights, start them. They're just for you.

Above all, keep putting energy into your partnership. Be committed to the commitment. It's vital. Create good times. Spend time together and make future plans. One of the most accurate barometers of a relationship is your sex life. If life changes have led you to stop or drastically reduce your love-making, you should work on this. It's all about communicating with each other, and sex is the most powerful communicator. While Chapter 8 focuses solely on this area, you may also need external help from a couples therapist. Why not? Invest in your relationship.

So, what's not changing?

Changes rarely affect all aspects of our relationship. If we're feeling overwhelmed, it can help to focus on what is staying the same.

Can you change?

In many cases, a relationship ends because one partner believes the other is incapable of change. The fact is that most people can change once they see and accept the need to do so. Even a minor shift can be a major turning point in a relationship, so don't give up hope. However, some people just cannot develop and will not change. And you need the wisdom at this point to really have a good look at your partner and think, 'Are you in this? Are you willing to change, or are you just paying me lip service?' If you believe this is the case, you need to check this out thoroughly with them because it's all well and good for somebody to pay you lip service, but if they're not walking the walk by this point, it's alarm bells for me.

If you are aware that you need to change, start with a small change in either your thoughts, approach, or behavior that you are able to maintain for a week. Just try it. For example, it could be that you don't handwash the dishes for a week and you use the dishwasher like your partner keeps on asking you to do. Just a small change like that. See how it is, and at the end of the week, discuss how it was. You might realize that you prefer using the dishwasher after all because it's easier on your back, or you might decide that you still prefer handwashing. It's amazing if you can come up with a compromise. Perhaps you could take responsibility for putting the dishes in the sink while your partner puts them in the dishwasher.

Just start off with one change that is very real, manageable and will involve both of you. Of course, there are more serious issues than how to load a dishwasher, but I'm giving you an example of how you can start with something simple. It could be something to do with cooking or making the morning coffee.

Be aware: we can't change somebody else even if we see their attitude or behavior as the main reason for our relationship problems. But we can change somebody else by changing ourselves. If we make changes, it impacts them.

Think of three things that really annoy you in this relationship, perhaps the dishwasher scenario, and think about how we could manage safe and reasonable change.

Either way, be realistic and accept that there is unlikely to be a dramatic overnight shift. And enforcing change is work. It takes up time, energy, and emotions. So, it is best to start with one of the biggest areas where you would like to see change, and work through the skills in the remainder of this book (communication, meeting each others' needs, handling emotions, etc.)

Real change takes time, so stick with this process with me and remind yourself that you are not trying to recreate your early romance; you are moving forward into a new, improved phase of your relationship.

In a nutshell

Task 4: How do I manage change going forward?

- Talk about an upcoming change with your partner. How will it impact them? Tell them how it will impact you. How do you see the change differently? Does one of you feel threatened? Recognize how that mutual understanding has already led to a change in your relationship. Monitor feelings, ideas, attitudes, and thoughts. Don't forget to pop these down in your journal as a reminder of what you experienced.

- What change-related fears have we uncovered. How can we prove to each other that those fears are unfounded?

- Can we make changes to direct more energy into our relationship. Avoid one-sided changes and absolutes. Asking your partner to give up watching sports or baking shows is not going to be as successful as suggesting you both cut down on your favorite shows and invest the extra time into your relationship.

- For an expected change, list three ways in which your relationship won't change.

- Is one of you more resistant to change? Will they consider one small, positive change that will benefit you? Like not cutting their toenails in the bedroom.

- If there is no evidence of intent to change from your partner, consider professional help or just point out that they haven't changed and ask them directly if they are going to put in the effort. Revisit whether you are willing to continue along the make up route with them.

For more guidance, read:

Acton, M. (2022). *Raw facts from real parents.* Life Logic Publishing

Clear, J. (2018). *Atomic habits.* Random House Business

Wilde McCormick, E. (2008). *Change for the better: self-help through practical psychotherapy.* Sage Publications Ltd.

PART II: MAKING UP

CHAPTER 5

DON'T LISTEN, HEAR: HOW TO BEST TALK TO EACH OTHER

All healthy relationships are founded on effective communication. It is through communication that we share thoughts, goals, ideas, fears, and feelings. This is how we express our needs and understand our partner's. Through talking, we negotiate shifts in our approach and discuss whether these changes are working.

Quick wins by improving communication
One of the best ways we can boost our communication skills is by asking our partner more questions, especially open questions that require more than a yes/no answer. When answering our partner's questions, give fuller answers. Make it a date night game. Earlier, I mentioned the timer when talking to each other. It is an amazing tool.

Communication blockers
If you find it difficult to talk, or you tend to avoid or skirt around an issue, explore why that might be. Was talking openly frowned upon in your childhood home? Were you punished for speaking your mind or criticized as selfish for expressing your wants and needs?

Did you once say something you instantly regretted because it hurt someone else? Are you still carrying that guilt around with you? Do you now avoid saying anything that might cause offense or be misinterpreted?
If we have any insecurities about voicing ourselves because of previous

issues, we need to challenge these blocks. They're not going to help us moving forward. An exercise at this point would be to think back to three times when we were glad that we said something; when we made a positive difference by expressing ourselves.

Sometimes we all put our feet in our mouths and make faux-pax or wish we hadn't said something. And if you've been treading on egg shells for a number of years, this can add to our confidence issues. So, list the three things and remind yourself that you intend to be good, to help, and to be positive. Just occasionally, we've messed up. Give yourself permission to mess up because no human is perfect. Start speaking up your truth, especially in your relationships. This is how we get rewards: by communicating clearly with each other.

Talking about these early life experiences is often difficult, but the roots of our challenging emotions and behaviors are found here. Only by understanding and sharing our pain can we develop mutual empathy and move past obstacles to change our communication style.

We can practice open communication by writing a letter to our partner. We don't have to send it, but the exercise of expressing what happened, who was involved and, most importantly, how you felt is gold dust. Avoid being negative about your partner, but highlight anything positive they did to support you. Sometimes couples get into an attack mode. We can be hurt, scared, and defensive. If you nit-pick each other, or have got into a negative trend of judging or putting down your partner, pull yourself back by your breeches and just stand there and look at yourself for a second because that doesn't work.

Consider why you are attacking and putting your partner down. Is it to defend some painful thing in your shadow. Are you embarrassed by your partner? Be honest here. And how does this reflect on your childhood? Were you forced to fight for your place in your childhood home? Was there a lot of bickering and putting down of each other? How did it work then? How does it work now?

If you are committed to staying together, you must temper your honesty with empathy. You must understand what is annoying you, be honest about it, but frame and voice it with care and love. It's very important to bring kindness into our relationships.

Active listening and its power
The whole role of a therapist is active listening. It is one of the key skills that we're trained in. Learning to actively listen to one another can transform our relationship. It's not easy, it takes training, and here are some tips on how you can do it:
- Encourage your partner to speak using both verbal and non-verbal cues. For example, maintain eye contact and an open posture, and use, "mmm," "yes," and "OK" to signal your attention. This is a great exercise to combine with the timed talk sessions I introduced in Chapter 4.
- Don't disconnect when you hear something you don't like. If you look away or blank out, your partner will sense you are not listening and will either stop talking or react angrily. Deliberately turning off is a form of aggression. So, what you need to do here is be non-judgmental, and very respectful, and understand it's your partner's way. This is how they feel and think.
- Stop your internal chatter. Are you listening or preparing your words for when it's your turn to speak (or doing your shopping

list). You can't react honestly to your partner's words until you hear them. So, do your best to turn off your inner voice, listen attentively, and be in the now. Listen to every single word that comes from your partner's lips. A helpful tip for maintaining attention is to focus on what your partner looks and sounds like as they talk. Observe how they're sitting and what's happening with their face.

- Wait before speaking. Breathe slowly, count to three, and take time to really absorb what your partner just said. Then formulate a measured response. If you are tempted to interrupt or rubbish what your partner's saying, understand that this is your fear-based motivation. On a deep level, you may be scared that backing down will cause you or your relationship to fall apart. In fact, your partner will realize that you have given them space to express themselves, and this can be enough to dispel any strong, negative emotions that they might have been holding on to. This is your arena for being in your truth. Hear their truth and speak your truth, but do it in a compassionate way.

- If you are unsure what your partner has communicated, don't assume. You may feel more comfortable responding to a 'straw man', but if you have misunderstood your partner, this will only frustrate them. To clarify their position, summarize what you think your partner has just said, and give them a chance to correct any misunderstandings. Or simply say, "I'm not quite sure I understand what you're trying to say. Could you say that again." Always be kind, always be engaging, and above all else, always be interested. And if you're not that interested at this time, you may not want the relationship to continue. Think about that. You really need to check in with yourself at every stage of this process.

As with any new skill, you are unlikely to master effective listening in one session. Start with scheduling in a 15m 'active listening' slot twice a week, and gradually increase the time and/or frequency until it becomes a natural way to communicate. If one of you keeps interrupting the other, choose an object and make it a rule that only the person holding the object can speak.

Practicing skills such as maintaining eye contact and turning towards your partner will pay off, even if you don't fully have your heart in it at first. You may want to avoid talking about your relationship issues until you have mastered the basics of effective listening.

If you are really struggling with this, consider some couples counseling sessions. A therapist can model effective listening skills for you.

As you become more comfortable with effective listening, you can move on to developing more subtle skills. For example, your partner may repeat certain words that are particularly relevant to how they're feeling, or their body language may tell a different story to their words.

For example, you could say, "You keep repeating that you're not really bothered, but I can see that you're gripping tightly to the arms of the chair. I think this might be bothering you. Tell me how exactly it makes you feel."
This level of communication can trigger intense emotions, but we will cover how to handle these in Chapter 7.

How to ace communication in your relationship:

- Understand how you push each other's buttons, and avoid this behavior.
- Instead of blaming your partner, take responsibility for your contribution to the relationship.
- Acknowledge your partner's feelings without engaging in a 'tit-for-tat.'
- Don't moan at or boss around your partner. Give them specific requests for improvement. Clear communication always wins.
- If you are unable to fulfill a request, just say "no" and suggest an alternative plan.
- Focus on one issue at a time - dumping doesn't help.
- Avoid shouting or cowering at all costs. Use a clear, calm voice and steady eye contact. And if at any time you feel unsafe, leave.
- Keep up the momentum. Once you've resolved a relationship issue, it is important to keep up the habit of good communication. Thoughts and feelings about an issue can change, sometimes daily, so we need to keep updating our data to reflect the current state of our relationship. Make sure you use your journal. It is your friend.

If finding the balance in a relationship is hard, then being in our truth is harder still. And if speaking our truth while holding our balance is tough, then it's tougher still to ensure that the other person hearing our words takes them as intended. It's like a dance.

It's messy, but if we can be in our truth as much as we are able to and work on balancing our approach, both before and during a conversation with self or other, then we will feel whole lot more at peace, and our dance moves will be smooth and in sync.

It's important at this point not to walk on eggshells. Walking on eggshells is not moving forward.

Relationship communication masters: lessons to be learned

In a longitudinal field simulation study (Gottman, 2018) (which means a real experiment involving real people which was conducted over a long period of time) researchers from the University of Washington set up a fake bed and breakfast scenario and observed couples interacting. They also took blood samples, urine samples, etc., to measure stress levels, immunity, and other biochemical reactions.

The study findings enabled the researchers to make surprisingly accurate predictions about how specific relationships would develop. They could predict divorce with an over 90% accuracy rate (and with 85% accuracy after just 15 minutes of observation). After 40 years of studying a cohort, they could even predict exactly when an unhappy couple would divorce!

More positively, the results revealed three principles that united those relationships that succeeded (where the couples not only stayed together but were satisfied in their relationships). These were:
• Quality friendship
• Conflict resolution
• Shared meaning

So, it's just these three qualities and principles that we need to work on in order to move forward in a loving and lasting relationship. So, let's go through these one at a time:

Quality friendship

This research team were able to dissect the vague notion of a 'quality friendship' into three specific areas, as follows:
- Strong 'love mapping.'
- Expressed fondness and admiration.
- Response to 'bids' for emotional connection.

Love mapping refers to the involvement both parties have with the other's inner psychic world. In a quality friendship, we want to know about each other's goals, motivations, and pain points without being abusive. The best way we can do that is to ask open-ended questions. Dr. Gottman recommends testing this by turning 50% of our statements into open questions and noting the effect.

While we may feel fondness and admiration for our friends and partners, they won't know this unless we - in the words of Billy Joel - 'Tell Her (or Him) About It!'

The researchers found that people in healthy relationships would respond to bids for emotional connection. This could be a simple statement such as, "Isn't that bird song lovely?" A lack of response (turning away) would often lead to clear evidence of hurt, including self-soothing behaviors. It would also reduce the likelihood of a 're-bid' for attention to almost zero!

While all couples mess up, every interaction can be thought of as a deposit to or withdrawal from an emotional bank account. A healthy bank account leads to 'positive sentiment override' which can act as a buffer during tough times. Conversely, 'negative sentiment override' will lead to hyper-vigilance to criticism. If your partner appears to have a 'chip on their shoulder,' could it be that you have made few deposits into their emotional bank account? Maybe it's time to take an interest in them. Yes, I'm talking to you reading this; maybe you haven't.

The study actually measured the ratio between the number of kind and positive statements exchanged between couples and the number of critical and negative statements. They found that couples with a 0.8:1 ratio or worse were headed for divorce. The most stable relationships presented a 5:1 ratio: that's five positive statements for every one negative statement made! It's not rocket science. It's like putting gas in a car. If you don't put enough gas in, or you put bad gas in versus good gas, it's going to stop working.

Conflict resolution

So, how do we resolve conflict? A surprising finding from the field research was that 69% of conflicts in the relationships studied were never resolved. Wow! In healthy relationships, those areas of conflict were tolerated. However, underneath the apparent 'gridlock' was often a key to the partner's deepest life dreams. Unblocking this area could strengthen a couple's love maps.

Of the 31% of conflicts that were resolved, the researchers identified three key strategies:
- Gentle approach (i.e., being kind, empathic)
- Accepting influence from the partner (something violent males were particularly bad at).
- Compromise. Yes, that old beauty.

Working against conflict resolution was emotional 'flooding' because adrenaline impairs creativity and logical thinking. The researchers tested this by intervening in a heated conflict and then allowing it to resume once each of the couple's heart rates had fallen below 100bpm. This led to more successful outcomes, including more shared humor.

Shared meaning
Partners in successful relationships felt that they were building something important together. They saw their relationship as something that was continually growing, developing, and contributing to their own sense of self.

Avoiding the four horsemen
Dr. Gottman labels the negative attitudes that cause the most damage to relationships the 'four horsemen' (named after the horsemen of the apocalypse). These are:
- Criticism of the personality.
- Defensiveness (manifesting as righteous indignation or whining).
- Contempt (disrespect from a position of superiority).
- Stonewalling (emotional withdrawal from conflict).

Of the four, contempt was the greatest predictor of divorce, and the polemic state of contempt would be compromise. So, compromise is our friend in whatever we do going forward. Compromise is an act of kindness, understanding, and leveling out.

According to the researchers, the key to escaping the four horsemen, and all they bring with them, was cultivating a positive habit of mind. Rather than scanning the environment for things to criticize, look for those things that you can appreciate. Instead of name-calling and focusing on their mistakes, catch your beautiful partner doing good things and praise them for it.

Just imagine, we all have our inner child. When a child's doing something, we encourage them, we are supportive of them, we are in awe of them. All of us in relationships have our inner child. Be mindful to treat each other's inner children with the same respect, encouragement, love, and warmth. It's vital.

Rather than being defensive, take responsibility for your part in the problem (no matter how small that may be). Rather than stonewalling (which merely leads to escalation of the complaint,) practice showing engagement through eye contact, vocalizations, and non-verbal body language (such as nodding, appropriate facial expressions, or even a hug.)

No war on negativity
There is a caveat to all of this positivity: if something in a relationship isn't working, it is necessary to bring this up. Only then can the relationship change and develop. In fact, according to Dr. Gottman, relationships naturally cycle through periods of distance and closeness. Sadness can stimulate renewed courtship, so don't be too hasty to 'declare war on negativity.' Be wise, observe, and embrace.

In a nutshell

Task 5: Improve your communication skills:

- Ask your partner more questions about them, and answer their questions more fully when asked.
- If you struggle to talk, explore possible reasons for this. It could

be historical factors, bullying, parents and family. Just have a little look at why this might be. Journal it.

- Think of three times when you were glad that you did speak out. What difference did this make? Think about how exploring that could help you speak out now. Carry out an experiment. Go to a store or a bus stop and maybe say to somebody, "Good morning. Isn't it a nice day."

- Practice active listening. Start with 10m together a week, 5m each, with a timer. Remember during these times to be respectful and hear each other and keep with the boundaries. Be respectful of boundaries. This is not a time to 'bitch and beer.' It's a time to express each of us and what's going on in our world.

  ◊ Encourage your partner, verbally and non-verbally. Seem interested.

  ◊ Don't disconnect when you disagree.

  ◊ Turn off your inner chatter. Focus on what your partner looks and sounds like.

  ◊ Count to three before responding.

  ◊ Don't assume you understand what your partner has communicated. Summarize it and check it out with them.

- Follow the advice of the 'relationship masters:'

  ◊ Be interested in each other's goals.

  ◊ Express your fondness.

  ◊ Respond to bids for attention.

  ◊ Be gentle and kind in conflict.

  ◊ Accept your partner's influence.

  ◊ Look to compromise.

  ◊ Develop shared meaning as a couple.

  ◊ Avoid the four horsemen: personal attack, defensiveness, contempt, and stonewalling, at all costs

For more guidance, read:
Basterfield, B. C. (2023). *The effective communication method: 9 keys to master communication skills.* 365 Self-Growth Publishing

Leal III, B. C. (2017). *4 essential keys to effective communication in love, life, work - anywhere!* CreateSpace

Shaw, G. (2020). *7 winning conflict resolution techniques.* Communication Excellence

Reference:
Gottman, Dr. J. (2018, January 30). *Making Marriage Work* [Video]. YouTube. https://www.youtube.com/watch?v=AKTyPgwfPgg

PART II: MAKING UP

CHAPTER 6

WHAT EXACTLY DO WE WANT? IT'S TIME TO AGREE

If you want something, you damn well have to ask for it. That's what this world is about.

We all have needs: some are physical (food, drink, and warmth), others, like a need for love, affection, and support, are emotional in nature. These higher level needs vary a lot depending upon our personal make-up, our past experiences, and our present situation.

We may or may not need a hug when we're upset. Some people need to express their emotions openly, whether crying or whooping in celebration. Others prefer to curl up in quiet pain or enjoyment. Our needs often contradict each other. We want to laugh and talk with our friends, but we also want to rest at home with a good book.

It is impossible to meet all of our needs all the time, and it is even more difficult to meet others' needs - even our partner's. We may not know what their needs are, or we may be unable to meet them because of our own personality or because of a conflict with our own needs. And don't forget, some partners may never share what they need or want, and that's a dangerous flag right there.

In the heady days of a new romance, it's easy to sacrifice some of our deeper needs for the fulfillment of other, more superficial ones, but as a relationship develops, our unmet needs can become a burden to us.

Sometimes, we are aware of a clash of needs from very early in the relationship. Sometimes, these become clear only after a particular life event. You become pregnant and your partner tells you that they never wanted children. You get a full-time job and your partner takes a year out to travel.

Becoming aware of our needs

It is very difficult for our relationships to meet our needs if we don't know what those needs are.

Let's spend some time writing up a 'wish list' of our needs. Just think about where those needs come from and how important they are to us. Which of our needs are fundamental to our relationship? What agreements must our partner make? What are our deal-breakers - those red lines that, if crossed, would prevent our successful reunion?

And it's mindful here to talk about the difference between wants and needs.
- A need is something that will fundamentally contribute to our life and make it sustainable. We have to justify our needs. A need is 'because of... .'
- Wants are more of a personal addition to life. It's something we desire. We don't have to justify our wants.

If this exercise is tough, you may have cut yourself off from your own needs. And if you've cut yourself off from your own needs, you're clearly not doing very well. You're not in a healthy spot.

If you focus too much on fulfilling other people's needs and expectations, refusing to accept gifts for yourself, you will deny yourself access to lasting happiness and deep enjoyment. You are drowning. You may be able to ignore your needs, but you will still feel a nagging dissatisfaction with your life. This is not sustainable.

As with most of our personality traits, refusing to value our needs usually stems from our childhood, or at the very least from how others have treated us in life. We may have been taught that our needs are not important and that we should focus our energy on 'being good' - i.e., meeting the needs of others. As such, we may have never taken the time to really ask ourselves what we want out of life.

In relationships, we naturally carry that mentality into serving our partner's needs, blurring the boundary between what they want and what we want. Just choosing a holiday is a good example of this. Do we always err on the side of caution and book something we know our partner will like. Is booking a two week hang-gliding adventure for our partner while we sit on the beach with a book really meeting both of our needs?

So, just pause here. What do we want out of life that we're not necessarily getting now?

We can use dissatisfaction to identify some of these hidden needs. Why aren't we happy? What is it that our life is missing?

If you can work out your core needs and communicate them to your partner, you have taken a huge step towards getting those needs fulfilled in your relationship.

Let's revisit the holiday example. Imagine sitting with your partner saying, "OK, we've got two weeks vacation and enough money to go towards it, where should we go that will be mutually beneficial for us." That's a good way of starting out. We can then make our choice based on each other's wants, needs, hopes, safety and sustainability.

Simple ways to meet each other's needs
Share our needs with our partner and work on fulfilling both of your needs where possible. Start small and simple to establish trust, before building up to more significant and challenging needs.

Now consider this carefully: your partner may not be reading this book. They may not be doing work on themselves. So, don't surprise them by all of a sudden talking in psychobabble and running experiments. Explain carefully that you're reading this book or you're thinking about the relationship, and slowly introduce something nice such as, "Oh, it's a nice day. Let's go for a walk in the woods and see if we can track down those birds you like." Just start with taking baby steps towards considering their needs together with your own needs. If your ideas are met with a resounding, "No!" just respond with something like, "I'm going to go, and I thought you might like to come with me. If you change your mind, that's fine." Gently does it. These are changes, and changes are tough.

Meeting each other's needs does not have to involve grand gestures. Even something simple such as helping each other with the dishes fulfills much more than a practical function. It is a way to provide companionship and demonstrate a willingness to share responsibilities and support one another. And don't forget, doing things together like washing the dishes, tidying up, or doing the gardening is the perfect time to have a conversation and talk about things.

Now, even if we've lived with them for 20 years we might not know what our partner's needs are. They change over time. Maybe now's the time to use some of the communication skills I presented in the previous chapter.

Socrates walked around markets, trying to understand people by asking lots of open questions. To discover our partner's needs, we could try Socratic questions such as:

- "I'm thinking of starting a new hobby. If you were to do a new hobby, what do you think that would be, and why?"

- "I think you're telling me that you want us to go out together as a couple more. Is that right?"

- "I've noticed you're watching more nature programs on TV. I'm wondering if you would be interested in taking out a membership for a nature group. Is that something you would be interested in."

- "I really like it that you are holding my hand when we're walking. It makes me feel close to you. I was thinking of cooking a nice meal one evening and we could have an early night together. Would you like that?"

Do you ignore your partner's requests because the issue doesn't seem important to you or the timing is wrong? Perhaps you don't understand the need to call them when you're on your way home from work. Maybe you don't feel like taking a walk to the seaside after work. Maybe you're not in the mood for intimacy.

Be more open to meeting your partner's needs. They will feel heard and respected.

They might be worried about your safety on the roads. They might have been stuck at home all day and crave some fresh air. They may feel lonely and in need of physical connection.

Sometimes we have to do things that our partner wants to do even though we might not really want to at that time. Be open to new things, even if they seem mundane or scary. You might end up enjoying it more than you think.

Help our partner. Be kind to them. Just imagine for a moment that they're a very dear friend. Would you just sack off a friend's offer to go to the pub or a walk. Probably not. So, stop doing it to your partner. Start engaging with them.

You are building bridges.

Most relationships include certain expectations about meeting each other's needs. For example, most couples expect to be able to rely on each other for companionship, financial support, certain types of practical support (parenting, housework, etc.,) and sexual intimacy. If you are struggling to make the necessary commitments, try to understand why.

With a flexible mindset, practical obstacles can usually be worked around. But could your reasons actually be excuses based on fear (of intimacy, of being controlled, etc.) Or more than likely, there could be underlying resentment (i.e., unprocessed anger) that you need to work out in order to be open and to be able to support and love your partner again. Bear this in mind: are you treating them with contempt?

If either of you are unable to honor agreements that are fundamental to your relationship, then it may well be worth your while getting in touch with couples therapy. Make certain that the therapist is qualified to work with couples. If they're not, it can be a disaster. The beauty about couples therapy is that there's nowhere for either of you to hide. You will need to face facts. The spotlight is on you at all times, and it can bring about positive change.

If you're really struggling at this point, and feel that the making up of this relationship isn't working, there is always the exit strategy of moving on (Part III), but be mindful of how to do that. If you are thinking about moving on at this point, and leaving your partner, do it at a time that's right for you. Take care of yourself, and be safe.

We are not joined at the hip: satisfying needs outside of your relationship

It is hugely unrealistic - and terribly unhealthy - to expect to have all of our needs satisfied within our relationship. We all have unique personalities, upbringings, attitudes, strengths, and weaknesses. This is reflected in the diversity of interests we enjoy: baking, playing tennis, running, watching sport, Scuba diving, watching nature programs...It would be a miracle if our partners enjoyed exactly the same activities as us.

In reality, there is likely to be a basic clash of need in one or more areas of life.

For example, we may need to experience the thrill of an adrenalin rush every now and then, whilst our partner prefers to avoid scary experiences. Rather than forcing our partner into activities they hate, or missing out and feeling bitter, we may have to accept their "No!" and take responsibility for meeting that specific need for ourselves. Perhaps we can join a club of fellow thrill-seekers or hook up with a friend or family member who shares our daring nature.

One of the easiest ways to meet our need for comfort, security and pleasure is to give ourselves an occasional gift. Take a leaf out of Miley Cyrus's book and buy yourself a bunch of flowers. Treat yourself to an indulgent meal, take a long, luxurious bath, or play a tape of affirmations to remind yourself how special you are.

Hold your own hand. Parent yourself. Pleasure yourself.

In a nutshell

Task 6: Identifying each others' needs:

- What are your needs? What do we really like. What do we really get off on. Get together with your partner and divide a sheet of paper (or screen) into three columns headed: Must Have, Nice To Have, and Let Go. This only works if you're absolutely honest. Your partner should do the same. Come up with at least ten needs each and put them in the appropriate columns. Compare sheets. Can you meet each other's most important needs? Are you surprised about some of your partner's needs? Are you shocked that your partner didn't know about your important needs? Parents can often tune in to their children's needs but we can't rely on our partners to do the same. This is usually because our partners aren't as open and clear as children. They're more filtered.

- Are you a people-pleaser who meets everybody else's needs bar your own? What does your partner do in this respect?
- Start using active listening skills, including summarizing, to clarify your partner's needs. And make it fun. This can be fun!
- Do you ever refuse to satisfy a request because you don't see why it's important to your partner? Make an effort to meet their need. Discuss how you both felt afterwards.
- When was the last time you gave yourself a treat? Make it a regular occurrence going forward, as long as it's healthy and sustainable. If you are plagued by negative self-talk, record a tape of positive affirmations and listen to it regularly. This is a very powerful thing to do.
- Are you expecting too much from your partner? Are you expecting too much from yourself? What needs could you meet outside of your relationship?
- Is your partner asking for a commitment you can't make or asking you to do something you don't really want to do? Consider couples counseling or accept that reunion may not be achievable and consider moving on at the right time for you.

For more guidance, read:
Chapman, G. (2015). *The 5 love languages: the secret to love that lasts.* Moody Publishers.

Power A. (2022). *Contented couples: magic, logic or luck.* Confer Ltd.

Harley, W. F. (2011) *His needs, her needs: building an affair-proof marriage.* Monarch Books.

PART II: MAKING UP

CHAPTER 7

THE BUTTONS WE PUSH AND MANAGING THESE

Learning to cope with difficult emotions is often the key to a successful make up. If you're not able to do this, you must change. It's as simple as that.

How fear impacts us

Fear can sometimes feel overwhelming and stop us in our tracks. This may create a self-fulfilling prophecy. We either bury these fears so deeply that we lose connection with them completely or we hold on to them for too long until they over-boil and spill out everywhere. Our motives may be loving. We want to protect our partner from our emotions. Often we want to protect ourselves from harm by covering up our vulnerabilities. Sadly, the result is that we cause greater harm with our outbursts or by shutting out our partners. It's a shame that we couldn't express our emotions in a healthy way rather than treating them disrespectfully.

Going back to the lessons of Part I, Chapter 5, when we repress our difficult emotions, we also lock away some of our positive qualities. Into the closet, alongside our vulnerabilities, goes our empathy, our honesty, our sympathy, and our ability to feel remorse. This lack of a rich emotional life can lead to depression underpinned by a deep, unfathomable sadness, hopefulness. What do our partners see when they look at us? A blank face. What do they hear? A toneless voice. Is there any wonder our relationship broke?

It also takes a lot of effort to pin down our emotions. As a result, we lose the ability to concentrate. We experience chronic stress, which causes its own pain to us and all those in our lives.

On the other hand, letting our emotions loose at every opportunity provides only a one-sided, short-term fix. Over the long term, it will put the other party on the defensive. If they respond in like manner, you have the recipe for escalation into abuse and violence. On the other hand, one emotionally expressive partner could be taking on the role of expressing everyone's emotions. They have the responsibility given to them. This is fine when you are both on the same page, but often means that the less expressive partner feels unable to make their voice heard when there are relationship problems. Sound familiar?

The root of poor coping skills

We don't have to be too hard on ourselves when it comes to our sub-par coping skills. We have to give ourselves permission to be imperfect. We all are imperfect. It's highly likely that we have simply never learned the skills.

As we're developing through life, we pick up ideas, manners, and ways of coping with crisis. In life, our first instructors are our parents or guardians - and they are not always the best examples of how to do things. Sometimes our parents can be dismissive of problems; sometimes they can catastrophize as we're growing up; sometimes they can be 'drama queens'; sometimes they can be aggressive and try to punch out any challenges. Yes, we pick these up as we go along. I'm wondering if we can reflect now and think, 'Well, do I behave like any of them, the influencers in my life growing up?'

It's OK to change what they did. We can change.

If we feel possessive over a partner, we may have grown up competing for the attention of our parents or our guardians. If we feel overwhelmed by situations, our parents may have always fought our battles for us. And if even the smallest detail of things going wrong causes a huge explosion, it could be that our parents over-reacted to situations and catastrophized. Whatever the situation is, we can only look at what works for us and what doesn't. What parts of our parents or guardians bringing us up works for us and what parts could we modify because it doesn't work?

The following task is one of the most powerful tasks I will present to you in our work together in this book. Take time with it. It's vital to understanding you, your partner, your past, how we cope with things, and how we communicate.

Task 7: Developing emotional coping skills:

Be transparent and work with your partner on this task. Each of you should choose a painful emotion you are wary of working with (anger, sadness, shame, guilt, etc.) Think back to your childhood home, and answer the following questions in your journals:

- How did your parents/guardians handle this emotion or not?
- How did your siblings handle it?
- Did you discuss these feelings as a family? What did you learn from that?
- How did you handle this emotion coming from your parents/guardians and siblings?
- Do you notice a connection between these childhood experiences and how you and your partner handle this emotion?
- Swap notes with your partner and discuss them.

Escaping the drama triangle: From childhood roles to equal partners

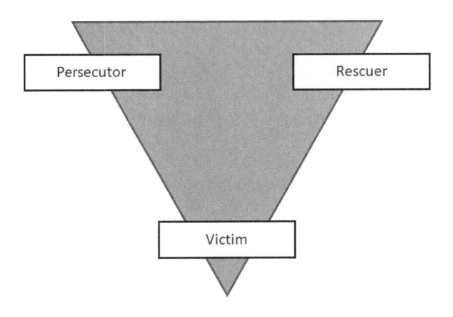

Graphic created by 1000Faces and licensed under Creative Commons 4.0.

The Karpman Drama Triangle (Karpman, 1968) is a therapeutic tool designed by psychiatrist Stephen Karpman. It brings together the work of Eric Berne, founder of Transactional Analysis, and Murray Bowen, who developed the concept of triangulation in systemic therapy. Karpman was also a keen actor, hence his use of drama and role-playing to clarify his concepts.

Karpman's triangle is a negative system because it keeps the 'actors' locked into patterns which seem to be solving relationship problems, but in reality keeps things the same. The payback for the actors is that comfortable feeling of familiarity.

Despite the emotional distress and pain of the drama, everyone gets to play the role they've rehearsed since birth, and everyone remains in control of their little world. However, they never move beyond these childhood patterns to achieve the ideal of equal power-sharing enjoyed by adults.

So, what are the three roles?

1. Victim. This role takes the 'one down' position in the drama. They disown their power and seek to manipulate others into achieving their needs.

2. Rescuer. This role takes a 'one up' position, with the actor using their power to meet the needs of the victim. In doing so, they ignore their own needs and the victim becomes dependent on them.

3. Persecutor. The villain of the triangle. They also take a 'one up' position by dominating the victim.

It is important to remember that these are three *roles*, not necessarily three actors. So, the drama triangle is often played out by couples.

In fact, when couples are in an unequal relationship, they have to use the drama triangle to achieve balance. This is where Bowen's triangulation concept comes in. If a couple only stuck to the roles of Rescuer or Perpetrator and Victim, the strength of their unmet needs would eventually cause the relationship (or the individuals) to break apart.

However, the third point of the triangle provides an escape lane. When the Rescuer gets overwhelmed by the frustration of their unmet needs, they can choose to either lash out as a Perpetrator or collapse as a Victim. In the second case, the Victim has two choices: they can counter-attack (switching role to become the Perpetrator) or try to restore calm by meeting their partner's needs (becoming the Rescuer). Having released their bottled up emotions, the original Rescuer will resume their rescuing role to make up for their moment of 'weakness.' The Victim is happy to hand the power back as they settle back into their most comfortable role. The board is reset with everyone a winner in the short-term - and a loser in the long game.

This is just one type of game that psychologists from the Transactional Analysis perspective are trained to recognize. Berne presented many other scenarios in his popular book *Games People Play*.

Using Karpman's triangle, think back to the task you've just done. Can you identify the different roles you played within your childhood family? You may have stuck to one familiar role or switched between them depending on the people involved. You may have even played two roles at the same time (e.g., persecuting yourself for 'getting it wrong.')

These patterns often persist into our early adult relationships, compounding the problem as our story becomes complicated by breakups and heartache.

Beware! One of the hooks that could keep you trapped in the drama triangle is the need to resolve conflicts from before your initial breakup. William Worden (1991) said that successful grieving is learning to live without the answers. This is also true when negotiating a relationship makeup because success depends upon you making new agreements and, to a large degree, letting go of some of the loose ends from what happened before.

This is a balancing act because you also need to be alert to the potential risks of being blindsided by false promises.

We will now move on to healthy emotional management, and your work as a couple is to move on from recreating these childhood drama triangles to relating to one another as equal adults.

Emotional management: three stages
We can break healthy emotional management strategies into three parts: awareness/acceptance, investigation/interpretation, and appropriate expression.

Let's put it another way: We can only express emotions appropriately if we know what lies behind them, and we can only find that out once we have accepted that we are feeling the emotion in the first place.

Awareness: Try to catch an emotion as soon as it bites. Be as clear as possible when describing it. Are you anxious? Angry? Sad? Naming an emotion can often reduce its intensity. Where in the body can you feel it? What does it make you want to do?

Acceptance: Remind yourself that it is natural to feel emotions. It is part of being human. Give it a name because this will help you to gain control over it. You can then choose to feel it and let it go. Over time, you will usually find that the emotion loses its intensity.

If your emotions continue to overwhelm you, consider talking to a therapist before continuing this work.

Investigation: When you face your emotions, you can start pulling them apart. You will often find that thoughts are bundled up with those emotions. You feel sad (emotion), tell yourself you're not good enough (thought) and then feel angry at yourself (emotion). You then tell yourself you shouldn't feel angry (thought), leading to guilt (emotion).

If this wasn't complicated enough, we often read emotions in our partner and match them with thoughts we think they might be having. We might even offload our own emotions and thoughts on to them. It is easy to misinterpret signals when we are in the grip of strong emotions. Even if we do read the emotion correctly, we might get the thoughts all wrong. Your partner may be thinking angrily about a road rage incident on the way home rather than reacting to your admission that you forgot to pick up milk!

Investigating each other's emotions can stir up deep feelings and bring up painful memories of past events. We must be prepared for this and apply the lessons of the previous chapters. What are you both feeling and thinking? What do they need from us? What do you need from them? If they ask for your reassurance, don't just give them your words, show them how important they are in your actions. Help them to build their self-confidence and independence.

Moving forward, how can you both show each other that you have changed since the breakup? If you betrayed your partner, words may not be enough to generate the trust 'glue' to repair your fractures.

How can you demonstrate you are doing the work? What would you expect from your partner if the shoe were on the other foot?

If you were the betrayed one, what will it take to earn back your trust? Are you able to forgive your partner and refuse to allow their misdeed to affect your future relationship?

Expression: When you can recognize, accept, and understand the reason for an emotion, it becomes easier to choose how you express that emotion.

The number one rule is that you must not choose to physically or mentally hurt each other. If you are able to talk, focus on expressing what each of you are feeling without blaming the other for 'making' you feel that way. This can take practice, so don't worry too much if your first attempts blow up. As long as you both prioritize safety, you can always reset and try again later. Be sensitive to timing. People often need to wind down after work or prepare their mind ahead of an important task or event. Wait until you are both in a relatively relaxed place.

As explained in the previous chapter, difficult emotions are often the result of unmet needs. Hopefully, you will now be clear on what your needs are. Once you have expressed your feelings, ask for what you need using clear and positive language. Let's wrap that up with some examples:

Poor emotional expression: "I'm angry because you always treat me like a skivvy. Stop being so lazy and give me some help."

Good emotional expression: "I am feeling angry right now. There's so much housework to do. I would really appreciate some help. Would you dry the dishes if I wash up?"

Can you see how the second example does not force the listener onto the defensive? They are being made aware of their partner's anger without being openly blamed for it. Note also that they have been given the option of fulfilling a need rather than a command.

If you are listening to your partner's feelings, are you prepared to accept them? It can be tough to hear that they are angry or disappointed, even if they don't directly blame you. Assure your partner that you can handle what comes up. Your goal is to understand where their emotions come from, not to argue your position. Use effective listening skills from Chapter 5, such as summarizing, to clarify exactly what your partner is communicating. If you can meet their needs, follow through on the actions requested. If you can't or won't, explain why and come up with an alternative plan. By changing your behaviors to support one another, you can start building that mutual trust you will need for the long-haul.

When you just can't talk
You have the right to choose not to talk or outwardly express an emotion. This is not the same as denying your feelings or trying to cover them up. You can allow yourself to feel grief without bursting into tears. You can feel the heat of your anger without verbally or physically hitting out. Expressing your anger can simply be calmly saying, "I don't feel ready to talk about this right now," and then removing yourself from the situation.

Some couples come up with a special word that they can use to indicate the need for a timeout. Note that a request for a timeout is for the purpose of reducing 'emotional flooding,' not to end the conversation. If you can, allocate a specific time to resume talking.

When taking a timeout, let your feelings flow through you without acting. If the intensity of the emotion demands immediate action, channel that energy into something constructive (at least avoid destructive actions). For example, if you feel intensely sad, give yourself half an hour to lie down, relax, slow your breathing, and cry.

If you are furious, take a brisk walk, kick a ball about, or weed the garden. That might be all you need to take the edge off of your anger and enable you to think rationally about the situation. As explained in Chapter 5, reducing emotional flooding has been proven to improve conflict resolution.

Even hitting a pillow or shouting at an empty chair is fine, but make sure you are out of your partner's way. Expressing anger in their presence, even if not directed at them, is likely to stop them wanting to open up to you. Used as a method of control, this could even be regarded as a form of abuse.

If you are struggling with this part of the work, consider getting some couples counseling. A good therapist will model healthy emotional expression and can support you as you gradually learn to manage your feelings. Don't worry. They will never force you to express your feelings in front of your partner, and they won't trap you into making agreements you can't keep. They will help you to realize that you don't need to fear your emotions because they can't destroy you and will naturally fade.

Dealing with traumatic issues

Difficult emotions that are particularly strong or persistent are often rooted in experiences of trauma, bereavement, abuse, or neglect. You may feel that your emotions don't match the situation or you recall situations or people from the past.

I recommend you explore this with a professional therapist before tackling this part of the book. Whatever your story, you won't shock a professional therapist, and they will respect your confidentiality unless there is a risk of harm to you or somebody else.

In a nutshell

Task 7: If you haven't already, carry out the Drama Triangle exercise above.

For more guidance, read:
Berne, E. (1964). *Games people play: the psychology of human relations.* Grove Press

West, C. (1991). *The Karpman drama triangle explained.* CWTK Publications

Worden, J.W. (1991). *Grief Counselling and Grief Therapy (3rd ed.).* Brunner-Routledge

References:
Berne, E. (1964). *Games people play: the psychology of human relations.* Grove Press

Karpman, S. (1968). Fairy tales and script drama analysis. *Transactional Analysis Bulletin.* 26(7): 39–43.

Worden, J.W. (1991). *Grief Counselling and Grief Therapy (3rd ed.).* p. 141. Brunner-Routledge

PART II: MAKING UP

CHAPTER 8

HEALTHY INTIMACY: WHAT HAPPENS IN THE SACK?

One of the most reliable symptoms of unhealthy relationship issues is a reduction in sexual intimacy. This shouldn't be a surprise. If we don't feel supported or relaxed in our relationship, how can we ever create the right conditions for love-making?

If you've progressed well to this point, your sexual activity may have naturally increased. But if your sex life could be better, I recommend taking this chapter seriously. In the event there is abuse in your relationship, and your partner punishes you through sexual withdrawal, this isn't what we're talking about here. That is cruelty. That is abuse.

What we're talking about here is where sexuality wanes, the libido becomes depleted because of anxiety, low mood, depression, or other factors of course, hormonal, biological factors. But, more importantly, we have to make the distinction now between natural issues affecting sexual intimacy within a relationship and behaviors that are abusive. If you do feel you're being abused by withdrawal of sex as punishment, then please revert back to Part I, Chapter 6, the domestic violence chapter.

Creating a supportive environment
For many couples, discussing sexual matters can be uncomfortable. It's always been a taboo, the 's' word. Therefore, the first step is to create a supportive environment where you both commit to

discussing sex in a relaxed, non-judgmental manner using language and terminology you both feel happy with.

Ruling out physical and psychological causes

Many medical conditions - and/or the medications used to treat them - can directly lower libido or affect sexual performance. Diabetes patients may struggle to maintain erection, while multiple sclerosis (MS) can reduce the feeling of sexual pleasure. Also, amputees can have circulation issues which impacts on their sexual activity. Other conditions get in the way of sex indirectly. For example, you may have an illness or disability that affects how you look, move, or smell. Pain and scarring following surgery can also leave us afraid or ashamed of our bodies.

Hormonal changes are another common culprit whether due to menopause, the contraceptive pill, pregnancy, or childbirth.

Psychological issues such as stress and burnout can make us too tired and distracted to enjoy each other sexually. Alcohol and some recreational drugs are another potential source of sexual problems. In this case, simply taking some time off, catching up on lost sleep, eating healthy food, moderating alcohol, and exercising regularly can bring our sex lives back on line.

However, if our sex life is suffering because of relationship issues, we mustn't use tiredness, hormones, or pain as an excuse for your lack of intimacy. The old proverbial, "I've got a headache" does not help. It does not work. Throughout this book, you have been learning to act and react from a place of honesty. This same approach will help you to get to the root of your sexual problems and change things for the better.

Are we giving ourselves enough time to have sex?
In the early stages of a relationship - and throughout Hollywood movies - sheer passion is enough to overcome the practical barriers to love-making. People are seen in cupboards having amazing passionate sex - cars, sheds, bus stops, fields, you name it.

But in the real world, the time-consuming activities of work, household chores, hobbies, rest, and sleep can prevent us from taking the time to enjoy sex, especially for those of us who take a little while to 'get in the mood,' or have to have the situation or environment 'just so' to make us feel safe and secure.

If the opportunity to sneak off together eludes us, schedule in a convenient time to work on your sexual skills. Treat this slot as a priority. Organize childcare, if needed, disconnect from social media, and commit to only accepting emergency calls. And don't forget, if an emergency doctor can turn their phone off for half an hour, so can you.

So, what of exploring sexual needs and fantasies?
In Chapter 6, we learned how to communicate our needs and respond to requests from our partner. Our sexual needs are just an extension of that.

Sexual needs encompass everything from holding hands to hugging to kissing, mutual massage, sexual touching, and intercourse.

Sexual fantasies are a creative way to explore and meet our sexual needs. While we need to be open about our fantasies and fetishes, we must remember that all sexual activity must be consensual and safe. It is important to be clear about boundaries and to respect them. Trusting one another is crucial when learning about our mutual sexual needs and desires.

If our fantasies are likely to shock our partner, we can consider stripping them down a little bit to a more basic level to avoid potential misunderstandings. For example, if we have never been open about our S&M fetish, we can start by talking about our desire to control or to be controlled sexually. This is what exploration is all about. If our needs match, we can deepen our mutual understanding of our needs and enjoy a richer, more fulfilling love life.

If our needs conflict, we may need to compromise, perhaps by watering down scenarios to a level that we are both comfortable with. And remember, comfort is the most important thing during sex alongside communication. Sex is the most intimate way in which two people can communicate. Even if our partner's fantasy does nothing for us, we can still share in the pleasure they feel. Sex is about giving and taking; sharing.

If you are concerned about your fantasies, consider speaking to a therapist with experience in sexual issues. Or look this up online. There are lots of help pages available now. Just check out their authenticity. Professionals are ethically obliged to protect your confidence unless there is a risk of harm to you or other people.

Where did our sexuality come from?
While sexual attraction and reproduction are rooted in our biology, the ways we express (or repress) our sexuality are strongly influenced by our childhood experiences and early family environment.

Direct and indirect messages we receive as children influence whether we believe we deserve to have our sexual needs met. Receiving and giving pleasure through sexual intimacy is a wonderful thing, but if we grew up understanding that we only deserve pleasure if we are 'good,' a lack of self-esteem can negatively impact our libido. Add into this religious and cultural beliefs, and boom! We've got a perfect storm.

In many households, sex is treated as a taboo. If we were scolded for talking about sex or looking at explicit images or videos, we may feel unable to tell our partner about our deepest desires. We might struggle to let go and enjoy the moment, fearing that we are doing something bad.

Again, religious and cultural beliefs often proscribe what is normal when it comes to sex. For example, sex may be treated purely as a means of procreation. In this context, the idea of experimenting with sexual positions may seem weird. Other messages you or your partner might have absorbed include:

- Men must make the first move.
- Women who have a lot of sex are sex workers.
- Big penises are better than small ones.
- Being 'good at sex' is a natural attribute (in reality, it is a mixture of knowledge, experience, and sharing).
- Men always (and only) want intercourse.
- Women only come during intercourse.
- Good sex means simultaneous orgasms.
- Every time we have sex, we must have an orgasm.

Learning from previous sexual experiences
In healthy environments, people form their first sexual relationships as adolescents or adults. Those early experiences add another layer of complexity to our sexual education. For the first time, there are performance expectations all round.

Later relationships are profoundly affected by all of the above, and it can be difficult to identify the source of specific sexual problems. But if you are struggling to enjoy sex, despite being in a good physical condition, you may benefit from a few sessions with a qualified and experienced psychosexual therapist. Once you are comfortable with the idea of sexual intimacy, you can move on to developing those all-important sexual skills.

Important note: If you have suffered sexual abuse or trauma, either during childhood or as an adult, you should consult with a therapist or therapist who specializes in this field.

From a personal point of view, there are ways that we can become more comfortable with the sexual act if previous sexual abuse is interfering with us being comfortable with sex. I know there can be a lot of shame involved when we have been sexually abused, but maybe this is the time when we need to look at that, embrace it, and find out how it can stop impacting our life in a negative way. You will find helplines online.

Sexual skills and common issues
Learning and improving our sexual skills is a never-ending journey, and it can be fun. However, there are some key issues that we may need to address first.

Are you prioritizing your own enjoyment and fulfillment over that of your partner? Are you a people-pleaser. A successful sex life can only result from compromise.

The inability to achieve or maintain an erection is a common issue and is divided into primary and secondary erectile dysfunction. Primary erectile dysfunction is when you are never able to get an erection. This is usually a physical medical condition, so you should see your GP in the first instance and get referred. Secondary erectile dysfunction is often psychological or contextual in nature. Start by ruling out lifestyle factors (e.g., alcohol, recreational drugs, poor diet, etc.) If your situation doesn't improve, use the skills you developed in Chapter 7 to identify any emotional needs that may be getting in the way. Do this together if you can. Do you feel ashamed? Pressurized? Repeated inability to get an erection can cause performance anxiety, leading to a vicious cycle of disappointment. Once we've identified unhelpful emotions, we can use the skills we learned in the past three chapters to manage our emotions and communicate our needs to your partner.

Vaginismus is another common sexual issue whereby the muscles of the vagina contract making love-making painful or impossible. It can have complex physical and psychological foundations, and it is best to deal with or rule out any physical factors before focusing on potential psychological causes. What emotions do you feel before and during intercourse? Have you had traumatic sexual experiences in the past? If so, consider going to see a therapist with training and experience in trauma. They will work with you at your own pace. And it's an important time to pause here and question our sexuality. It may be that we're trying to be in a sexual relationship that doesn't quite fit us. It may be that you are gay, bisexual, or trans. It's been reported over and over again how trans males, when they were in relationships before transitioning, felt like they were raped each time they were in an intimate bond with their partners. And likewise with trans females, they felt like they had to perform in a way they hated, and they hated the relationship with their penises.

At this stage, if this is a problem for you, it's very important that you take very careful steps towards being comfortable with yourself, and maybe accessing professional help for sexuality and gender issues. Maybe start Googling, and see what you can do to feel more comfortable.

Do you find it difficult to achieve orgasm? This is often due to a lack of clitoral stimulation. Managing sexual stimulation is a vital skill that both partners can work on to enhance their enjoyment.

Sexual issues are often caused by a lack of arousal or by not recognizing our own arousal. Rather than focusing on the mechanics of sex or worrying about performance, spend time getting to know your body and what activities you each find pleasurable, and how to manage the intensity of pleasurable sensations for a shared positive experience.

For example, mutual full body massage, exploring each other's sexual arousal, playing with different parts of each other's body. This is all natural and very welcome in the sexual arena. Experimenting with different sexual positions or using the tongue, fingers, vibrators or other sex toys can help with clitoral or anal stimulation, while gently squeezing the penis behind the glans can delay ejaculation while maintaining an erection.

Think beyond intercourse itself. What types of genital and non-genital stimulation do you enjoy? It could be your ears being tickled, your feet being stroked. It could be all manner of things. Don't forget, sex is intimacy. It is not an aggressive, purely orgasm-related experience. Sex is two people being intimate, loving, and erotic together.

If you think you would benefit from face-to-face support in developing your sexual skills, consider looking online and seeing what other people are doing for this, or book some sessions with a fully trained psychosexual therapist. A psychosexual therapist will provide you with carefully chosen 'homework' activities to suit your unique situation. They will then discuss with you your experiences, and focus on how you both felt and how you can both improve. Baby steps.

In a nutshell

Task 8: Improving our sexual skills:
- To develop sexual skills in a relaxed environment, agree on the terminology you will use when talking about intimate matters. Some people prefer to stick to the scientific names for sexual organs and body parts, while other people feel more comfortable using everyday language. Decide with your partner on the terms you will use.
- Rule out physical causes of sexual problems by investigating how specific conditions, medications, substances, and hormonal changes can impact sexual appetite and performance. Book an appointment with your doctor if you suspect a physical cause to your sexual issues.
- Set aside some protected time to focus solely on your sexual skills; together or individually.

- Explore your sexual needs and fantasies, watering them down if necessary.
- Think about the messages we received from parents and siblings about sex. How has this affected our adult relationships?
- How much are you influenced by myths about sex (see earlier in the chapter for some common myths)? How do we get to the truth about sex? How do we feel more comfortable about sex? Start pleasuring and exploring ourselves and our partners. Let's dispel some of these unhelpful myths.
- If there is an experience of erectile dysfunction or vaginismus, again, speak to a specialist or medical doctor to identify and work with physical, lifestyle, and emotional factors.
- Do we struggle to reach orgasm? Some people do. Try different sexual techniques and positions. Share what pleasures you.
- Are you over-stimulated during sex? Prioritize pleasure over performance and non-genital over genital stimulation. Embrace each other.

For more guidance, read:
Barker, M.J. (2018). *The psychology of sex.* Routledge

Campbell, C. (2022). *Sex therapy: the basics.* Routledge

Litvinoff, S. (2001). *The Relate guide to sex in loving relationships.* Vermilion

PART II: MAKING UP

CHAPTER 9

STEPS TO A REWARDING AND SUPER FUTURE: PRACTICAL SKILLS

Always remember that we are building a new relationship. This is a new relationship; the old one didn't work. So, we're done, dusted and we're moving forward. So, our eyes must be firmly set on the road ahead. While it's fine to think back to the good times we had together, our work up to this point will have revealed how our memories like to edit out the bad stuff.

Although we will need to let go of the romantic notion of 'everything' being good back then, we can still focus on understanding specific positive experiences and recreating these in the present.

It is important that we both are honest and truthful about what we enjoyed doing together. Perhaps you really enjoyed going to rock concerts and dancing all night, or having quiet walks along the beach, or reading together on a bench. But if they were only going along to make us happy, there is a danger that we will force our new relationship down old roads that our ex won't want to return to that. It's very important, at this moment, to check out what's real, what happened for both of you, and how you can do it better, going forward. This is just about doing it better.

Spend quality time together
A new relationship must be pressure tested, so make sure you spend enough time together to enable issues to naturally arise. This will help

you to develop your communication and emotional coping skills. If you are not sharing a home, you should aim to spend quality time together on at least a weekly basis. Remember we reap as we sow. What we put in, we get out. We have to nourish, feed and cultivate these new beginnings.

While we still need to have personal space, include each other as much as possible. If important work and caring commitments are reducing our time together, we may need to cut down on individual hobbies and other activities. Make sure this is fair and reasonable; one person shouldn't make all the sacrifices. This is not sustainable moving forward. For example, if one of you plays football once a week and the other attends a book club, perhaps you could switch to fortnightly and spend the second week together instead.

Compliment each other to reinforce positive relationship behaviors. How has your partner demonstrated their support? What did they do that you appreciated? And say this to them. This may feel unnatural at first, and the recipient of the praise may react awkwardly, but persist. Consider sitting down together once a week and recalling three positive interactions from the previous seven days.

Compliment yourself too. This work is hard, and every success deserves congratulating. Give yourself an occasional treat: an hour of meditation time, a scented bath, a new pair of shoes, a steak pie from the local baker...whatever it is, treat yourself.

Above all, we need to plan our future together, sharing our dreams and building a practical way forwards that works for us both. This will bring in healing and security even if our visions are not fully aligned. As long as we are committed to moving forward together (i.e., committed to the commitment), we will probably be able to hammer out a workable compromise.

It is always good to have at least one short-term and one long-term project on the go. List your resources, clarify your timeframe, and create a 'To Do' list.

Staying on track
Just as with a new relationship, couples who get back together often experience a honeymoon period. To avoid slipping back into old habits (beware that comfy hygge energy), it is important to keep checking in with one another. How is life through your partner's eyes? Has anything changed that may need talking through?

Finally, remember to have fun. Even if there are still issues to resolve, laughter is healing in itself. And if we are recovering from an affair or deceit, we have to park that. Of course, we must be aware of the facts and any lessons to be learned, but we have to be willing to release our attachment to this as we move forward.

In a nutshell

Task 9: Focussing on the road ahead
- Keep reminding each other that we are building a new relationship, not resurrecting the old one.
- Consider bringing back activities we both used to enjoy, but check out what we *both* used to enjoy. Refer back to Chapter 6 if you need to work more on understanding each other's needs.
- Spend sufficient time together to 'pressure test' your new skills. Aim to set aside at least three periods of thirty minutes each week.

- Reinforce positive relationship behaviors with compliments.
- Praise and treat yourself.
- Plan your future destination as a couple. Invest in some short-term and long-term projects.
- Check in with each other regularly, especially if your situation has changed.
- Above all else, have fun!

For more guidance, read:

Christensen, A., Jocobson, N., and Doss, B. D. (2014). *Reconcilable differences.* Guilford Press

Matheson, C. (2009). *The art of the compliment: how to use kind words with grace and style.* Skyhorse Publishing

Ocean, J. A. (2024). *99 dates to remember: the couple's adventure guide.* Independently published

PART II: MAKING UP

CHAPTER 10

PROTECTING AND EXPANDING: NEW HORIZONS

Well, we've made it this far. Wherever you are in your relationship breakup recovery journey right now, my hope is that you now have hope for the future. But we still have some wrap-up tasks to complete before I will feel comfortable releasing you back into the world:

How do we clarify what we want for our future?
Although this chapter is in the 'Making Up' section of this book, I am opening it up to also include those who may be thinking about moving on.

Our long-term success must depend upon us stepping back and painting a clear picture of what a fulfilling future life means to us.

Now, if we've done work on ourselves through this book, and we've rethought ourselves, looked at ourselves in the mirror, and pulled ourselves inside out, it might be that we're looking for something new.

Even if we are committed to making up with our ex, we might have repositioned and rethought what a successful relationship is for us. 'Successful' is a good word for this because it encompasses all aspects of a relationship working out well for us. And successful is also a good umbrella term for what's uniquely special, precious, and necessary for us.

So, stepping back and painting a clear picture of what a fulfilling life means to us is very important right now: Where do I see myself in 10 years? Where will I be living? Will I have children or pets? What job will I have? Where will I go on holiday? What kind of lifestyle do I want? What will I do in my spare time?

We don't need to flesh out all the details; an outline will do, but we must avoid thinking in vague, romantic terms of love, happiness, and satisfaction. This is a dangerous attitude in a world where abusers lurk. We don't want to be 'ripe for the picking.'

Now let's move on to thinking specifically about our future relationship - whether with your ex or somebody else.

We've already done the work to separate the story of our past relationships from the reality, so let's use that wisdom to clarify how we will know when a partner is not measuring up (i.e., what are our boundaries; boundaries are essential at this stage).

Mark out our red lines: what we will not put up with, what is a deal-breaker for us. And yes, that does mean being prepared to walk away if those red lines are crossed. We need to set the bar high enough so that a few nice words and crumbs of affection will not be enough for our ex (or future partner) to charm us and stride over our boundaries.

Ideally, we should get our future vision in place before we renew our relationship (or start a new one). For instance, if we don't know what we're going to the store for, why go the store? We have to do a shopping list first, right? Otherwise, we just come out with a lot of stuff we don't want. Same in relationships.

It's equally important to not rely upon friends, family, etc. to tell us what we should have. Otherwise, we will be coming out of that store with all the things they want, not what you want.

A weak or unformed vision is at risk of being dominated by a stronger one. A lack of rules - boundaries - about what language and behavior is acceptable to you can quickly deteriorate into humiliation, disrespect, and being used. You may start convincing yourself that this is what 'real love' is and blaming yourself for messing things up.

In the worst case scenario, you will start saying, "Oh my gosh, I've got somebody interested in me. I'm so unloveable, I am going to grab this person because nobody might have me and I will be alone for the rest of my life." Not true. There are people out there for everyone; we just have to look and make ourselves available.

Conversely, if your partner doesn't make their rules clear, they could change them at the drop of a hat. They might disappear on a whim, leaving you in turmoil, wondering where they are, what you've done wrong, and what's in store for tomorrow. Your life is in danger of becoming a fruitless quest to make them happy. This is called coercive control and it is the worst form of cruelty. This state can last for months - even years - until you find yourself back in that storm.

For those who are thinking about moving on, it can take three or four dates before you find somebody you really want to be with and you can trust.

Don't let your self-respect crumble. Be ready to nip a relationship in the bud, especially if your previous experiences are to grab something because it is interesting you. Nip it in the bud while your self-worth is still intact. If you're grabbing hold of somebody that's paying you interest, and it feels too good to be true, step back and think about it. Take a week's break. Think about where you are.

Once an abuser has got the thin end of the wedge in, they will keep on twisting. Remember that. It can take three or four

Monitoring progress
Unless your boundaries - those red lines - have been crossed, it is better to assess the progress of your relationship by looking at overall patterns rather than individual incidents.

Having said that, at any stage of your evolving relationship, you are entitled to leave if it doesn't feel right to you. Give yourself permission to do this.

Our partnership may improve rapidly as superficial differences are resolved or a new skill is mastered. Then our progress may slow as we tackle deeper issues in our relationship. We may struggle to learn more advanced skills.

Other relationships show a slow but gradual improvement over time. These relationships often benefit the most from conscious efforts to praise and show appreciation to each other; otherwise, the steady incline can turn into a decline.

It's the same as nurturing a plant. Unless we feed it, tend to it, and pay attention to it, the plant is not going to do well. But if you are looking after it and it's not rewarding you by growing well, maybe it's a dud. Maybe you have to pluck it out and replant something else. It's that simple.

Again, if fear is keeping you in an unhealthy relationship or a relationship that is not serving you, then leave (Acton, 2021).

Then there are the erratic relationships punctuated by heated arguments and passionate makeups. If this is your general pattern, it is vital you reflect on what extra work is needed. Do you both need to revisit one or more of the relationship skills? Are you still hanging on to fake stories? Is a demon from the past haunting your present life? Remember that professional couples therapy is always an option if you need extra support during a rough patch.

Whatever your pattern, you can boost your chances of success by reminding yourselves of the problems you have solved and the situations you have handled well. During easy times, continue to practice your newfound skills and scan the road ahead for upcoming obstacles.

If you're working through this book by yourself, you may decide, at some point, to introduce it to your partner. You can revisit the book as a couple and work through all the tasks together, especially those in Parts I and II.

Keep in mind that significant life events are often going to be triggers for relationship issues (such as redundancies, menopause, children leaving home, bereavement, etc.) We need to weather these storms.

Anticipate challenges and be attentive to your partner's need to talk - even if they don't ask for a conversation. Are there any practical steps you can take to make the journey easier for you both? Again, professional couples therapy is always an option.

Work diligently at how to spot potential problems early (revisiting Chapter 2 would be a good idea.) Discuss how you will communicate your ongoing feelings about your relationship with your partner and vice versa. This doesn't have to be verbal. A smile and a hug could be the way you tell your partner that everything between you is OK, even if you're having a bad day. We all get grumpy. We all snap. This is being human. Don't beat yourself up for being imperfect. Be imperfect together, but only where it's safe and where there are sincere apologies and respect.

So, what happens if we come across a problem that cannot be solved? What if we feel uninspired by the future or a general malaise about our lives set in?

Ultimately, the hard truth could be found in Chapter 6. You simply may not meet each other's fundamental needs. If this is the case, honesty is paramount. You will need to return to the beginning of this book, and maybe walk through it again with different eyes and a different vision. Maybe you need to revisit the decision about whether to make up or move on. At this moment in time, keep in mind that your partner is not supposed to fix your life. They're not meant to make your life successful and enduring.

Your partner is there to go on the journey with you, not to make the journey for you. You have just as much right and responsibility to make your life the best it can possibly be, with or without a partner.

Consider this carefully: a successful partnership is one that complements and enriches our life, anchors us, and gives us so much sustainability that we can achieve in life. In turn, we are to complement them. This is why choosing a partner is very important. They must complement us. And in turn, we complement them.

The most important thing is: if you want to fix your relationship, fix it from within the relationship. Don't make the mistake of going elsewhere to fix it, by having an affair or wandering. It doesn't work.

Important: Keep in mind that fleeting emotions can be misleading! The best barometer of progress is our overall feelings about the future. If we are both generally positive about where we are in this relationship and where it is heading, it is likely we will handle the bumps in the road. Feeling generally happy about our health, career, appearance, and home projects, etc. is also an indication that our relationship is in a good place. Celebrate these things. Be mindful of what's not working and work on that. Remember, no relationship is perfect. It is always a work in progress.

Friends or foes: the influence of other people
At this stage, it is worth mentioning that your new relationship will affect everyone that has a connection to you both. And their reactions, opinions, and priorities will have an impact on your relationship - for better or for worse.

It could be a controlling or jealous mother who has always disapproved of your ex. She may become hostile or withdraw from your life, feeling you are betraying her by going back.
If you used to enjoy going to the gym with your partner's energetic

and positive sister, reconnecting with her could transform your fitness levels for the better.

Be wary of those with a strong interest in keeping you together or, conversely, breaking you apart. They do exist. They will be around. Are there any skeletons left in the closet that another party could reveal? If you or your partner have children, how will they react to another change in their lives? Be sure to keep them involved but don't burden them with your problems (my book *Raw Facts From Real Parents* (2022) can help you to navigate any issues you might be experiencing with your young or adult children). It's important, at this stage, to have everything on the table before going forward. Everything! Affairs, deceit, lies, etc. Otherwise these things will come back and bite you.

Friends and relatives are rarely trained therapists, so always be wary of false or biased data about how your relationship is progressing. They may mean well, but they can ultimately cause damage. Some connections may even act out their own past or current relationship dramas, and project these onto your life. Some may even be living their lives through you. This is very inappropriate and can be dangerous. If you use their information to justify staying together - or initiating another breakup - you could end up confused and stuck in a mire of blame and self-blame. You should only stay in your relationship, or leave it, if it is the best thing for you. You are important.

Every relationship is unique, and this is where our red lines - our boundaries - come in. Hold on to your deal-breakers because they *are* deal breakers!

If agreements about acceptable behavior are broken, your firm stance makes it harder for your partner to shift the blame on to you, even if their friends or family members rally behind them or plead with you to give them another chance or to attend professional help. If you are bowing to third party pressure rather than following your own North Star, you will probably sabotage therapy with resentment.

If a deal-breaker has been hit, it's over. This is why it's so important to really think about your boundaries and deal-breakers. If they were created in your truth, you can walk on and rest assured that the relationship wasn't for you.

If you feel that friends or relatives - yours or your partner's - are pushing an agenda, minimize contact for a while, at least until they get the message that your relationship is none of their business. For some very pushy people, you might have to use language such as, "We really appreciate your concern and interest, but at the moment, we are really trying to work out things for ourselves."

There is one important caveat: if your friends or family members raise concerns about domestic abuse, or what doesn't seem to be sitting right, it would be wise to reflect upon their words. Remember, you can always visit Part I, Chapter 6 for more guidance.

Celebrate the new 'us'
My final piece of advice to you is to mark your success with a makeup ritual. You could plant a tree; buy a set of new rings; write some faux nuptials or organize a special ceremony (for just the two of you or with friends).

Agree on the date you formally got back together and celebrate your first and subsequent anniversaries with a card and gifts. This is a great time to reflect on the profound journey you have both been on and to recharge your relationship with energy. It is part of the all-important glue that can keep you together through the tough times.

Feel free to celebrate additional milestones - maybe with a special meal or a glass of wine: a week without an argument, first sex since getting back together, six months together. There are no rules about what to include, but to celebrate each other is a sign of an amazing accomplishment. As you commit yourself to the future, you are breaking free from the past, creating your own traditions as you head off into the sunset, endless new paths expanding in front of you.

Every day, see your cup as half full. Every day be grateful that you have a partner that was willing, able, and motivated to treasure your relationship as much as you do. Don't judge others. Some partners are unable to, or don't want to make up with their exes. It rarely happens permanently. Although the stats say that a large proportion of people get back together again, there are not the longitudinal studies to show how long their reunion lasted. And if we take into account that divorce rates are way over 50% worldwide, that's an indicator of how many relationships fail. And maybe it's like careers. In the 21st Century, people don't have one career through their whole lives anymore. In the present socio-economic environment, people have to move from job to job.

Maybe this is a new relationship model moving forward: that people don't generally get together for 60 years. Maybe we are meant to have multiple relationships through different stages of our lives; and this is OK, too.

Remember, you are important. And ultimately, whether you are staying with your ex or embarking on a new relationship, it is to complement you. It is for you to be happy and peaceful. And consider this carefully: if you have come from a toxic, unhealthy relationship before this wonderful one, then you may feel a little bit bored at times because you are not living on a knife edge, wondering what's going to happen next. Embrace peace. Embrace moments of boredom. It's really good to think about and restructure life.

I wish you all the success in the world moving forward, and I'd like to think there's a little piece of me and this book and my work in your future lives together. Thank you.

John: *I feel free. I've got my power back.*

In a nutshell

Task 10: Future proofing your relationship:
- Note down some answers to the following questions: Where do you see yourself in 10 years? Where will you be living? Will you have children or pets? What job will you have? Where will you go on holiday? What will you do in your spare time?
- Note down at least three deal-breakers: What are your relationship red lines? What language and behavior will you not put up with?
- Ask yourself, 'What does success look like in a relationship?' 'What does a complementary relationship look like to me?'
- Ask your partner to specify their red lines.
- What is your relationship healing pattern? Slow, gradual improvement or heated arguments followed by reconciliation? Did things get better quickly before deeper issues reared their heads? Revisit how you can do this better.

- How will you 'troubleshoot' your relationship to keep things on track?
- Scan the earlier chapters of Part II. Do you need to brush up on any of the relationship skills?
- Are you generally happy with your life and relationship?
- List 10 important people in your lives (five from each partner). Note down whether you feel they will support, oppose, or be neutral about your relationship. Who stays and who goes? Decide between you how you will handle their influence (e.g., not see them, only see them as a couple, talk through your differences, etc.)?
- Has any friend or relative suggested you may be in an abusive relationship (as abusee or perpetrator)? This is a red flag. Re-read Part I, Chapter 6, and be kind to yourself and your partner. This needs to be addressed. There is usually a fragment of truth in a suggestion.
- Who will be your source/s of support outside your relationship? How will you access that support?
- If you have children, how do they feel about your reunion? How about your partner's children? Are you giving the children a voice? Are you providing them with love and security?
- How will you celebrate your success and milestones?

For more guidance, read:
Acton. M. (2021). *Learning how to leave.* Life Logic Publishing

Acton. M. (2022). *Raw facts from real parents.* Life Logic Publishing

Vision Board Book. (2024). *Our future, our dreams.* Independently published

Dr. Michael Acton

References:
Acton. M. (2021). *Learning how to leave.* Life Logic Publishing

Acton. M. (2022). *Raw facts from real parents.* Life Logic Publishing

"When we forgive, we heal. When we let go, we grow."

- Dr. Michael Acton -

12 Signs we are Being Toxic to Ourselves

1. In our life, people put us down and we let this happen.
2. We are too thin-skinned and vulnerable to other's people's opinions of us.
3. All we want is for people to love us, so we have no boundaries in case we lose them.
4. We are worried we are 'too much' and feel we are not allowed to voice our opinions and ideas
5. We don't know ourselves enough, so we don't see there is much to take care of. We do things for others not ourselves.
6. When we try to stand up for our needs, people get angry and turn tables on us. So, we don't, we let people walk over us.
7. As humans, we are all perfectly imperfect. However, we want people to understand that we are perfect by being strong, masking emotions, and trying to take care of others. By doing so, we reject and throw ourselves under the bus. Because we are ultimately imperfect. And of course, us people-pleasers and do-gooders may hate that about ourselves.
8. We feel we've made so many mistakes that we don't trust our instincts/opinions
9. We are frightened to be successful, so we attract people who feel safe but are the opposite. They are not our people. We settle for less in money, people, love, work, etc.
10. We always put others first and feel we need to fix them. Our own hard knocks make us feel we need to do this for others and protect them instead of us.
11. We are shit at boundaries. We don't have enough knowledge or understanding of what they are or what they are for.
12. We take everything too personally and don't trust ourselves or others. We pay far too much attention to what others think about us.

PART III

MOVING ON

PART III: MOVING ON

CHAPTER 1

TOUGHEST DECISION TO MAKE

"Be mindful: we only heal if we were to forgive, and we only grow if we were to let go."
- Dr. Michael Acton -

Whichever way we talk about it, leaving someone we love or have a history with, or are invested with, is probably one of the most difficult things we could ever do in our lifetime because it is completely against human nature and how we form bonds and attachments.

It can be absolutely heart-wrenching, raw, inconceivable, overwhelming, and hopeless. But what a relief it can be, too!

Our first task in breaking up with our ex is to pull ourselves off the path, pause life, and have a good look at what we're doing and go over what our life's been so far. It's so important to pause: no knee-jerk reactions.

While we are pausing, it's so important to use this time to get ourselves ready for the journey ahead. It's going to take health, balance, determination, understanding, very good parenting of self, and a lot of grit.

During this pause, it's also important to stretch our legs a little bit, make sure we're hydrated and eating good food, and we have to put ourselves in the right headspace for the journey ahead. We're not going to get there if we don't take care of ourselves, and this is probably going to be the most stressful time of our lives.

When someone dies, we have to deal with it because they died. When we leave somebody, we're making an elective choice to change our lives. We are putting ourselves in a position of change.

I can't emphasize enough that our priority, at this point in time, is our personal safety and the safety of all those that depend upon us (children, parents, pets, whoever that might be.) If there is violence of any kind, or a stalking risk, please re-read Part I, Chapter 6, and take steps to protect yourself.

I explain to everyone who crosses my path, listens to my lectures, reads my books, or sees me as a patient: only leave when it's the right time for you and in a safe way (Acton, 2021).

Remember: if you are in physical danger, or if you feel you could be a danger to yourself, seek emergency help.

In all other cases, it is better to take a measured approach to maximizing our safety.

Self-care tips for moving
Safety includes making provision for self-care. While some of the chapters ahead will focus specifically on certain aspects of self-care, here are some general tips to ensure you are in as good a place as possible as you progress towards moving on permanently.

• Be mindful to stay connected with others. Phone a person every day (see Chapter 8).
• Allow yourself to feel the pain (see Chapter 7).
• Stick to sleep, healthy meals, and hygiene routines (see next section and Chapter 4).

- Be in nature. Get fresh air (see next section).
- If you have children, check in with them during this time. Understand they are going through their own journey of grief. With the exception of education, health, and wellbeing, they are the CEOs of their own lives, in many ways (Acton, 2022)
- Limit social media and depressing news. Really! Laugh every day. Play a funny YouTube video. Enjoy a good hour of cheerful content every day (See Chapter 9).
- Most of all, be tolerant and kind to yourself.

Physical self-care moving on: medication and physical health
Once we accept that relationship breakup can be as intense as bereavement, we have to consider that it might be bad for our health. According to studies cited by Skinner (2021), high scores on grief assessments have been linked to systemic inflammation, blood clots, and other risk factors for heart disease. Don't be alarmed, but this is real research. It is important we take it one step at a time and take care of ourselves through this process.

Protective factors against this risk include paying attention to eating well, getting adequate sleep and rest, exercising, attending to personal hygiene, and spending time in nature and/or with animals - in short, have a simple life and take care of yourself. If you have to work excessive hours, if you have no time to yourself in many ways, make the time. Everyone can make one hour a day.

SSRIs/anti-depressants can ruin lives!
Most people when they first go through a breakup and are moving on from a relationship can exhibit signs similar to depression, and they may even get depression. Anxiety is a large part of depression. In this day and age, most people go to their GP/family doctor if they

can't cope, and the doctor's MO is to subscribe Selective Serotonin Reuptake Inhibitors (SSRIs) when that happens. SSRIs have their place, but unfortunately, they are over-prescribed and prescribed wrongly for grief With grief, we have to move through a process, and SSRIs arrest and delay that process.

Those involved in the manufacture, design, and prescribing of SSRIs for people grieving a relationship loss - whether through breakup or bereavement - should be sued, in my mind!

While anti-depressants, as with many types of medication, have their place, supporting people through relationship loss is not it. SSRIs may, if they do work, simply help to arrest the grieving process. Once the person comes off the medication, which they will have to do at some point, the loss still has to be processed.

Unfortunately, SSRIs have huge numbers of side effects. One of these is loss of libido (sexual drive), which can be a problem if you are in a situation where you are trying to repair your relationship. Anther common side effect is weight gain. If you are prescribed SSRIs, always read the patient information leaflet that comes with the medication. If you have any questions, go back to your GP or family doctor and talk to them. SSRIs are only supposed to be prescribed as an adjunct to psychotherapy and only for a short period of time (three to six months) whilst being monitored all the way through.

Unfortunately, GPS/doctors and other medical health professionals are prescribing SSRIs without any of this follow-up and without ensuring the patient is undergoing psychotherapy.

Menopause, medication, and moving on
Some women in their forties have even been prescribed anti-depressants for what turned out to be menopausal symptoms.

An ABC show that was aired on 13th May 2022 on the topic of women's health, menopause, and depression highlighted the use of SSRIs in treating menopausal symptoms. The program featured a woman who found that anti-depressants worsened her symptoms in marked contrast to the hormone replacement therapy (HRT) she tried afterwards.

Mental and physiological health issues, in all their forms, can contribute to a relationship breakdown, which can then, of course, lead to a relationship breakup. If your relationship is going through a rocky patch and you're considering leaving, it is always worth checking this out if you are in this age bracket or if there are mental health issues.

In a nutshell

Task 1: Attend to your safety and wellbeing:
- If violence or stalking are a risk, re-read the relevant Part I chapters and take appropriate action.
- Talk to a friend or relative every day. Do not hibernate. Push yourself out there.
- Slow down and allow yourself to feel the pain. Yes, it is tough, but this too shall pass.
- Follow healthy sleep, meal, and hygiene routines.
- Get plenty of fresh air and be in nature.
- Check in with children and other family members.

- Limit social media and depressing news.
- Be tolerant and kind to yourself.
- If you are on SSRIs, have a rethink with your GP/doctor or health provider about what you're taking and why.

For more guidance, read:
Acton. M. (2022). *Raw facts from real parents.* Life Logic Publishing

Acton, M. (2021). *Learning how to leave.* Life Logic Publishing

Thompson, K. (2007). *Medicines for mental health: the ultimate guide to psychiatric medication.* Booksurge Publishing

References:
Acton. M. (2022). *Raw facts from real parents.* Life Logic Publishing

Acton. M. (2021). *Learning how to leave.* Life Logic Publishing

Skinner, Q. (2021, November 18). *The sixth stage of grief.* Life Time. https://experiencelife.lifetime.life/article/the-sixth-stage-of-grief/

PART III: MOVING ON

CHAPTER 2

HOW 'DO' WE BEST DO THIS: RESOURCES

Ensuring our safety goes hand in hand with managing our resources. Just as we need fuel, water, life jackets, map, etc. to ensure a safe and comfortable boat trip, so we need to gather everything we might possibly need before moving on to some of the practical matters in Chapter 3 (securing child custody, dividing assets, managing the legal separation process, etc.)

First, let's see what we're already carrying with us.

There are many things that can affect our journey right now. For most people, a financial change can happen during the process of moving on. It could be that we've worked our whole lives to contribute, and our partner's not sharing what was ours in the relationship, what we built together. This can leave us in a difficult position.

We could be looking at health, age, reputation, work, juggling children, etc. Many factors affect how well we do at this time. Some are protective, helping us to cope with the changes we are going through. Others create risks that we need to manage.
Some of these factors will partly dictate how we move forward, but we must protect our rights.

As Thema Bryant said in her book *Homecoming* (2022), never let anyone take the food from your table or the money from your pocket, but this can be expanded. We must make sure people don't take away our right to privacy, our safety at home, and our future opportunities.

If you need to find more about protective factors when moving on from toxic relationships, please see my book *Learning how to Leave* (Acton, 2021).

These resources mentioned above include 'things' (such as money, car, a place to stay, medicines, plane or train tickets, etc.), services (school places, health services) and emotional and psychological support (psychotherapy, friends, family members). Resources even include drugs or alcohol (if you are managing an addiction). And if you have healthcare issues and disabilities, we need to also consider what you need for those. If you've had to move, your new home may not be as suitable for your needs. Accessing your new GP/family doctor surgery could be fraught with difficulties.

So, spend some real time investigating what resources are available to you in your local community, whether it's the same one you were in or whether you have had to move to a new one. Some grief-related services may be appropriate at this point because we are moving on, and we are realizing that there has been a loss of many things including identity, relationship, safety, and security. Change automatically brings a feeling of grief. Many of these have sprung up to meet the needs of people who have rejected professional therapy, so you may be surprised with what support you can find with a simple Google search. Nowadays, fortunately, it's even easier to access resources, in some respects, because we can do online psychotherapy and support without being in a specific geographical area. Sometimes this is important. For example, if you have a job or known position in the local area, you can choose to access services in a different area to avoid being the subject of local gossip.

In a nutshell

Task 2: We need to take stock of our resources and note, in our journals, what we need:
- What physical resources can we draw upon?
- What services can we access?
- Who will provide us with emotional support?
- How are we going to take care of and parent ourselves better? What can we do to laugh once a day, take time out once a day, and be with ourselves once a day?
- Try a 15m guided meditation once a day. Having someone talk you through something can be enough to quieten our minds during this unpredictable stage.
- Above all else, be kind to yourself.

For more guidance, read:
Acton. M. (2021). *Learning how to leave.* Life Logic Publishing

Bryant, T. S. (2022). *Homecoming.* TarcherPerigee.

Pollard, J. K. (1987). *Self parenting: the complete guide to your inner conversations.* The SELF-PARENTING Program.

References:

Acton. M. (2021). *Learning how to leave.* Life Logic Publishing

Bryant, T. S. (2022). *Homecoming.* TarcherPerigee.

"IT'S NOT ABOUT THE LAW, ITS ABOUT
DOING WHAT'S RIGHT"
- DR. MICHAEL ACTON -

PART III: MOVING ON

CHAPTER 3

HOLD ON BOYS, IT'S GOING TO BE A BUMPY RIDE: THE BATTLEGROUND

"We can't glue wings on a caterpillar and expect it to fly like a butterfly. We must change from within."
(Keep in mind, we cannot change others, but we *can* change ourselves)

A famous saying from Bette Davis is quite fitting here: "Fasten your seatbelts, it's going to be a bumpy ride."

Every journey towards permanent breakup is different, but many begin on a busy highway with aggressive driving, flashing lights and blaring horns... welcome to 'The Battleground!'

As my study confirmed (see Part I, Chapter I and Appendix A), the process of separation involves many practical considerations. These usually need immediate attention and cover everything from buying and selling property to arranging child custody to signing divorce papers to negotiating new relationships to getting ourselves back in shape for dating.

During the breakup process, one or both of us might act out our pain in this practical sphere. I call this 'The Battleground' because it is a war full of politics, allies, and enemies, and some of these people even shift camp, something you are probably already aware of. I very rarely come across a relationship breakup (even outside of my patient population) that doesn't involve some tension and conflict. *

Unless we are one of the few people who either have limited shared assets or a mutual amicable approach to everything practical, we must quickly steel ourselves for this imminent battle. We don't have the luxury of time. And guess what, now is the time to choose our battles wisely.

Fortunately, no-fault divorces are now legal in some countries, and some divorce coaches have even created models to help their clients navigate their way to an agreeable solution, as illustrated on the next page (Hope, 2023). However, irrespective of how easy the law is now making it for people to make decisions based on their personal experiences, wants and needs, it doesn't take away from the process of disentangling ourselves from what the relationship was and who the person was within it.

Assets and Agency

A lot of our stress during relationship breakup is related to the dividing of assets. This is one massive area that falls outside of the scope of grief models. Yet when our ex turns up unexpectedly outside our former shared home with a trailer, it can almost feel like a corpse has returned from the grave.

If we feel that another's agency threatens our own freedom (e.g., our ex pursues our property, money, or custody over children), we can experience reactance - an unpleasant sensation that motivates us to fight to protect or reclaim that freedom. Similarly, if our ex is not reasonably and thoughtfully sharing what our assets are from that relationship, it can create a further feeling of abuse, disempowerment and the need to fight to reclaim what's rightfully ours.

Agreeable
one couple + one team

The Agreeable Pathway - what your journey will look like

AGREE
Assemble → Gather → Review → Evaluate → Enable

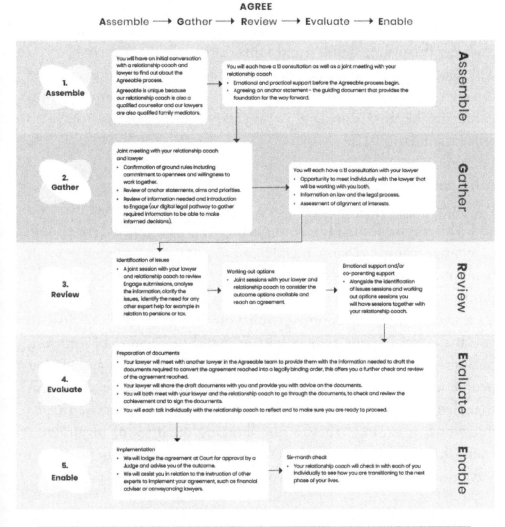

1. Assemble

You will have an initial conversation with a relationship coach and lawyer to find out about the Agreeable process.

Agreeable is unique because our relationship coach is also a qualified counsellor and our lawyers are also qualified family mediators.

You will each have a 1:1 consultation as well as a joint meeting with your relationship coach
- Emotional and practical support before the Agreeable process begin.
- Agreeing on anchor statement – the guiding document that provides the foundation for the way forward.

Assemble

2. Gather

Joint meeting with your relationship coach and lawyer
- Confirmation of ground rules including commitment to openness and willingness to work together.
- Review of anchor statements, aims and priorities.
- Review of information needed and introduction to Engage (our digital legal pathway to gather required information to be able to make informed decisions).

You will each have a 1:1 consultation with your lawyer
- Opportunity to meet individually with the lawyer that will be working with you both.
- Information on law and the legal process.
- Assessment of alignment of interests.

Gather

3. Review

Identification of issues
- A joint session with your lawyer and relationship coach to review Engage submissions, analyse the information, clarify the issues, identify the need for any other expert help for example in relation to pensions or tax.

Working out options
- Joint sessions with your lawyer and relationship coach to consider the outcome options available and reach an agreement.

Emotional support and/or co-parenting support
- Alongside the identification of issues sessions and working out options sessions you will have sessions together with your relationship coach.

Review

4. Evaluate

Preparation of documents
- Your lawyer will meet with another lawyer in the Agreeable team to provide them with the information needed to draft the documents required to convert the agreement reached into a legally binding order, this offers you a further check and review of the agreement reached.
- Your lawyer will share the draft documents with you and provide you with advice on the documents.
- You will both meet with your lawyer and the relationship coach to go through the documents, to check and review the achievement and to sign the documents.
- You will each talk individually with the relationship coach to reflect and to make sure you are ready to proceed.

Evaluate

5. Enable

Implementation
- We will lodge the agreement at Court for approval by a Judge and advise you of the outcome.
- We will assist you in relation to the instruction of other experts to implement your agreement, such as financial adviser or conveyancing lawyers.

Six-month check
- Your relationship coach will check in with each of you individually to see how you are transitioning to the next phase of your lives.

Enable

If there is any gaslighting or abuse at any time during the breakup, do not throw the ball back. Unless there is reasonable communication, stay away. If there are disputes over money, custody, education, property, etc., you may need to instruct a mediator. Find someone whom you trust to be a mediator because you will not be able to take on that role yourself. If you don't know of a mediator, and this is a serious situation where you could lose a lot of your assets (money, furniture, family heirlooms, clothes, whatever it is), you will need to consider instructing a lawyer and settle your disputes through the courts. This can get expensive, time-consuming, and damaging because during this process, you are going to have to relive the relationship.

Allies and enemies

If things were to get nasty, how do we work out who is a true friend and who might be an ally of our partner? It's not unusual for people to change camps. Many people only support coupledom, so in breakup, those who used to do things with you as a couple might dump one or both of you as individuals because you no longer fit their needs and wants. Some people you thought were very close to you may choose your ex over you. It could be because of location, business opportunity, greed, whatever it is. We have to accept that people do choose, for whatever reason, and we have to accept that this is them now. If they are willing to do this, maybe they're not worth pursuing. They're not showing qualities of loyalty and friendship, irrespective of who's saying what, when and how. Best to leave them in the rearview mirror.

It is important, at this point, to let go of the need to know. It is natural to want to control the actions of those around us, especially our ex. We want our ex to be reasonable, our relatives to side with us, our friends to have our back, but none of this is within our control and sometimes it just plain doesn't happen.

When I tell a person that there is nothing they can do to change their partner, mother, brother, sister, friend, boss, coworker, etc., they often look at me as if I were crazy, but it's a fact. We can only choose our own attitude and behavior, and others will either fall in or out of line with that. We must find ways of taking small but strategic steps towards a better life, with or without the support of our ex or the blessings of our family and friends.

Bear in mind, if we were in a relationship where we were trying to make changes and sometimes our ex showed some promise that they might change, but didn't, they were never going to change because they didn't see the need to change. They didn't have the motivation to change. We can change ourselves; that's our power. Here is an adaptation from my favorite prayer, the Serenity Prayer:

Give me the serenity (patience, understanding, etc.) to stay with what I cannot change,
Give me the strength to change what I can,
And the wisdom to know the difference.

That is our absolute gift right now to understand that. The strength to change ourselves and what we can change; the patience, understanding, and serenity to be with what we cannot change (i.e., our ex) and the wisdom to know the difference.

Be selective of which of your ex's connections you keep in your life. Some people will be helpful, some people won't be. Consider cutting off some of the significant people that would do nothing but remind you of your ex or shield you from the truth about them.

The worst thing we can have is disingenuous people around us, and that includes people that pretend they haven't seen our ex when they have or pretend they're not supportive of our ex when they are. That's a betrayal in itself, and who needs to make excuses for friends who aren't supporting us or being real. If they are open about spending time with and supporting your ex, that can be fine, but they must lay it all out on the table. We don't want any surprises.

Thin line between love and hate
Consider this carefully: in a court of law, the lawyers fight to win. There is no such thing as pure justice. But when it comes to child protection, we have to do everything within our power to make sure our children and anyone that is dependent upon us (geriatric adults, disabled siblings, etc.) are visible, have a voice and are OK.

Unfortunately, one of the biggest battlegrounds in a breakup is that around children and dependents. It's been my life's work to protect children and give them a voice. Annie Lennox aptly sang, "It's a thin line between love and hate." (Poindexter, Poindexter & Members, 1971). When hate is part of a relationship, it seems that some people will justify using anything to hurt their ex, and this will include using dependents for personal retribution and to play games, etc.

The biggest problem with human beings is that we kid ourselves in times of pain and crisis. Be honest with yourself. Look at the children and other dependents involved and consider, 'What's the best outcome for you, right now? What could I let go of or fight further for to make you OK?' Too often, children are made to be with abusive parents, so fight as much as you can to make sure they are safe. Do this legally, carefully, and kindly.

Be mindful, at this stage we must make sure we're safe by locking down every bank account. If we have children at school, we must make sure that reception understands about access and who has custody. Chapters 22, 23, and 29 of my book Raw Facts for Real Parents will provide you with additional support when protecting children following your decision to move on (Acton, 2022).

In a nutshell

Task 3: Start preparing yourself for practical matters that have arisen due to your breakup:
- Take a measured approach and be practical when getting what's rightfully yours.
- Resist the urge to get involved in emotional arguments with your ex.
- Find an impartial third party who can play the role of mediator.
- Plan for the possibility of court.
- Make a list of people whom you and your ex are personally connected to. Who can you trust?
- If you are unsure of a contact's allegiance, arrange a meeting with them to gain clarity.
- Who must you cut out of your life? Don't try to change them. Let them go.
- What is the best outcome for children and other dependents? What could you let go of or fight further for to secure their health and wellbeing.

For more guidance, read:
Acton, M. (2022). *Raw facts from real parents.* Life Logic Publishing

Caine, T., Leigh, S., Lister, M., Nettleton, C., McCann, K., and Bell, D. (2021). *Your divorce handbook.* Stellar Books LLP.

Woodall, K., and Woodall, N. (2009). *The guide for separated parents: putting children first.* Piatkus

References:
Acton. M. (2022). *Raw facts from real parents.* Life Logic Publishing

Hope, G. (2023, January 01). Our Agreeable model: utilizing our mediation skills in a new way. https://www.familylawpartners. co.uk/blog/our-agreeable-model-utilising-our-mediation-skills-in-a-new-way

Poindexter, Richard, Poindexter, Robert, and Members J. (1971). Thin Line Between Love and Hate [Song]. Atco Records

"There's a difference between being patient and wasting your time."

- Dr. Michael Acton -

PART III: MOVING ON

CHAPTER 4

EASY DOES IT: NO KNEE-JERK REACTIONS

As humans, whenever we're cornered we are going to react, but when we are trying to sort things out and move forward, this is the worst time to have sporadic, knee-jerk reactions.

This chapter is not rocket science. It provides very practical ways of being in our truth and not getting caught up in the chaos of a breakup.

We've battled our way through a noisy and very difficult times with ringing in our ears and chaos all around us.

Whatever reasons led to us leaving or being left, now is the time to be quieter, more considered, and more open and aware of what's going on because believe it or not, we're not out of the woods yet. This is still a treacherous path we're taking, with many bumps, twists, and turns.

Despite the recent disruption, now is not the time to engage in speeding along in life being reckless and crazy. We need to stick to the rules of the road in many ways to keep us and those we love safe. An don't forget, this too shall pass; we just need to get through this bumpy part of the ride.

We all need to go to our place of comfort sometimes, but try not to overeat or drink too much or take drugs. If you do recreational drugs, keep them to a minimum and bear in mind the fallout time. Our mind is going through massive changes. We must drink lots of water for the shock, get out and exercise as much as possible, and keep everything else in moderation.

We have to keep everything going, so please be focused at work - or in the activities that bring us money. We have to be sustainable during this process. We have to take care of ourselves. Yes, life is tough but we also have to be practical.

Unless we have to at this stage (e.g., due to divorce, safety, etc.), this isn't the time to make massive, significant life changes (like selling our home, moving overseas, adopting a pet, etc.) This may initially seem a good way to escape our pain and do things differently, but it can make us feel even more lost and insecure when we make bad choices. We can't make decisions about what's for dinner when the kitchen's on fire. It's just impossible. Let's put out each of the fires in the kitchen and let the smoke die down before we start writing the menu. Only at this time can we work out what to cook for dinner. We have to keep things going as they are for a year or two to let the ashes settle. We need to spend that time on reflection, and only make decisions once we're well on the way to healing and the skies are clearer (See Chapter 6).

Should we find somebody else?
As explained in Part I, most of us have an innate drive to seek fellow humans when we are in crisis. Although we have patched ourselves up following our relationship wreck, we are not yet fully healed. While you may feel ready to meet other people by, for example, joining a dating app, be careful because screwing around or jumping

into another serious relationship this soon after a breakup may not help us to permanently heal. Yes, there are amazing success stories of staying with somebody we had an affair with or finding true love right after, but this is very rare. Instead, you could well be jumping from the frying pan into the fire!

At this point, we have spent time, in Part I, ruthlessly pulling apart the story of our former relationship, so we must be careful not to create new fake stories featuring our latest romantic interest. If we've already hooked up with somebody new, we may be telling ourselves that we've moved on to something better, but at this stage of our work, it could just be a temporary band aid. No relationship is perfect, nor can we replace someone instantly; it takes time. If you hurry into a new relationship you are unlikely to have processed the fallout from your previous one. This is the definition of a risky 'rebound relationship.'

Rebound relationships may seem to work out at first, but often end up being unhappy and toxic. Now, rebound relationships can be healthy, they can help somebody move on from grief. However, usually, in my experience of being a relationship specialist for three decades, the person has not had time to adjust, and the people in the relationship have not had time to learn about each other before grabbing hold of each other, with everything they have, to make it work. We need more longitudinal studies looking at the long-term effects of rebound relationships (i.e., relationships that happen very quickly after a breakup).

Even those who stay together often find themselves trapped in an unfulfilling, unhealthy relationship because one or both partners hasn't grieved properly.

It's very important to learn from our mistakes, and allow ourselves time to recover from the heartbreak and the trauma. If our ex went off with somebody new, don't put them or their new relationship on a pedestal. Everything might seem rosy, but all may not be good in paradise because nothing is ever perfect in this world.

On the other hand, dating can help you to understand more about your present truth and future needs. We may realize that we miss our ex more than we realized or that we want to be on our own.

Really think about what you want before you bring something new in. Thinking about what we want usually reflects what we didn't get from the last relationship. It might also illuminate those hooks of familiarity and security we explored in Part I of this book.

Again, my message is moderation rather than abstinence. Be kind in everything we do, especially to ourselves, and think about there being no ceiling to what we want to achieve.

In a nutshell

Task 4: Balance your life as much as possible by:
- Sticking to a healthy life plan (diet, exercise, etc.)
- Minimizing alcohol and drug use.
- Drinking plenty of water. Your body is in shock.
- Keeping our work and home life steady.
- Taking new relationships slowly - friendships and romance interests.

For more guidance, read:
Castenskiold, E. (2013) *Restored lives: recovery from divorce and separation.* Monarch books

Leckie, T. (2023) *Don't be desperate: get over your breakup with clarity and dignity.* Trina Leckie

McFadden, W. (2022). *Painkiller: everything you need to know about rebound relationships.* Independently published

PART III: MOVING ON

CHAPTER 5

KEEP OUT OF THEIR HEAD: YOU ONLY THINK YOU KNOW THEM

Depended upon the circumstances, of course, but continued exchanges with our ex are likely to slow down our journey to a healthy permanent breakup. It will reduce our ability to move on fully and to regain control over our new, exciting life. It will create difficulty in our ability focus clearly on what the road ahead looks like, and we also might even make a wrong turn, depending upon what the dialogue is about and how it may change us. Sometimes it fills us with false hope, sometimes it's full of challenges, sometimes it's a continuation of abuse.

If the exchanges are about child welfare or other issues that are going on, of course that is natural and acceptable. But they are more than likely going to be of one of the types I mentioned before, so beware. Maybe consider safe times to talk. If your ex is struggling because you left or if you are struggling because your ex left, maybe talk about that in a controlled environment. Most relationship psychotherapists will do 'breakdown of relationship' work with you, and it usually takes only five to ten sessions to clearly mark that with somebody and help practically. So, a relationship coach or psychotherapist is something you might want to look at.

Keep in mind that communication channels don't always need to be completely shut down, but I recommend turning down the noise by limiting contact - at least for a while. Let go. Don't stalk. Don't fixate on their social media profiles.

I don't agree with those who say that we should unfollow or unfriend as a knee-jerk reaction. You may need to know broadly what they are doing for reasons of safety (e.g., if they are on a trip with the children) or strategy (e.g., if they are claiming poverty in court while living it up on Instagram). It can even be useful to test your progress along the breakup route. Look at one of their recent Facebook posts and ask yourself, 'Are my feelings the same for you? Do I miss this?' If you do feel yourself getting hooked back in, remind yourself why you left. Why was there not enough glue. Or, if they left, remind yourself why they left and maybe of what has been better since they left.

It is so vital at this stage to not to troll your ex. This can be very difficult, but it's important. You've loved them; at the very least, you've been with them for a long time. Don't trash them and don't trash yourself. Be kind to yourself and them. Remember, life unfolds as it's meant to.

If you've been in a relationship for a number of years in which you have both been invested, the worst thing one of you can do is ghost the other. It shows more about their inability to be adult and reasonable moving forward. After so many years together, there will be things that need to be ironed out. There will be parts of your lives that are entangled that need to be disentangled. And there are bound to be assets of some description to divide between you.

Bear in mind, whatever the reason for your breakup, it's important to be thoughtful to self and other. Even if this may seem so alien to you right now, it's important to forgive, forget, and move on with kindness and compassion. And remember, this too shall past.

In a nutshell

Task 5:

- Whether you left or were left, reduce or cease communication with your ex, but be polite and reasonable about it. Clearly you see no hope of reconciliation at this time, otherwise you wouldn't be in this part of the book. This strategy will help you avoid the hooks and binds.
- Your journal is your friend. Whatever you would want to say to your ex or share, say it to your journal first. Sometimes sharing something with your journal is enough because what you really needed was to share it with yourself.
- If there are children or animals involved and you really don't want to talk to your ex, at the very least make sure your ex knows about their wellbeing via a third party. And if there are any court issues going on regarding care and control of children or animals, you have to be mindful to abide by those court rulings even though they may seem to be unfair.
- Above all else be reasonable, otherwise it can come back and bite you.

For more guidance, read:
Gershon, I. M. (2010). *The breakup 2.0: disconnecting over new media.* Cornell University Press

Kruse, C. J. (2017). *A guide on how to stop arguing.* CreateSpace

Zahariades, D. (2022). *The art of letting go.* Independently published

PART III: MOVING ON

CHAPTER 6

WHAT DO WE REALLY, REALLY WANT?

So, let's recap:

We're safe, we have most of the resources we need, we're back in control of practical matters, we've moderated our comforts and reduced communication with our ex to a minimum, we've realized that seriously difficult relationships do pass, and we are considering our amazing future.

Whenever the sky ahead is clear, it's a good time to take stock and check our bearings. This is our life to live; it's that simple. We're living in this amazing world of natural beauty.

It's time to let our truth - our authentic story that we told in Part I, Chapter 4 - be our guiding North Star. Whenever we act, we must make sure we are being fair and reasonable and not using our story as ammunition for residual anger about what happened back then in the rearview mirror.

Being in our truth is both the most important and the hardest thing to do in the world because we, as humans, are our own worst enemies in times. We made a good start with the tasks in Part I, Chapter 4, but this work is ongoing and it takes most of us a very long time to master it.

Our core is naturally geared for survival, and that leads us to distort facts to protect our self-esteem. The best way to combat this is journaling. Make your journal your best friend ever, which is why which is why I made keeping a journal the very first task in this book.

If you have been brushing over this, start now. You might want to open your journal with the date of the breakup and what's happened since then, and where you are now. Also, by reading our journal and going back to different times - maybe this time last month or this time last year - we will see our progress. It is a reminder of how we were, not how we are.

Whether you prefer to journal in the morning or just before bed, on a bus ride to work, or sitting on the loo, don't just write; challenge what you're writing. Re-read older entries and ask yourself, 'Is that the truth now?' As time goes on, we will find ourselves thinking, 'Oh gosh! I said that, but that wasn't actually quite right. This is what I think happened, now. This is how I am. My feelings are completely different now.'

Staying in our truth is affected by how cruel, damaging, disrespectful, or harmful our ex was. It also depends on how we were in that relationship. There's no kidding here, this is work, and it does take time, so log what happens during this time. I can't emphasize this enough.

Am I on the right track?
Ask yourself: is moving on permanently really what I want? I called it quits for a reason (or my ex did), but have I turned over every stone and determined that this is a relationship I should leave behind and stay out of permanently?

Sometimes revisiting this and realizing that part of us wants to go back or rekindle is OK. It doesn't mean we have to. This is just us owning those feelings that it wasn't all doom and gloom and rejection. There are silver linings in everything we do, and it is important to be grateful every day for what we do have.

If we have any doubt at all about whether we are happy about the relationship ending or not, we can always go back to Part I (Chapters 4 and 5) and revisit the work. This is a work in progress, and sometimes we have to go back and have reminders. This isn't a running race; this is a journey to exit beautifully.

Now, if our ex reaches out to us at some point (either directly or through a third party), we have to ask ourselves this: 'If they were to walk through my door right now, would I engage them and try again? What would they need to do in order for me to try? Are they capable of that? Would I want them back now considering all of the damage that has been done? Can I unthink and unremember what has happened to this point?'

If you are sure moving on is the right way forward, think of all the ways in which your life is better now, and remind yourself why it was a good idea to leave (or if you were left, why you now believe it's a good idea to leave that relationship in the rearview mirror). Yes, we all miss some things, but also consider what we won't miss. Journaling at this stage is very important. In fact, it's vital for your wellbeing and to achieve the most, moving forward.

Unfortunately, the only way to do this is to put to bed what could have been: our hopes, aspirations, and dreams. Now is the time to truly understand the reality of what was. Perhaps our futures didn't align, or our safety was at risk, or there was disrespect to a level of demeaning or controlling behavior that made us and the relationship toxic and unhealthy.

We must make sure we pat ourselves on the back. We need to celebrate the benefits that freedom will bring us and allow ourselves to feel relief for having escaped the negative impact of staying in the wrong relationship, whether we left or our ex left us. Doors closed in order for others to open. This has happened, and we are accepting it and we are moving on.

It's time to consider our worth
In this present moment, have we started valuing ourselves again? We may have lost sight of our worth in our previous relationship. If this were the case, we have to come home to ourselves and say, 'I am of value.'

It may be an idea to start with the simple realization that we are here. We are breathing. We survived. So they had affairs and were nasty to us. That's nothing to do with us. That's their problem. Look what they've lost. They've lost us and our kindness and our value. What else have they lost in us? What else did they leave behind? What else can they never replace?

Reaffirming our worth is a very important step towards finding ourselves again following a relationship breakup, whether we were together for a month, 5 years or 25 years.

We have to find ourselves again. We have to search and turn ourselves inside out. It's raw work, but we have to do it. We have to work out who and what we are and what we want, moving forward. We have to have hope, ambition, and purpose in life.

So, what's the next stage of our journey? We need to really think about our passion, purpose, and what we want our future life to be. What are our goals? More importantly, what is success to us?

Future relationships
In terms of future relationships, if we're valuing ourselves, we'll bring in someone to respect us. If we're not valuing ourselves, we may bring in somebody that will do more harm than good, disrespect us, and fulfill our prophecy.

Now is a good time to think about what you might want from a future relationship. And if you're saying, "I never want a relationship again," that's not human, that's not natural. So, think about it, irrespective of where we are right now.

In your journal, let's write down a list of 10 things we really want from our next partner. Include everything from attractiveness to holding hands in public to faithfulness to honesty to keeping agreements to making us feel like we matter.... Whatever it is, we will find that writing this down will reinforce how lacking our previous relationship was and how what we hoped for was very different from what we actually got. This can be very healing in itself.

The main reasons relationships fail include trust issues; partners moving through life at different speeds; having different expectations;

communication issues; abuse; financial issues; health issues, and simply growing apart. The main point we have to understand is that we didn't fail: the relationship failed, not us. We cannot fail. That relationship just did not give us what we needed. It was just a learning experience we had on our journey through life.

Healthy relationships require give and take: compromise. Ask yourself how much you compromised and how much you sacrificed in your previous relationship because there is a difference between the two.

Trust is also vital - both in ourselves and in our future partner. How do we trust ourselves to make a healthy choice next time? Can we really trust somebody else implicitly? No because all humans naturally have the capacity to lie and betray. It's in our core. Instead, we must ask ourselves, 'What are my deal-breakers?' We must think about the deals that our ex partner broke because that will help us to heal. Then we can focus on what deal-breakers we will need to put in place in the future to guarantee our physical, emotional, spiritual, and psychological safety.

The most important thing is always to be in our truth. Accept our new situation and ask the universe - the higher power - for what we need in order to create the future we want.

Be mindful; we are worth it

In a nutshell

Task 6:
Take stock of your current situation by:
- Revisiting your journal, especially the early tasks of Part I. Reflect on and challenge (by adding notes) anything that no longer rings true.
- Double checking we are still committed to the moving on route. Do we need to go back to the watershed moment of deciding whether to make up or move on, or are we on the right road?

Reaffirm our self worth by:
- Rewarding ourselves for our progress so far.
- Thinking seriously about our passion and our future life goals.
- Asking the universe/higher power/God to give us what you need

Think about healthy future relationships by
- Listing 10 things we really want from our next partner.
- Reflecting on the difference between compromise and sacrifice.
- Setting out our deal-breakers.
- Having a shuffle up of our friendships. and family members, seeing who is in our inner circle and who may be moved to the outer circle.

These are all important moves.

For more guidance, read:

Hinds, D., and Hinds, T. (2005). *Countdown to love: find your ideal partner - this time for good.* Arcturus Publishing

Starfire, A. L. (2019). *Journaling through relationships: writing to heal and reconnect.* MoonSkye Publishing

Walker, R. (2019). *The art of noticing: rediscover what's really important to you.* Ebury Digital

PART III: MOVING ON

CHAPTER 7

THIS TOO SHALL PASS: GRIEF

The moving on route will not always have clear skies above. Sometimes the clouds will gather and we will need to work hard to stay in control. I am reaching out my hand to you now. I hope you feel me with you on this journey as a co-traveler and also as a person who has experienced this deep, dark place. There are no words for it. Each of us experiences it slightly differently. But it is something we have to work through in order to get to the other side.

Grief following breakup is a painful but normal part of life. It affects all aspects of a person: their body, thoughts, and other relationships. Whether it was you who planned your exit or you were the one who was left behind, you're still going to go through a grieving process which is likely to include shock, anger, rage, depression, and negotiating all the ifs, buts, wheres, wherefores and other questions that you will probably never get answers to. Only after fully processing these feelings will we be able to move on towards some kind of closure.

We have made good progress in Part I of this book, but we will probably need to return to the beginning at times (especially Chapters 4 and 5) because working out what life will be like without that ex significant other can be tough, and we might struggle to cope with that concept and reality.

Although coping with the grief of relationship loss is one of the most difficult tasks to complete, with time and support, most people can learn to understand and accept these emotions and thought patterns and to express them without becoming overwhelmed. Eventually, these emotions will - I promise you - lose their intensity and the thoughts that generate them will become less frequent and disturbing. A wonderful book, at this point, is *Mind Over Mood* by Dennis Greenberger and Christine Padesky (2016). It's a practical workbook that can help change our thought processes.

In the Dual Process grief paradigm, mentioned earlier, returning to where we started - our decision-making process in this breakup - is a great example of loss-oriented processing. It may feel like we're going backwards for a time, but it's still progress. Even in our darkest day, when we feel like we've gone back to ground zero, we haven't. We're simply going through the treadmill of recovery from separation. The additional work we do will enable us to return to the moving on route feeling lighter and freer.

We have to be especially mindful of our thoughts during these times because our thoughts can be very intrusive, frightening, traumatic, and unhelpful. We can experience strong feelings of guilt, loss, and longing, so we have to just make sure we keep them in check. By keeping them in check, I mean occupying ourselves with other things, and if a thought comes in, start challenging it: is this story really true or am I twisting it because I'm feeling lonely right now or I've just found out something about them.

Accept how we're feeling. Let it flow through us. Keep the emotions in motion. They will go away.

We have to understand that everyone experiences similar feelings and there are people out there who want to help us through it. These include myself, of course, friends and family, but also your doctor, religious groups, charities, helpline volunteers, etc. See the next chapter for more guidance on retaining social connections during this stormy time. You might also want, at this point, to seek some professional help for managing the aftermath of a breakup.

Complex grief and relationship loss

Would you believe that 10-15% of people may experience a state similar to complex grief (Howard, 2011; Neimeyer, 2009)? In this case, the symptoms may not fade over time. Complex grief is debated but is usually considered after six months of symptoms. Symptoms can include:

- Ongoing denial and an extreme longing for the person who has left.
- Preoccupation with memories, thoughts, and pictures that interfere with new activities.
- Persistent guilt, anger, and/or bitterness.
- Avoidance of grief triggers.
- Struggling with a sense of purpose and joy.

Getting stuck in the grief process can and does lead to suicides, so please remember to get immediate emergency help if you feel you might be a danger to yourself or others.

On the other hand, many people may hardly need to work through this grief stage at all. They may even experience a post-traumatic growth where the sun bursts through the silver-lined clouds, and their motivation to develop overwhelms any lingering symptoms of loss. This is common where there has been domestic abuse or where they were a full-time carer for their ex-partner.

There's no one right way to get over a breakup
I have personally found that, despite its flaws, the Kubler-Ross and Kessler model of grief can help with many of the distressing symptoms of the post-relationship experience.

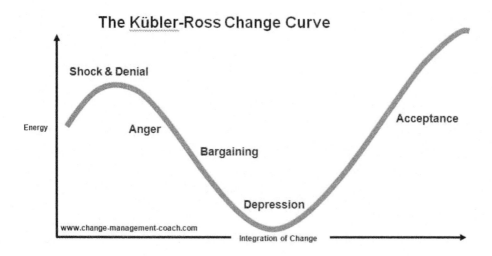

However, it is important to understand that everyone's route through grief is different. Are you worrying that you aren't dealing with a breakup the way you should be? According to relationship nonprofit Relate (2018), you're not alone.

Perhaps you sense that friends and family members are expecting you to 'snap out of it.'

The truth is that the post-relationship experience is unique for each of us: there is no one right way to handle it. The important thing is that you give yourself the time and support you need to feel better. And I mean parent yourself in a kind, loving, and patient way.

Shock symptoms

A breakup, whether you initiated it or not, is a shock to the system. This is a bigger deal than many people realize. Shock dehydrates the system and keeps it on alert, so we need to drink lots of water. We can't drink enough water during this stage.

'Depression' symptoms

This part of the breakup road is often disappointing, like driving through miles and miles of desert or urban sprawl.

John: For a long time I was in a wasteland, a no-man's land, and this made me vulnerable to the hooks.

I put depression in inverted commas because this stage of a relationship breakup is not necessarily clinical depression although it may present some symptoms that are similar. We cannot treat relationship breakup in the same way as we do clinical depression. Symptoms of depression defined in the DSM-5 (2013) and ICD-11 (World Health Organization, 2022), such as sadness, fatigue, sleep disturbance, appetite loss, and difficulty concentration can overlap with grief though. Google clinical depressive symptoms and check in with your own experience, and if you are experiencing these, it may be time to seek medical help from somebody such as a GP/ family doctor, psychologist, or psychiatrist.

What am I really missing?

We can't beat ourselves up just because we find ourselves thinking back to the good times we spent with our ex. We did have good times. We can't ignore that. We can't state that we never did. What is important right now is to balance out the good times with the not so good times, and remind ourselves why it was an unhealthy, toxic relationship, or why the relationship just didn't work out. But getting a balance between the good stuff - and holding on dear to that - and letting go of the bad stuff is a really good way forward. But keep this in mind; learn from the bad stuff. It's important not to repeat bad habits.

At this stage, it would be an idea to go back to Part I, Chapter 4 and make this a good time to ponder what you are truly grieving for.

We may be grieving for our own self-image. We may be grieving for our ex. What do we miss about them? How much are we missing them, and how much are we missing the money, home, status, friends, etc. we had? How much are we missing our identity as someone who is part of a relationship? How much are we missing the feeling of familiarity?

Always remember: there is no hard and fast rule for how long it will take you to get over a breakup. But if it's a fast 'get over,' then it's probably a fake 'get over' because healing takes time. Hence rebound relationships sometimes are counterproductive. They may feel like a great band-aid to put over a wound, but in time, we all have to process our loss, change, and difficulties.

In a nutshell

Task 7: Work with your challenging thoughts and feelings by:
- Getting *Mind Over Mood* by Christine Padesky. I trained with Christine many years ago, and this is a very good workbook on challenging our intrusive and negative thoughts.
- Returning to Part I, Chapter 4 and repeating the tasks there.
- Connecting with sources of support, including a psychotherapist if necessary.
- Drinking plenty of water to manage symptoms of shock. And believe me, this really works.
- Getting out into nature as much as you can, and breathing.
- When regretting our breakup, clarifying exactly what we miss about our former relationship. It may surprise you.

If you're feeling like you want to end your life, it's important to tell someone.

Help and support is available right now if you need it. You do not have to struggle with difficult feelings alone.

Crisis Helplines
UK: Samaritans - 116 123
US: National Suicide Prevention Lifeline - 988
Australia: Lifeline - 13 11 14
Elsewhere: Check your local resources and get immediate help.

For more guidance, read:

Greenberger, D. and Padesky, C. A. (2016). *Mind over mood: change how you feel by changing the way you think.* The Guilford Press.

Han, E. (2017). *Grieving the loss of a love.* Komorebi Press LLC.

Kubler-Ross, E., and Kessler, D. (2005). *On grief & grieving: finding the meaning of grief through the five stages of loss.* Scribner.

References:

American Psychiatric Association. (2013). *Diagnostic and statistical manual of mental disorders.* (5th ed.).

Greenberger, D. and Padesky, C. A. (2016). *Mind over mood: change how you feel by changing the way you think.* The Guidford Press.

Howarth, R. (2011). Concepts and controversies in grief and loss. *Journal of Mental Health Counseling.* 33:1, pp 4-10

Neimeyer, R. A. and Currier, J. M. (2009). Grief therapy: evidence of efficacy and emerging directions. *Current Directions in Psychological Science.* 18:6, pp 352-356

Relate. (2018). *Getting over a breakup.* https://www.relate.org.uk/getting-over-breakup

World Health Organization. (2022). ICD-11: *International classification of diseases* (11th revision)

PART III: MOVING ON

CHAPTER 8

PARENTING OURSELVES: JUST GET OUT THERE

Brad Brenner, Ph.D., posting in Therapygroupdc.com, said, "By avoiding the people who love and value you, you're depriving yourself of their love, support, and concern, which are essential for your recovery."

That deprivation can be more deadly than you might imagine.

It is natural for humans to want to go into their cave in order to recover and repair. It is a centuries-old tradition for humans. It doesn't work in the 21st Century where we need to work and engage with society. More importantly, we're not generally part of a village or close community. Modern day society is the most inhumane ever known to the human being, where we are put into concrete or wooden boxes and separated from each other.

The hidden dangers of isolation
A big motivation for me to write this book was to bring to the fore the dangers of the fallout from a relationship breakup, and also to explain what we need to empower ourselves with to move on and move forwards. So, I'm not going to mince words here. Loneliness (i.e., not being part of a community, family, or partnership) may be a silent killer! We must take note of any feelings of loneliness we experience after a breakup and work through these.

A recent study in the USA (Office of the Surgeon General, 2023) concluded that loneliness is as damaging to health as smoking fifteen cigarettes a day, while a series of studies and meta analyses (Steptoe *et al.* [2013]; Holt-Lunstad *et al.* [2015]; Foster *et al.* [2023]) have linked social isolation with a shorter life, hence the term 'silent killer' has been verified. Specifically, Foster *et al.* found that social isolation increases the risk of premature death by nearly a third through health issues such as dementia, diabetes, heart attacks, and insomnia. Julianne Holt-Lunstad and her colleagues (2015) concluded that loneliness is a greater risk to health than obesity, so since nearly half of Americans are thought to have experienced social isolation, it is no surprise that many health authorities there are asking for its treatment to be prioritized, just as I am in this book.

Another study (Kovacs *et al.*, 2021) discovered that the Covid lockdowns led to a 16% decrease in a person's average social network size. While the quality of our connections is more important than the quantity, this does suggest that there is an overall greater risk of isolation today, even compared with just a few years ago. This being said, we can understand how partnerships, relationships, and marriages take on a huge importance when we're isolated from the general public at large. We do not necessarily live in villages or small communities, and yet we're expected to go out there and make our own communities. If we've just broken up with somebody and we've decided to move on, it can be scary thinking, 'Where am I going to find my people again?' It's this simple: we need people in order to be healthy.

John: When I left my last dysfunctional relationship, I decided to be in my truth, and I kicked shame to the curb. I told my 'special twenty' in the world the truth about everything that had happened, and I received exactly what I needed. I received understanding, compassion, thought, care, love, and support, and each person in my twenty came to me, made time for me, and helped me heal and move on. It was such an amazing, miraculous experience. I dread to think what would have happened if I had been in my shame and not been honest. Where would I have been now?

So, how can we keep loneliness in check?

Sometimes, we lose contact with people that we love or that are important in our lives. Following a relationship breakup, don't be afraid to reach out to family and friends for support, but do not let shame disguise your problems, the issues in your relationship, or where you are right now. Healing from loss can be all-consuming, and it is natural for us to want to isolate ourselves as we process difficult thoughts and feelings.

To avoid this becoming a habit, we have to give ourselves a target of spending at least 15 minutes a day with loved ones. Today, this is a lot easier with FaceTime, WhatsApp and different ways of communicating. We all miss familiarity in a relationship breakup, so find some way of creating new traditions and more familiarity with family and those chosen friends.

Re-connecting with old friends can be a great relief for the stress and anxiety of a breakup. Take a day trip somewhere, or maybe even a mini-holiday, or a group vacation so that you feel that you are part of something outside of your breakup journey. In addition to finding friends and reaching out to family, purpose is very important in this time of our lives, when we're re-jigging and refinding a place for ourselves in the world. So, giving to a charity group or doing something within our local community would be a very good start to re-establishing ourselves.

It's very important to adopt a mindset of helping out other people because this can help with our own healing. As we receive support and empathy from others, we will begin to feel grateful again - a powerful state of being for healing. Always look at our cup as being half full and be grateful every day for what we do have.

We can seek out groups and services in your local community. By finding things to do and places to go, we will find other people to talk to. Some communities provide more support than others, so if we're struggling to find resources, we can consider setting up our own group or peer network. And be mindful that in the 21st Century, our group can be online.

If we are immersing ourselves in work or study to manage the pain of relationship breakup, ponder this: loneliness has also been linked to reduced performance at school and work.

When we are with people physically, make sure we are fully present. That means avoiding distractions such as mobile devices when socializing. If we feel ourselves drifting off in our thoughts, we must pull ourselves back, tell ourselves off, and remind ourselves that we have to be in the moment. That's very important.

We must make sure we don't neglect our need for human companionship and support. Isolation can become entrenched, and people may even start avoiding us unless we make the effort to stay connected. Some people may be getting bored of our repeated stories of woe, toil, and trouble. Remember, even though we are going through our darkest moments and biggest challenges, other people have their own stories too. We may unintentionally be neglecting our friendship groups or our family by putting our own issues to the forefront. Pick up on other people's clues.

Looking for an escape lane?

If we're not ready to reach out to friends and family members, it's still important to express our vulnerability to someone. Remember, be in our truth. The end of a relationship can leave us searching for a new place to live, determining the custody of children or pets, and explaining our breakup to people in our circle—all while accepting a future without our ex. This is a formidable task. It can be physically, mentally, emotionally, and financially stressful. A psychotherapist can provide a neutral perspective that your close friends and family members may not be able to, so don't be afraid to ask for professional help. As Dinah Mears (2022) explains , counseling is like an escape lane off the side of a busy dual carriageway. Ultimately, it can help us build self-esteem and regain strength.

We should also consider therapy if we are not functioning properly. A breakup can make you feel like your life is falling apart, and it generally is. We might get into trouble at work, fall out with family members, or find it difficult to eat or sleep properly. Coping with the pain might involve unhealthy coping mechanisms, such as abusing alcohol or drugs, or becoming addicted to sex.

The right type of therapy can provide a safe place to explore pain from the breakup while learning how to build our resilience and embrace our independence. Years and years of research have shown that therapy is a valuable component of the healing process, especially when mental health concerns such as depression, low self-esteem, substance abuse, or PTSD arise after the end of a relationship.

Finding a suitable psychotherapist

Whether you're starting therapy for the first time or searching for a new therapist, it's essential to find the right mental health professional for you. Opening up about relationship issues is never easy, but forming a positive therapeutic relationship can help us feel more comfortable during our sessions. As Brenner of Therapy Group DC says, "Above all else, you should feel like your therapist listens, expresses empathy, and has your best interests in mind."

Keep in mind: not every psychotherapist will be suitably qualified to help you, especially in some countries - like the UK - where 'psychologist' is not a protected title. There is a strong case for protecting this title, and I would go further and introduce a revamp of the teachings, practice protocol, and monitoring of psychological practice in all contexts: NHS, private practice, courts, university settings, hospitals, etc.

In a nutshell

Task 8: It's vital we protect ourselves from social isolation:
- Be honest, with ourselves and others, about any feelings of loneliness we have.
- Reach out to someone every day - aim for at least 15 minutes

contact, and be fully present (not distracted by anything else). Tell people what you're doing and why you're doing it.

- Consider going on a trip with some old friends.
- Connect with your local community if you have one. If not, connect with a community online. Give to others. Find purpose in life again.
- Accept gratitude when people thank you for helping.
- Avoid using work or study as an excuse to avoid contact. Negation does not work in the long run.
- Seek a psychotherapist if you are struggling.
- Go to https://www.mentalhealthacademy.com.au/team/michael-acton and look for my video course titled Silent Killer. This was due to be made available by the Mental Health Academy shortly after this book was published. You may also benefit from reading my book on leaving toxic relationships: *Learning how to leave* (Acton, 2021)

For more guidance, read:
Acton. M. (2021). *Learning how to leave.* Life Logic Publishing

Borthwick. D. (2022). *How to talk to anybody.* Independently published

Gavrani. R. (2021). **The art of being alone.** Independently published

References:
Acton. M. (2021). *Learning how to leave.* Life Logic Publishing

Foster, H. M. E., Gill, J. M. R., Mair, F. S. ., Celis-Morales, C. A., Jani, B. D., Nicholl, B. I., Lee, D., and O'Donnell, C. A. (2023). Social connection and mortality in UK Biobank: a prospective cohort analysis. *BMC Medicine.* 21, p 384

Holt-Lunstad, J., Smith, T. B., Baker, M., Harris, T., and Stephenson, D. (2015). Loneliness and social isolation as risk factors for mortality: a meta-analytic review. *Perspectives on Psychological Science.* March. 10:2, pp 227-37

Kovacs, B., Caplan, N., Grob, S., and King, M. (2021). Social networks and loneliness during the Covid-19 pandemic. *Socius: Sociological Research for a Dynamic World.* 7

Mears, D. (2022). Choosing Life or Death. *Therapy Today.* Jul/Aug, pp 38-41)

Office of the Surgeon General (OSG) (2023). Our epidemic of loneliness and isolation: the U.S. Surgeon General's advisory on the healing effects of social connection and community. *US Department of Health and Human Services.*

Steptoe, A., Shankar, A., Demakakos, P., and Wardle, J. (2013). Social isolation, loneliness, and all-cause mortality in older men and women. *Proceedings of the Natural Academy of Sciences.* 110:15, pp 5797-5801

"Joy - A pinpoint of light across a violent gorge. "

- William Bortz -

PART III: MOVING ON

CHAPTER 9

LIGHTEN THE LOAD FOR FULL SPEED AHEAD

Although there may still be some blips, by this stage you should be experiencing more peace, and even periods of happiness and joy.

Embrace and build on these moments in the sun. Let the wind flow through your hair. Every moment we connect with our natural world can be celebrated, so get out in nature. See the good in things. If you come across an obstacle, see it as a challenge. Turn it around, it does work.

Choose happiness
How can we anchor this positivity in our lives and attract more of it? Part of the solution is drugs! That is, those healthy, natural drugs that build up in the brain after certain activities.

Four chemical keys to feeling good
The four drugs that you need to focus on are dopamine, oxytocin, endorphins, and serotonin. This lesson in our brain activity is vital for your future success.

Dopamine is a chemical that gives us that satisfying feeling of being rewarded. We get it when we've achieved a goal we've set for ourselves, but we can also enjoy its benefits by through bodily pleasures such as eating a hearty meal, getting adequate sleep, and relaxing in a warm bath. It's that easy. Try it.

Oxytocin is a hormone that is stimulated through bonding with significant others. We can be lacking in this when we decide to leave or a relationship breaks up against our will. Oxytocin can be stimulated by physical touch (including petting animals) and through helping others and taking part in social activities. Just holding hands and having a hug can fill us with oxytocin. Find the opportunity and do it.

Endorphins are those well-known painkillers that kick in after exercise. They can also be boosted through listening to music and even by laughing, dancing, and watching a funny movie. So, make time to play and have fun. Endorphins are your gateways to a happy future. Feed yourself. Think of them as pills.

Serotonin is another often mentioned neurochemical due to its function in stabilizing mood. To increase serotonin levels, we can go for a walk in nature and get some sun on our skin. Sunlight is the best natural source for serotonin-boosting Vitamin D, which is also essential for overall health. Even if we use suncream, enough light will usually get in through our eyes and our skin.

If we aren't lucky enough to live in a sunny country, get a seasonal affective disorder (SAD) lamp. Many manufacturers make them, and they have come down in price. Having just one hour a day with a SAD lamp lighted in the room can be amazing for serotonin release. If you're finding it difficult to wake up and get into a routine in your life, a SAD lamp in the morning will adjust your whole body clock.

In general, we have to take charge of our new life by embracing new things. Say yes to these healthy, naturally-produced chemicals. Stimulate the body to produce them and you will be your own best friend.

Say yes to healthy invitations. We have to build our life and be grateful for everything that's good in it.

After our difficult, winding road to recovery, we need to pay attention to self-care. We have to stay physically fit and boost our mental health by giving time to friends, speakers, and social media influencers that are wonderful, strong individuals that bring us encouragement to live our best life.

Think about our character, our personality. Guess what: we can reinvent ourselves right now, in this moment. How can we make our personality shine? Remember to smile. Others reflect our inner worlds, so if we're smiling at people in the street, we will often get a smile back. Make an effort to be a happy person, too, and show this to the world.

Make sure we say, "yes" every day to getting outside that door and doing something, whether that's just going out to buy a loaf of bread or walk our dog or a neighbor's dog (borrow one, why not?) Be part of the world. Maybe even go and get a coffee by yourself. You'd be surprised at how many people will talk to you if you're drinking your coffee with a smile on your face. No I'm not being ridiculous. This is a true and proven phenomenon, worldwide.

Watch upbeat movies, nature documentaries or anything that makes you laugh. Laughter is a really good tonic.

If you need to do some fine-tuning, read self-help books (such as this one; well done!) People knock them, but the self-help model is often about taking practical steps that work, and through my work and personal experience, I know that a good self-help book can work wonders even if the theories behind some of them are contentious.

Breakup and moving on is an opportunity for growth, self-discovery, and reinvention. Never view it as a failure. It is a stepping stone to an amazing future.

In a nutshell

Task 9: Build up your stores of natural neurochemicals by:
- Taking care of your physical needs (diet, sleep, comfort, etc.)
- Maintaining physical touch with people or animals, and making sure you hug friends or hold hands.
- Getting out in the fresh air and sunlight. Connecting with nature.
- Getting a SAD lamp if you're having difficulty with routine, or you're not anywhere with sunshine.
- Laughing with friends.
- Absorbing yourself in positive influences (music, movies, books, etc.)

For more guidance, read:
Guduza, A. (2021). *Saying yes to life in spite of everything!* Independently published.

Modern Psychology Publishing (2018). *Happiness habits: habits to increase serotonin, dopamine, oxytocin and endorphins.* Independently published.

Rosenthal, N. E. (2023). *Defeating SAD (seasonal affective disorder).* G&D Medi

*"Everything is going to be okay.
Actually, it's probably going to be better than okay"*

- Prophetess Lashandra Graves -

PART III: MOVING ON

CHAPTER 10

OUR ULTIMATE GOAL: KIND INDIFFERENCE

"We shall not cease from exploration
And the end of all our exploring
Will be to arrive where we started
And know the place for the first time."
- T.S. Eliot -

So, this is a stage of your rebirth. Not being corny with you, wooly cardigan, white socks and sandals sort of thing. But what I am saying to you is that to get to this stage of a relationship breakup is peace, is resolution, is knowing one's self again, finding our place in the world again, understanding the good and bad, the great, the not so good, and all the gray area of our last relationship.

This is our time. To, yes, occasionally feel the pangs, to feel the relief. There still may be some regret, but we're no longer in that storm, that turmoil, that downpour, that darkness. Sometimes, it's good to go through this book again and again, and even again. Maybe get it on Audible if you haven't already. Remind ourselves of the different stages, the different work we need to do. Remind us of where we are now.

And our journals: never underrate a journal. It is our best friend being us. It's a reminder. It's a barometer of where we are and how well we're doing. It's a reminder of how well we can do. It's a testament to what we're able to do in life, what we're able to achieve, what we're able to overcome, see, do, experience, champion.

We have the whole world and all its beauty at our feet. We can do and be anything at this stage. Doesn't matter about our abilities, our age, gender, sexuality, geographical position, financial situation, education. In this moment, we can step forward and be anything. Do anything.

This is the moment where we have to revisit success. A favorite mantra of mine is Emerson's *What is Success?*

What is Success?

To laugh often and much;
To win the respect of intelligent people and
the affection of children;
To earn the approbation of honest critics and endure
the betrayal of false friends;
To appreciate beauty;
To find the best in others;
To give of one's self;
To leave the world a bit better, whether by a healthy child,
a garden patch, or a redeemed social condition;
To have played and laughed with enthusiasm and
sung with exultation;
To know even one life has breathed easier because you
have lived -
This is to have succeeded.

- Ralph Waldo Emerson -

Success in the 21st century is rammed down our throats as materialistic things: diamonds, looks, travel, private jets, etc. But if we look at the very, very successful people in the world who have done very well, such as Richard Branson, J. Lo, Warren Buffett, Keanu Reeves, Oprah Winfrey, Paul McCartney, Michelle Obama, LeBron James, Dolly Parton, Tom Hanks, Emma Watson, David Attenborough, Meryl Streep, Malala Yousafzai, Barack Obama, Ratan Tata, Jack Dorsey, Serena Williams, Jennifer Lawrence, Steve Carell, Chris Hemsworth, and Maya Angelou, they all revert back to basic human needs. They draw water, they build fires, they have friends, and they have a very basic, good, healthy living. We all can make our own private islands. All of us. We just have to visualize what it is that we like and want.

Kind indifference is where we want to be. T.S. Eliot is one of my favorite writers. He always said that home was where we started from. I never quite understood that statement for many, many years, but I felt akin to it in some way. Having personally traveled the world and lived in Australia, the Middle East, the Americas. France, UK, Ireland, it's difficult for me to pinpoint where my home is exactly. So, home is where one starts from. It's been very confusing to me for many, many years. I think I've personally found that spot now. Home is where one starts from when one works through the myriad layers of stories and experiences in life and comes back to the raw meaning of where we started (i.e., who we are, what we like, what we need, and what we do to help ourselves and others). It's our true, authentic self.

In therapy, there's a thing called actualisation which means we get to be the best version of ourselves possible. And that best version of ourselves possible can manifest when we've cleaned out and pushed out a lot of the conflicts that grow over a lifetime. When we sort out our battles and our grievances, and our fears. I'm hoping that our work together in this book has helped you to purge some of these unnecessary and redundant facets of being human, and helped you get back to basics. We can stand in our truth.

Stand up now, put both feet firmly on the ground with both arms next to you, point your arms to the ground and Earth yourself. Say, "This is me. This is who I am. I am strong. I am confident. I have managed to get through so much in my life. And now I'm going to be kind, compassionate, loving to myself and to others. I have no ceiling on life. I'm going to bring in people that compliment me, people that have my back, people that love me, people that want me, and I'm going to accept that all people are different, but I'm going to stand in my truth from this moment onwards. There's a battle to stay in my truth, but I'm going to battle it because it's how I can get what I want. It's how I tell people what I like. That's how I tell myself what's important, and what's not." Always from this day forward, choose your battles very carefully. We can get sucked in very quickly.

Forgiveness
Forgiving, truly forgiving, is the gateway to peace. It's essential, at this moment, that we really take a good look at ourselves, take a good look at our ex and all the people that have been impacted by this breakup, and face our true feelings about what took place, what the aftermath was about, and where we are now.

If someone's hurt us, it's only understandable that we hold on to some pain and bitterness. However, if we really look at what's happening with resentment, anger and rage, we're only really hurting ourselves. If we think about our feelings and what forgiveness is doing for us, it can bring in peace and resolution. It keeps our energy within us. If we don't forgive someone or people or a situation, we're just using all of that toxic energy on what? We're not hurting anybody. We're not doing anything to anybody apart from ourselves. And don't forget, it's all too easy to say that we forgive someone, but then we dwell on it in dreams, we dwell on it in daytime thoughts, and if we don't truly forgive someone, then it can open wounds again. It can hurt us all the more.

If you're reading this, and you're thinking, do you know what: I can't get this person unhooked for me, it could be that you haven't forgiven, truly. I know it might sound crazy and silly and stupid and weak to admit that they did all that to you and then they did all that with your social circles, all that with your family, etc., but we are the ones that have to take control in our lives. We are the ones that need to move on. We are the ones that need to gather in all of ourselves, revisit ourselves, do the work and walk on into our future. So, we can forgive them. We won't forget; we'll be mindful. We'll never make that mistake again. We may never want to be like them. We may not understand how they can be like that. But the one thing we have to do is we have to forgive to get rid of that line that's hooked deep in our body.

And sometimes, a ritual can help with this. Write down all the things you feel are difficult not to forgive a person for. Really ruminate over them and then burn them and bury the ashes or put them off in a bottle somewhere. Just take care not to put your name to anything. If somebody finds it, they won't be able to trace it back to you. But do a ritual.

I left organized religion many, many decades ago, but I didn't leave behind some of the essence of the teachings of the Bible, and I've since studied the Qur'an, Judaism, Shamanism, Lutheran, and all of the teaching, the wise teachings of the world talk about forgiveness as the key to peace. And I'm telling you now, it's tried and proven, over the years, with my patients and myself and my loved ones, that the only true way to moving on and peace is forgiveness.

Yes, we need to protect ourselves, but we also have to forgive ourselves. Yes, we were part of it all. Resentment has no place. No place for others, and no place for ourselves. What do we have to forgive ourselves for? What hurt may we have caused someone else? What hurt could we have done to our ex? To people that used to be our friends? To loved ones? What hurt have we caused ourselves? How have we betrayed ourselves?

Look long and hard at yourself and your ex and all that went down. Write it down on a piece of paper. What aren't you proud about? We are all perfectly imperfect as human beings. And we all have the right to forgive ourselves and others. We all have the right to let go of toxic darkness; bad energy.

Let go. Take a deep breath, and let go.

Use all of that energy for something positive. Every time you think those nasty thoughts or resentment or shame, turn it into something positive. Think about something great that's happening. Think about something good that you want to do.

Move that energy forward.

Growth

It is so important that we understand growth, and how we can grow every minute, every hour, every day, every month, every year. It all looks different but all looks the same. As long as we're moving forward. Hope is part of growth. Vision is part of growth. And purpose is part of growth.

We've just left behind all of our resentments and battles that are no longer our business. We have freed ourselves from those which gives us the ability to propel ourselves forward and develop even more. Just letting go of things is growth. Letting go of things is wisdom. As we progress through life, our experiences do increase and deepen, and give us a much better understanding of our world and of ourselves within it. What is our place? Who are we in this world, and what do we want to bring in, what do we want to manifest?

Even suffering plays an important role in our Soul's journey. My teaching is just that. Compassion, empathy, and wisdom for others. Every loving experience feeds us. It gives our inner being all the nurturing we need, and now we're ready to bring in new love, whether that be by family members that we're reconnecting with, or connecting with for the first time; bringing you social group; friendship group, or maybe even bringing a new lover; a new romantic interest.

We must sit, be quiet, and give the space for all of our ideas about our growing to process and take hold. It's important we give ourselves just a moment every day. Just sit and be. Now, if you can't meditate, not many people can, if you can't sit still, not many people can, we need to consider a way of just being quiet and thinking about how wonderful we are at this moment in time with all the work we've done. Try to clear our minds for ideas to come in on how we can be useful and purposeful in this world.

Understand, at this point, and have faith and vision that life does unfold as it's meant to. We are all here in this moment right now, and we're meant to be here at this moment in time.

Be curious. Don't be too hard on yourself. Be curious like a cat, padding around with a string ball, being curious. Be curious about life. Recognise when we're being judgmental and let it go. Recognise when we're being angry and let it go. Defend ourselves for sure, but give space for curious, give space for vision, insight, new routines, new traditions, and new healthy habits. And be kind. If we're kind to people, whether it's somebody we're passing in the street, somebody we're walking along a country lane with, somebody we open the door for, somebody, we help in some way, the rewards are amazing. They far outweigh any monetary reward or any other reward on the earth, apart from our kindness being repaid.

Trust in self and self-guidance

Finally, we have to believe in ourselves; we have to believe in our journey, and we have to believe that things are great and are going to be even greater. There has to be death. There have to be endings in life. We are all born to die. And there's a very true and haunting expression which is, 'That which we love, we must lose.' If we think about it, whatever we do love in life, we will lose eventually whether it's by death or changing circumstances. Our puppies, our cats, horses - whatever it is - each other, our lovers, our family. Everyone dies. Everything dies. It depends on our version of faith and our understanding of the higher power how we manage these losses, but it's true to say that this is part of evolution. This is part of us moving through life. This is normal.

And again I want to bring it to you that maybe the 21st century way of loving is very rare for people to now stay together for life. It's very rare for people to have one career and one job for life, which used to be the case. Now people have several jobs for life. They have several careers at times, and the new people coming through, the Millennials, Generation Z, Generation Alpha, etc. bet on changing their career, every two years, every four years - or changing their job, at least - maybe that's the same for romantic relationships. Maybe we are in the 21st century where we are serial monogamists (i.e., we have several relationships going through life) and this is normal. And where do we find love? What kind of idea is successful love these days? Has it changed from years gone by?

Wherever we are right now, whatever we're thinking right now, we are the manifestors of our future. Whatever we want to be, there are stepping stones to getting to that vision. We must have a vision in life and a motivation for change. As I've said throughout this book, being in our truth is so important in order to bring in the correct vision for what we like and want. And we're all different. We're all individual, and we're all unique. So, endings are new beginnings. However tragic your ending was, this is your new beginning.

Take time to really think about what you've always wanted. Go back to your childhood and think about what you wanted to be when you grew up? Have an idea of what it is that would rock your boat. What kind of people do you want to be around? What kind of environment do you want to live in? There are some restrictions in life, but even with restrictions, if we have a vision of what would best serve us, we can make it happen. It doesn't matter what our situation is. We must be inspired, bring ideas in, and work towards our vision, and find the motivation for it.

It's been wonderful walking through this with you. Through the hard times and the good times. I hope you felt my hand holding your hand tightly throughout this journey. I have nothing but respect for anyone wishing to work on themselves. It's very courageous wanting to heal ourselves, and it's very wise to forgive our past and ourselves and move on to an abundant future.

In a nutshell

Task 10:
- Be kind and honest to yourself at all times, even though this might be the most difficult thing to do.
- Go through this book again. Get it on Audible if you haven't already.
- Keep updating your journal. Remember; it is your friend for life.
- Who do you need to forgive? Consider a releasing ritual. Forgive yourself. Breathe deeply and transform toxic energies into positive actions.
- Who are we in this world, and what do we want to manifest? What is success for you?
- We would love to hear from you about your journey. If there's anything you would like to share about this book, your journey, or anything else, please email us at confidential@mpamind.com
- Help others by spreading the word. If you found this book helpful, please let the world know by leaving a review on Amazon, Goodreads, and anywhere else you can think of.

GLOSSARY OF TERMS

Acton Model for Gatekeepers of Domestic Violence (SOS DV8):
Dr. Michael Acton's 'first aid' style guidebook giving first responders eight simple rules for handling situations involving domestic violence.

Acton Post-relationship Experience Model (APREM):
Dr. Michael Acton's bottom-up model for navigating relationship breakup, whether the patient makes up with or moves on from their ex. It combines elements of stage-based, task-based, and dual process models of grief. It is the framework for *Weathering Relationships.*

American Psychiatric Association (APA): The largest professional association of psychiatrists and trainee psychiatrists in the world. The APA publish the Diagnostic and Statistical Manual of Mental Disorders.

Codependency (CD): A disorder characterized by enabling behavior in a relationship. The codependent takes responsibility for the other person's behavior and wellbeing. See my book: *Learning How To Leave: A Practical Guide to Stepping Away from Narcissistic and Toxic Relationships.*

Cognitive: Relating to the various information processing activities of the brain, including storage, retrieval, thinking, and understanding.

Cognitive Behavioral Therapy (CBT): An evidence-based form of psychotherapy that helps patients understand and change how thoughts, feelings, and behaviors interact. CBT is designed to change unhelpful thought patterns.

Dopamine: A brain chemical connected with reward-motivated behavior. Some drugs and addictive activities stimulate or block the absorption of dopamine.

DSM-5: The latest (2013) edition of the Diagnostic and Statistical Manual of Mental Disorders. Published by the APA, it standardizes and classifies mental disorders.

Dual process grief model: Theoretical models that frame grief as two separate processes - generally one of building for the future (restoration) and one of coping with loss (e.g., Stroebe and Schut's Dual Process Model of Coping with Bereavement).

Endorphins: Hormones that the body releases in response to pain or stress. They can be stimulated by exercise, sex, eating, and massage, and lead to pain and stress reduction, and a feeling of overall wellbeing.

General Practitioner (GP): The UK and Australian term for a Family Physician.

ICD-12: The latest (2022) edition of the International Classification of Diseases. Developed by the WHO, it provides diagnostic codes for the classification of diseases.

Karpman Triangle/Drama Triangle: Stephen Karpman's (1968) model used in Transactional Analysis to understand and work with relationship conflict. It defines the dynamics between three roles that are often adopted in relationships: persecutor, victim and rescuer.

Kubler-Ross Five Stages of Grief: A long-established model for understanding and working with patients facing death or loss. It proposes that patients experience stages of denial, anger, bargaining, depression, and acceptance.

Narcissistic Personality Disorder (NPD): A disorder characterised by exaggerated self-importance, lack of empathy and craving for admiration. See my book: *Learning How To Leave: A Practical Guide to Stepping Away from Narcissistic and Toxic Relationships.*

Oxytocin: Informally known as the 'love hormone,' oxytocin is a hormone and brain chemical released during physical contact (e.g., hugging, kissing, and breastfeeding).

Paradigm: A set of beliefs and assumptions that determines how a subject is approached and interpreted.

Post-Traumatic Stress Disorder (PTSD): A mental disorder caused by experiencing or witnessing traumatic events. Symptoms include re-experiencing the events (flashbacks), hyperarousal and mood changes.

Psychiatrist: A medically trained professional who specialises in the study, diagnosis and treatment of mental disorders. All psychiatrists hold a medical degree, but professional requirements vary by country.

Psychologist: A person trained in the workings of the mind. In many territories, the word is unprotected. It is therefore advisable for people to choose a psychologist who is an accredited member of one of the country's professional bodies.

Psychotherapist: A person who helps treat disorders of the mind and personality. In many territories, the word is unprotected. It is therefore advisable for people to choose a therapist who is an accredited member of one of the country's professional bodies.

Safeguarding: A term, used in the UK and Ireland, for the protection of individual health, wellbeing and human rights, especially those of children and vulnerable adults.

Selective Serotonin Reuptake Inhibitors (SSRIs): A class of antidepressants that work by increasing levels of serotonin in the brain. Prescribed for depression, anxiety, and other mood disorders.

Serotonin: A brain chemical associated with positive feelings such as happiness, calmness, and emotional stability. Stimulated by exercise, sunshine, social activity, meditation, and some foods.

Shadow: According to Jung's analytical psychology, the shadow is a psychological construct containing aspects of ourselves we find frightening or socially unacceptable.

Socratic questioning: A method of extracting information by the posing of carefully constructed open questions. Originally devised by the Greek philosopher Socrates.

Stage-based grief models: Theoretical models that frame the grief process as a series of inter-relates stages (e.g., the Kubler-Ross Five Stages of Grief model).

Suicidal ideation: A symptom of some mental disorders characterised by thoughts or fantasies about suicide. Suicidal ideation can progress from passive thoughts to active planning.

Stages of change (model): A five stage model used in the treatment of various addictions. Patients progress through the following stages: pre-contemplation, contemplation, preparation, action, and maintenance.

Task-based grief models: Theoretical models that frame the grief process as a series of tasks that need to be completed (e.g., Worden's Four Tasks of Mourning model).

Transactional Analysis (TA): A theory and therapeutic method, whereby social interactions are analysed by the ego state of the participants (whether this is parent-like, childlike, or adult-like). The concept was developed in the 1950s by Eric Berne.

World Health Organization (WHO): The United Nations agency dedicated to promoting global health.

FURTHER READING

PART I, CHAPTER 1

Casement, P. (1985). *On Learning from the Patient*, p.42. Tavistock/Routledge Publications.

Murray, J. (2016). *Understanding loss: A guide for caring for those facing adversity.* Routledge/Taylor & Francis Group

Rando, T. A., Nezu, C. M., Nezu, A. M., and Weiss, M. J. (1993). *Treatment of Complicated Mourning.* Research Press Publishers.

Worden, J.W. (1991). *Grief Counselling and Grief Therapy (3rd ed.).* p. 141. Brunner-Routledge.

PART I, CHAPTER 3

Burke, S. (2021). *In my defense - life after suicide.* Independently published.

Kaufman, D. (2016). *15 poems to healing & recovery.* CreateSpace.

O' Connor, R. (2021). *When it's darkest: why people die by suicide and what we can do to prevent it.* Ebury Digital.

PART I, CHAPTER 4

Greenberger, D. and Padesky, C. A. (2016). *Mind over mood: change how you feel by changing the way you think.* The Guidford Press.

Hill, C. (2019). *How to stop overthinking.* Independently published.

Kubler-Ross, E., and Kessler, D. (2005). *On grief & grieving: finding the meaning of grief through the five stages of loss.* Scribner.

PART I, CHAPTER 5

Banks, E. (2022). *Who the hell is Abraham Maslow?* Who the Hell is...?

Bryant, T. S. (2022). *Homecoming.* TarcherPerigee.

Krumwiede, A. (2014). *Attachment theory according to John Bowlby and Mary Ainsworth.* GRIN Verlag.

PART I, CHAPTER 6

Acton. M. (2022). *Raw facts from real parents.* Life Logic Publishing

Acton. M. (2021). *Learning how to leave.* Life Logic Publishing

Hobdey. C. (2022). *De-twat your life.* Ink! By The Author School

PART II, CHAPTER 1

Bee, B. (2024). *Speak your truth.* Independently published

Marshall, A. G. (2011). *How can I ever trust you again?* Bloomsbury Paperbacks

Schmidt, J. (2016). *Energetic boundaries 101.* CreateSpace

PART II, CHAPTER 2

Patterson, S. (2019). *The great compromise.* Independently published.

Smolarski, A. (2024) *Cooperative co-parenting for secure kids.* New Harbinger Publications.

Tagoe, B. A. (2023). *20 relationship red flags: understanding relationship warning signs.* Independently published.

PART II, CHAPTER 3

Acton, M. (2022). *Raw facts from real parents.* Life Logic Publishing

Christensen, A., and Jacobson, N. S. (2020). *Acceptance and change in couple therapy: a therapist's guide to transforming relationships.* W. W. Norton & Company

Usher, K., and Usher, N. (2024). *A couple's guide to menopause: managing the change together.* Hero

PART II, CHAPTER 4

Acton, M. (2022). *Raw facts from real parents.* Life Logic Publishing

Clear, J. (2018). *Atomic habits.* Random House Business

Wilde McCormick, E. (2008). *Change for the better: self-help through practical psychotherapy.* Sage Publications Ltd.

PART II, CHAPTER 5

Basterfield, B. C. (2023). *The effective communication method: 9 keys to master communication skills.* 365 Self-Growth Publishing

Leal III, B. C. (2017). *4 essential keys to effective communication in love, life, work - anywhere!* CreateSpace

Shaw, G. (2020). *7 winning conflict resolution techniques.* Communication Excellence

PART II, CHAPTER 6

Chapman, G. (2015). *The 5 love languages: the secret to love that lasts.* Moody Publishers.

Power A. (2022). *Contented couples: magic, logic or luck.* Confer Ltd.

Harley, W. F. (2011). *His needs, her needs: building an affair-proof marriage.* Monarch Books.

PART II, CHAPTER 7

Berne, E. (1964). *Games people play: the psychology of human relations.* Grove Press

West, C. (1991). *The Karpman drama triangle explained.* CWTK Publications

Worden, J.W. (1991). *Grief Counselling and Grief Therapy (3rd ed.).* Brunner-Routledge

PART II, CHAPTER 8
Barker, M.J. (2018). *The psychology of sex.* Routledge

Campbell, C. (2022). *Sex therapy: the basics.* Routledge

Litvinoff, S. (2001). *The Relate guide to sex in loving relationships.* Vermilion

PART II, CHAPTER 9
Christensen, A., Jocobson, N., and Doss, B. D. (2014). *Reconcilable differences.* Guilford Press

Matheson, C. (2009). *The art of the compliment: how to use kind words with grace and style.* Skyhorse Publishing

Ocean, J. A. (2024). *99 dates to remember: the couple's adventure guide.* Independently published

PART II, CHAPTER 10
Acton. M. (2021). *Learning how to leave.* Life Logic Publishing

Acton. M. (2022). *Raw facts from real parents.* Life Logic Publishing

Vision Board Book. (2024). *Our future, our dreams.* Independently published

PART III, CHAPTER 1
Acton. M. (2022). *Raw facts from real parents.* Life Logic Publishing

Acton, M. (2021). *Learning how to leave.* Life Logic Publishing

Thompson, K. (2007) *Medicines for mental health: the ultimate guide to psychiatric medication.* Booksurge Publishing

PART III, CHAPTER 2

Acton. M. (2021). *Learning how to leave.* Life Logic Publishing

Bryant, T. S. (2022). *Homecoming.* TarcherPerigee.

Pollard, J. K. (1987). *Self parenting: the complete guide to your inner conversations.* The SELF-PARENTING Program.

PART III, CHAPTER 3

Acton, M. (2022). *Raw facts from real parents.* Life Logic Publishing

Caine, T., Leigh, S., Lister, M., Nettleton, C., McCann, K., and Bell, D. (2021). *Your divorce handbook.* Stellar Books LLP.

Woodall, K., and Woodall, N. (2009). *The guide for separated parents: putting children first.* Piatkus

PART III, CHAPTER 4

Castenskiold, E. (2013) *Restored lives: recovery from divorce and separation.* Monarch books

Leckie, T. (2023) *Don't be desperate: get over your breakup with clarity and dignity.* Trina Leckie

McFadden, W. (2022). *Painkiller: everything you need to know about rebound relationships.* Independently published

PART III, CHAPTER 5

Gershon, I. M. (2010). *The breakup 2.0: disconnecting over new media.* Cornell University Press

Kruse, C. J. (2017). *A guide on how to stop arguing.* CreateSpace

Zahariades, D. (2022). *The art of letting go.* Independently published

PART III, CHAPTER 6

Hinds, D., and Hinds, T. (2005). *Countdown to love: find your ideal partner - this time for good.* Arcturus Publishing

Starfire, A. L. (2019). *Journaling through relationships: writing to heal and reconnect.* MoonSkye Publishing

Walker, R. (2019). *The art of noticing: rediscover what's really important to you.* Ebury Digital

PART III, CHAPTER 7

Greenberger, D. and Padesky, C. A. (2016). *Mind over mood: change how you feel by changing the way you think.* The Guilford Press.

Han, E. (2017). *Grieving the loss of a love.* Komorebi Press LLC.

Kubler-Ross, E., and Kessler, D. (2005). *On grief & grieving: finding the meaning of grief through the five stages of loss.* Scribner.

PART III, CHAPTER 8

Acton. M. (2021). *Learning how to leave.* Life Logic Publishing

Borthwick. D. (2022). *How to talk to anybody.* Independently published

Gavrani. R. (2021). *The art of being alone.* Independently published

PART III, CHAPTER 9
Guduza, A. (2021). *Saying yes to life in spite of everything!* Independently published.

Modern Psychology Publishing (2018). *Happiness habits: habits to increase serotonin, dopamine, oxytocin and endorphins.* Independently published.

Rosenthal, N. E. (2023). *Defeating SAD (seasonal affective disorder).* G&D Media

REFERENCES

Acton, M. [MPA Mind. (2023, May 31). #MPAMind - Expert panel discussion: 'What Would You Put in #MichaelasLaw ?' #MichaelaHallDay 2023 [Video]. YouTube. https://youtu.be/xR0ROex9TwE?si=7pSyyzbTdpw_ninI].

Acton, M. (2022). *Raw facts from real parents.* Life Logic Publishing

Acton, M. (2021). *Learning how to leave.* Life Logic Publishing

American Psychiatric Association. (2013). *Diagnostic and statistical manual of mental disorders.*(5th ed.).

Barford, D. (2022). Narcissism - the therapist's friend? *Therapy Today.* Dec 21/Jan 22, 32:10

Baryshnikov, I. and Isometsa, E. (2022). Psychological pain and suicidal behavior: a review. *Frontiers in Psychiatry*

Berne, E. (1964). *Games people play: the psychology of human relations.* Grove Press

Boroff, M. (2010). The art of asking questions in a narrative therapy. *Dissertation Abstracts International: Section B: The Sciences and Engineering.* 70(9-B). p5807.

Bryant, T. S. (2022). *Homecoming.* TarcherPerigee.

Cain, D. (2022). You are always the other person. *Raptitude*.
https://www.raptitude.com/2022/07/you-are-always-the-other-person/

Casement, P. (1985). *On Learning from the Patient,* p.42. Tavistock/
Routledge Publications.

Dailey, R. M., Zhong, L., Pett, R., and Varga, S. (2020). Post-dissolution ambivalence, breakup adjustment, and relationship reconciliation. *Journal of Social and Personal Relationships.* 37(5). pp 1604–1625.

Dailey, R. M., Rossetto, K. A., Pfiester, A., and Surra, C. A. (2009). A qualitative analysis of on-again/off-again romantic relationships: "It's up and down, all around". *Journal of Social and Personal Relationships.* 26(4). pp 443–466.

Dardis, C. M. and Gidycz, C. A. (2017). The frequency and perceived impact of engaging in in-person and cyber unwanted pursuit after relationship break-up among college men and women. *Sex Roles: A Journal of Research.* 76(1-2), pp 56–72.

DeGroot, J. M., and Carmack, H. J. (2022). Accidental and purposeful triggers of post-relationship grief. *Journal of Loss and Trauma.* Advance online publication.

Dennis, C. and Davis, R. (2000). Can't get you out of my head [Song]. EMI Music

Doka, K. (2008). Disenfranchised grief in historical and cultural perspective. In M. S. Stroebe, R. O., Edwards, K. M., Palmer, K. M., Lindemann, K. G., and Gidycz, C. A. (2018). Is the end really the end? Prevalence and correlates of college women's intentions to return to an abusive relationship. *Violence Against Women.* 24(2), 207–222.

Domestic Abuse Shelter, Inc. (2019) *Definition of domestic violence.* https://domesticabuseshelter.org/domestic-violence

Downe-Wamboldt, B., and Tamlyn, D. (1997). An international survey of death education trends in faculties of nursing and medicine. *Death Studies.* Mar-Apr; 21(2):177-88.

Foster, H. M. E., Gill, J. M. R., Mair, F. S. ., Celis-Morales, C. A., Jani, B. D., Nicholl, B. I., Lee, D., and O'Donnell, C. A. (2023). Social connection and mortality in UK Biobank: a prospective cohort analysis. *BMC Medicine.* 21, p 384

Frith C., and Frith, U. (2022). Reputation matters. *The Psychologist.* June

Greenberger, D. and Padesky, C. A. (2016). *Mind over mood: change how you feel by changing the way you think.* The Guidford Press.

Gottman, Dr. J. (2018, January 30). *Making Marriage Work* [Video]. YouTube. https://www.youtube.com/watch?v=AKTyPgwfPgg

Hall, C. (2011). Beyond Kubler-Ross: recent developments in our understanding of grief and bereavement. *InPsych.* Vol. 33:6 December

Halpin, Z. (2022). Working with the ultimate crisis. *Therapy Today.* Dec 21/Jan 22, 32:10, pp 34-36)

Holt-Lunstad, J., Smith, T. B., Baker, M., Harris, T., and Stephenson, D. (2015). Loneliness and social isolation as risk factors for mortality: a meta-analytic review. *Perspectives on Psychological Science.* March. 10:2, pp 227-37

Hope, G. (2023, January 01). Our Agreeable model: utilizing our mediation skills in a new way. https://www.familylawpartners.co.uk/blog/our-agreeable-model-utilising-our-mediation-skills-in-a-new-way

Howarth, R. (2011). Concepts and controversies in grief and loss. *Journal of Mental Health Counseling.* 33:1, pp 4-10

Jackson, C. (2022). Navigating complex grief. *Therapy Today.* Jul/Aug, pp 18-22)

Karpman, S. (1968). Fairy tales and script drama analysis. *Transactional Analysis Bulletin.* 26(7): 39–43.

Kovacs, B., Caplan, N., Grob, S., and King, M. (2021). Social networks and loneliness during the Covid-19 pandemic. *Socius: Sociological Research for a Dynamic World.* 7

Kubler-Ross, E., and Kessler, D. (2005). *On grief & grieving: finding the meaning of grief through the five stages of loss.* Scribner.

Maslow A. H. (1943). A theory of human motivation. *Psychological Review.* 50(4): 370–96.

Mears, D. (2022). Choosing Life or Death. *Therapy Today.* Jul/Aug, pp 38-41)

Morris, C. E., and Reiber, C. (2011). Frequency, intensity and expression of post-relationship grief. *EvoS Journal: The Journal of the Evolutionary Studies Consortium*. 3, 1–11.

Murray, J. (2016). *Understanding loss: A guide for caring for those facing adversity.* Routledge/Taylor & Francis Group

Needs, A. (2022). Change must engage a person's senses of identity, meaning, control, and belonging. *The Psychologist*. April.

Neimeyer, R. A. and Currier, J. M. (2009). Grief therapy: evidence of efficacy and emerging directions. *Current Directions in Psychological Science*. 18:6, pp 352-356

Office of the Surgeon General (OSG) (2023). Our epidemic of loneliness and isolation: the U.S. Surgeon General's advisory on the healing effects of social connection and community. *US Department of Health and Human Services*.

Parsons, A., Knopp, K., Rhoades, G., Markman, H., and Stanley, S. (2014). Let's try this again: the impact of breakups and renewals on dating relationships and marriage [conference session abstract]. *122nd American Psychological Association Annual Convention*, Washington D.C.

Plagaro, I. (2022). Healing the wounds of rejection. *EMDR Therapy Quarterly*. https://etq.emdrassociation.org.uk/case-study/healing-the-wounds-of-rejection/

Poindexter, Richard, Poindexter, Robert, and Members J. (1971). Thin Line Between Love and Hate [Song]. Atco Records
Potter, M. (2022). Spinal injury - finding strength for an unplanned future. *The Psychologist*. April

Rando, T. A., Nezu, C. M., Nezu, A. M., and Weiss, M. J. (1993). *Treatment of Complicated Mourning.* Research Press Publishers.

Relate. (2018). *Getting over a breakup.* https://www.relate.org.uk/getting-over-breakup

Skinner, Q. (2021, November 18). *The sixth stage of grief.* Life Time. https://experiencelife.lifetime.life/article/the-sixth-stage-of-grief/

Sobhani-Rad, D. (2014). A review on adult pragmatic assessments. *Iranian journal of neurology.* 13. pp113-118.

Steptoe, A., Shankar, A., Demakakos, P., and Wardle, J. (2013). Social isolation, loneliness, and all-cause mortality in older men and women. *Proceedings of the Natural Academy of Sciences.* 110:15, pp 5797-5801

Stroebe, M. (2008). Cautioning Health-Care Professionals: Bereaved Persons Are Misguided Through the Stages of Grief. *OMEGA - Journal of Death and Dying.* 74(4), 455–473.

Stroebe, M. S., Edwards, R. O., Palmer, K.M., Lindemann, K. G., and Gidycz, C. A. (2018). Is the end really the end? Prevalence and correlates of college women's intentions to return to an abusive relationship. *Violence Against Women.* 24:2, pp 207-222

Stroebe, M. and Schut, H. (2010). The Dual Process Model of Coping with Bereavement: A Decade On. *OMEGA - Journal of Death and Dying.* 61(4), 273-290.

Walker, J., and Gavin, H. (2011) Interpretations of domestic violence: defining intimate partner abuse. The 12th Conference of the International Academy of Investigative Psychology. Crime, Criminalistics & Criminal Psychology: *New Directions in Investigative Behavioural Science.* March/April.

Worden, J.W. (1991). *Grief Counselling and Grief Therapy (3rd ed.).* p. 141. Brunner-Routledge.

World Health Organization. (2022). *ICD-11: International classification of diseases* (11th revision)

WorldMetrics (2024). https://worldmetrics.org/reconciliation-after-separation-statistics/

Wright, S. (2022). The aftermath of traumatic loss. *Therapy Today.* May, pp 39-42.

APPENDIX A

DON'T FEEL ALONE, THIS IS WHAT OUR STUDY CAME UP WITH

To follow is an extract from the Methods and Results section of my research study. This study formed part of the foundation of the 'Acton Post-relationship Experience Model.'

All references and in-line citations have been removed to avoid confusion.

Methods and materials
This section will detail the methodology I used in this research study and rationale for choosing it; the source of the data and how I collected it; how data was recorded and managed, and how it was analyzed, validated, and presented. It also looks at the limitations of the research.

I designed this study to evaluate the use of the Kubler-Ross Stages of Loss model as a framework for working with patients presenting with Post-relationship grief (PRG). I wanted to look for evidence of themes that
showed the presence of the stages of Denial, Anger, Bargaining, Depression, Acceptance, and Meaning in PRG. I also wanted to see if patients were also dealing with PRG experiences which lay outside of the Kubler-Ross model's umbrella. In addition, I wanted to identify any qualitative differences between stages of loss experienced by patients with PRG and those experienced by patients who are terminally ill or grieving.

Type of design, rationale and assumptions

In accordance with convention, I refer to myself in the role of therapist in the third person throughout the rest of this chapter.

An interpretative phenomenological analysis (IPA) study was conducted on patient notes that had been written up by the researcher during their counseling sessions for PRG. IPA is a method for extracting rich qualitative (psychological, interpretative and idiographic) data from subjects. The analyst draws on double hermeneutic theory to make sense of the subject's sense making process. The use of IPA in research has increased between 2000 and 2010. The approach is most suitable for developing existing theories, hence my decision to use it to compare clinical PRG experiences with the grief stages defined by Kubler-Ross and Kessler.

Data sources and collection techniques

To be eligible for short-listing, a patient must have experienced a relationship break-up which had contributed to them seeking counseling. From those eligible, thirty (30) of the most challenging cases were selected using purposive sampling. The rationale for this was that they were likely to have expressed a wide range of emotions. This would provide a more robust test to the Kubler-Ross and Kessler model than a less challenging case where the patient's issues were resolved quickly.

The notes from these thirty cases were then separated into those who had left the relationships ('Leavers') and those who had been left by their former partners ('Lefts'). This was because the literature review suggested a unique 'Left' experience, and this study sought to highlight any differences in the PRG experience between these two groups. Due to time constraints, the final sample was limited to a total of six patients. Three each were picked, at random, from the Leavers and Lefts. This eliminated the risk of bias in the final selection. While some of the patients moved to different countries during the course of their therapy, all had experience of living in the UK and were predominantly based there during their therapy.

All data used in the study were collected from patient notes that had been recorded during
counseling sessions and stored securely on a computer hard drive following best practice
guidelines. The validity of the data was dependent on the patient's ability to express themselves authentically and the therapist's ability to correctly hear and transcribe those expressions. Due to time constraints, and to eliminate bias in which notes were subject to analysis, one in every five pages were used for the analysis. If the study were repeated and a different selection of pages was made, the themes revealed may have been different.

Data analysis procedure

To preserve anonymity, no patient names were used in any part of the analysis. To avoid any risk of unintentional disclosure, patients were referred to as simply Patient A, Patient B, etc., with Lefts given the initials A to C and Leavers given the initials D to F. For ease of reading, the six sets of patient notes were printed onto plain A4 paper. A spreadsheet
on Google Sheets was then created for the purpose of analyzing the data.

- Column A was headed 'Patient' and rows were created for each of patients A to F.
- Column B was headed 'Instigator' and Patients A to C were given the label Left and Patients D to F were given the label Leaver. The

'Merge Columns' command and color shading was used where necessary for clarity of presentation.

- Themes representing the Kubler-Ross and Kessler model (Denial, Anger, Bargaining, Depression, Acceptance, and Meaning) were recorded across the top of the spreadsheet in columns C to H.
- The remaining columns were left blank until the analysis had begun.

Starting with Patient A, and working down the page, line by line, the researcher went through the first page of notes, replicating the patient's comments and entering them into the relevant column. Where a comment introduced a theme that was deemed not to be covered by the Kubler-Ross and Kessler stages, it was entered into the next available column and labeled with a suggested theme. The table was adjusted over time with new themes merged or organized under superordinate themes as appropriate.

Knowledge of the Kubler-Ross and Kessler stage definitions was used to ensure patient comments were categorized as authentically as possible. For example, themes of panic and hurt were grouped under Anger because, according to Kubler-Ross and Kessler, "Anger is usually at the front of the line, as feelings of sadness, panic, hurt, and loneliness also appear, stronger than ever." Since Sadness and loneliness were associated more often with depression than anger, themes of sadness and loneliness were entered into the Depression column. Guilt was also included in the category of Anger because, according to Kubler-Ross and Kessler, guilt is, "anger turned inward on yourself." Identifying themes of Denial was complicated by the fact that reunion was always theoretically possible in any of the six relationship breakups studied.

It was decided to group any positive expressions of a return to the relationship as Denial with the caveat that these could equally have been grouped under a new theme of Hope. Acceptance was defined as any communication where the patient refers, in a factual manner, to the former relationship as being in the past. This does not imply that the stage of Acceptance was maintained for any length of time. Purely factual statements were omitted from the spreadsheet and analysis unless they reflected a clear theme. For example, Patient A's note stating, "Talking about Christmas plans,' was omitted because it is a factual statement that could reflect one of several themes. Do they imagine themselves and their former partner sharing a normal Christmas, which could come under the stage of Denial? Or are they talking about how to manage Christmas as separate people, which would be relevant to the theme of Acceptance? However, Patient C's note, 'Selling the house. The house sale is going through,' was included because it fits clearly under the theme of Security, an emergent theme which the researcher identified during the analysis.

Due to the ambiguity of communication and the complexity of human emotions and cognition, deciding which theme a particular note should be categorized under was not always straightforward. When Patient A said, 'I'm so angry,' this could clearly be categorized under the theme of Anger. However, when Patient D said, 'They haven't changed. They never did,' they could have been expressing anger or sadness. In these cases, the researcher made an arbitrary decision one way or the other, using the context of surrounding notes to help guide him.

Where the patient mentioned the name of their home city or town, these were replaced by the
generic noun 'city' or 'town' as appropriate to further reduce any risk

of unintentional disclosure of personally identifiable information. As patient gender was not applicable to this study, the pronouns 'they' and 'them' were chosen to replace 'he/him' and 'she/her.' The former partner was indicated in non-gendered terms (e.g., 'partner' or 'spouse' instead of 'boyfriend' or 'wife', etc.

Methods for verification/trustworthiness

To help ensure that the analysis was plausible, the researcher followed the advice of Smith et al. and contacted a third party psychology graduate who was not associated with the study but who was familiar with IPA procedures. The researcher read through the same pages of notes via a recorded Zoom session with the third party to whom he had previously presented copies of Kubler-Ross, Kubler-Ross and Kessler, and Kessler. This was to ensure that they were familiar with the Stages of Grief model. The third party was instructed to review the video in private, together with the IPA spreadsheet, and to highlight any areas of disagreement. The third party agreed with the themes chosen by the researcher and agreed that the patient comments had been added to the relevant themes.

Limitations

Due to the small size of the sample, this was not an exhaustive study, and the results cannot be generalized to the entire population of people experiencing PRG. Individual factors (e.g., personality disorders, inter-relational abuse, temperament, etc.) could have skewed results towards or away from specific themes.

In addition, time constraints meant that a random sample of pages from each patient's notes were analyzed. As described in the section on data sources and collection techniques, analyzing a different set of pages, or all case notes, could have revealed a different pattern of themes.

Results

This study was designed to help address the issue of a lack of models counselors can turn to when working with patients experiencing relationship break-up. The stated purpose of the research was to evaluate the use of the Kubler-Ross Stages of Loss model as a framework for post-relationship grief (PRG).

From this purpose, five research questions were generated, as follows:

1. In what ways is the Kubler-Ross model valid as a framework for working with post-relationship grief?'
2. In what ways is the Kubler-Ross model not valid as a framework for working with post-relationship grief?
3. What qualitative differences are there between the loss experiences of the bereaved and the loss experiences of those experiencing post-relationship grief?'
4. Which, if any, post-relationship grief experiences lie outside of the scope of the Kubler-Ross model?'
5. What differences are there between the loss experiences of those who have left a partner and the loss experiences of those who have been left by a partner?

Qualitative data, consisting of comments from case notes, were collected from six patients.

Research findings

<u>Stages of the Kubler-Ross model reflected in post-relationship grief themes</u>

The first research question in this study asks: 'In what ways is the Kubler-Ross model valid as a framework for working with post-relationship grief?' Suggesting an answer to that question involves querying the data for themes related to each of the six stages of grief as presented in the latest version of the Kubler-Ross model. All six patients brought up themes relating to Anger (including panic, hurt and guilt), directed at various parties, Bargaining and Depression (including sadness and loneliness). These findings suggest that the Kubler-Ross model may be valid for understanding these emotional and cognitive aspects of PRG.

Here are some example data:

Anger
Patient A said, "I'm so angry."
Patient B said, "Lots of people are pissing me off."
Patient C said, "I threw a glass of wine over them."
Patient D said, "I feel angry. How could they invite their family?"
Patient E said, "I'm angry because they often jump to conclusions."
Patient F said, "I'm full of resentment. I resent them."

Bargaining
Patient A asked, "How did this happen?"
Patient B said, "If only my dead brother were here"
Patient C said, "I'm praying to God for resolving this."
Patient D asked, "Who really made this relationship go bad?"
Patient E said, "I feel like I've messed up so many things in so many ways."
Patient F said, "If I had a million pounds, I would run away from everything and everyone"

Depression
Patient A said, "I'm not OK."
Patient B said, "My hope has died. That's why I'm grieving."
Patient C said, "I cried and cried and cried."
Patient D said, "I feel quite tearful. I don't know why. I'm mourning what could have been."

Patient E said, "I'm feeling very sad and disappointed in myself."
Patient F said, "I'm crying for my soul. This is my soul cry to the world."

All patients, with the exception of Patient E, expressed themes that could be categorized under the stage of Denial. Whether this conclusion can be justified from these findings is explored later in this extract.

Denial
Patient A said, "I feel that this could work again"
Patient B asked, "Was it all just a miscommunication?"
Patient C said, "Maybe they will come back."
Patient D said, "I keep on living in hope they will change."
Patient F said, "I'm willing to trust them one last time."

Stages of the Kubler-Ross model not reflected in post-relationship grief themes
The second research question in this study asked: In what ways is the Kubler-Ross model not valid as a framework for working with post-relationship grief? One reason why the Kubler-Ross model may not be valid as a framework for working with PRG is because there is no space on the model for a successful reunion of the separated partners. Indeed, at the time of writing, Patient F had returned to their partner. Hope of reunion clearly comes under the theme of Denial in post-bereavement grief because the fact of reunion is impossible. However, in PRG, the possibility, however slim, of reunion and rehabilitation suggests a separate role for Hope in a future model or theoretical framework for PRG. As I argue in the conclusion, working with Hope could be critical in supporting positive outcomes following a relationship break-up. I have elaborated on this thematic conflict in the Discussion section of this study [not included in this extract.]

While several patients expressed themes correlated to the Kubler-Ross and Kessler stages of Acceptance and Meaning, these were mainly in the 'Leavers' group. These findings will be elaborated on later in this chapter.

The strongest evidence against the validity of the Kubler-Ross model for PRG comes from the many themes that emerged from the analysis that had no correlation with the stages of grief as presented by Kubler-Ross and Kessler. These findings are detailed next:

<u>Post-relationship grief themes lying outside of the scope of the Kubler-Ross model</u>
The third research question in this study asked: 'What post-relationship grief experiences lie outside of the scope of the Kubler-Ross model?' While themes of intrapersonal conflict correlating with the Kubler-Ross and Kessler stages of Anger, Bargaining, and Depression were evident in the study, there were many themes of interpersonal conflict that lay outside of the Kubler-Ross and Kessler models. These are examples of 'secondary stressors,' which Stroebe, Schut, and Boerner, in their criticism of the Kubler-Ross and Kessler model, argued were not given consideration. It was decided to group these themes (Children's Welfare, Sex, Boundaries/Identity, Gaslighting/Abuse, Isolation/Neglect, Security [including finances, property and divorce proceedings], Physical Health, and Need for Closure) under a superordinate theme of Control, because they all had an impact on the amount of control that the patient had over their circumstances. The large amount of data recorded as relevant to these themes supports Stroebe, Schut, and Boerner's criticism of
the lack of account of secondary stressors in the Kubler-Ross and Kessler model.

Patient A asked, "How do we co-parent?" (Children's Welfare)

Patient B said, "They're making me question myself" (Gaslighting/Abuse)

Patient C asked, "Who am I?" (Boundaries/Identity)

Patient D said, "Sex is validating. Im seeing someone." (Sex)

Patient E said, "For financial reasons, I'm making the wrong decision." (Security)

Patient F said, "They reject me." (Isolation/Neglect)

In addition, there was some evidence of the inability to grieve properly that is characteristic of disenfranchised loss. Patient B, for example, says, "I need an emotional ending and a cognitive ending."

<u>Differences in PRG themes between those who have left a partner and those who have been left by a partner?</u>

The supplementary research question in this study asked: What differences are there between the loss experiences of those who have left a partner and the loss experiences of those who have been left by a partner?

The two main differences that have emerged from this analysis involve the stages and themes of Acceptance and Meaning. First, of the three patients who had been left by their partners, only one (Patient C) brought up themes that could be attributed to the Acceptance stage. In contrast, all three of the Leavers (Patients D, E, and F) expressed these themes to the counselor.

Second, none of the three patients who had been left by their partners expressed themes that could be attributed to the Meaning stage. In contrast, all three of the Leavers (Patients D, E, and F) brought up these themes. This suggests that people who have been left by their partners may have a more difficult time accepting the end of the relationship and finding meaning in that ending than those who have instigated the break-up.